D1614702

ACC. No: 05023764

Education, Asylum and the 'Non-Citizen' Child

Also by Madeleine Arnot

EDUCATING THE GENDERED CITIZEN: Sociological Engagements with National and Global Agendas

GENDER, EDUCATION AND EQUALITY IN A GLOBAL CONTEXT: Conceptual Frameworks and Policy Perspectives (co-edited)

KNOWLEDGE, POWER AND SOCIAL CHANGE: Applying the Sociology of Basil Bernstein (co-edited)

THE ROUTLEDGE-FALMER GENDER AND EDUCATION READER (co-edited)

CONSULTATION IN THE CLASSROOM: Developing Dialogue about Teaching and Learning (co-authored)

REPRODUCING GENDER? Essays on Educational Theory and Feminist Politics

CHALLENGING DEMOCRACY? International Perspectives on Gender, Education and Citizenship (co-edited)

CLOSING THE GENDER GAP: Post-War Education and Social Change (co-authored)

FEMINISM AND SOCIAL JUSTICE IN EDUCATION: International Perspectives (co-edited)

VOICING CONCERNS: Sociological Perspectives on Contemporary Education Reforms (co-edited)

Also by Halleli Pinson

CITIZENSHIP EDUCATION AND SOCIAL CONFLICT: Israeli Political Education in Global Perspective (co-edited)

Also by Mano Candappa

LOCAL AUTHORITIES, ETHNIC MINORITIES AND 'PLURALIST INTEGRATION' (co-authored)

Education, Asylum and the 'Non-Citizen' Child

The Politics of Compassion and Belonging

Halleli Pinson
Ben-Gurion University of the Negev, Israel

Madeleine Arnot
University of Cambridge, UK

Mano Candappa
University of London, UK
Institute of Education

371.826912

First published 2010 by
PALGRAVE MACMILLAN

Palgrave Macmillan in the UK is an imprint of Macmillan Publishers Limited, registered in England, company number 785998, of Houndmills, Basingstoke, Hampshire RG21 6XS.

Palgrave Macmillan in the US is a division of St Martin's Press LLC, 175 Fifth Avenue, New York, NY 10010.

Palgrave Macmillan is the global academic imprint of the above companies and has companies and representatives throughout the world.

Palgrave® and Macmillan® are registered trademarks in the United States, the United Kingdom, Europe and other countries

ISBN 978-0-230-52468-2   hardback

This book is printed on paper suitable for recycling and made from fully managed and sustained forest sources. Logging, pulping and manufacturing processes are expected to conform to the environmental regulations of the country of origin.

A catalogue record for this book is available from the British Library.

Library of Congress Cataloging-in-Publication Data
  Pinson, Halleli, 1973–
  Education, asylum and the non-citizen child : the politics of compassion and belonging / Halleli Pinson, Madeleine Arnot and Mano Candappa.
    p. cm.
  ISBN 978-0-230-52468-2 (hardback)
    1. Refugee children–Education–Government policy–Great Britain.
    2. Immigrant children–Education– Government policy–Great Britain.
    3. Stateless persons–Education–Government policy–Great Britain.
    4. Refugee children–Great Britain–Social conditions. 5. Immigrant children–Great Britain–Social conditions. 6. Stateless persons–Great Britain–Social conditions. I. Arnot, Madeleine. II. Candappa, Mano.
  III. Title.
  LC3665.G7P46 2010
  371.826'9140941–dc22   2010002709

10   9   8   7   6   5   4   3   2   1
19 18 17 16 15 14 13 12 11 10

'I have poured myself to the wind'

Where are you going from me where am I gone what does
this mean?

(From *Collage Poems* by Ziba Karbassi, an exiled Iranian poet,
translated by Stephen Watts, *Exiled Writers Ink*, 2009, p. 30)

Contents

Acknowledgments

There is always a reason why someone wants to write a book. In our case the reasons were both personal and political. All three of us had experiences of migration. Halleli's grandparents arrived in what was then Palestine from Ukraine and Poland in the 1920s and 1930s. One of her grandfathers and one of her grandmothers arrived without visas, the others arrived with a special certificate issued by the British Mandate. It was only when Israel was established as a nation in 1948 that all four grandparents acquired citizenship. When Madeleine's Jewish father came to England from Vienna in the 1920s, he avoided being classified as an 'enemy alien' since the family originated from what was then Czechoslovakia. He was naturalised British when he was 19. Her Polish mother lived as a refugee in Italy during the Second World War and received British citizenship on marriage in 1946. It was only after 12 years of having been brought up as a White colonial child in South Africa that Madeleine herself settled in Britain in 1962. Mano was classified as a migrant when she arrived in the UK in 1980 as a Commonwealth citizen from Sri Lanka. She acquired British citizenship much later in 2004. All three of us have lived in different countries and experienced the effects of migration, and of being strangers.

Our interest in the education of asylum-seekers and refugees was not therefore independent of our family histories. At the same time, the conditions under which our families were given citizenship in the UK and in Israel were substantially different from those affecting global refugees today. We have benefited in our lives from sustained formal education and stability of residence and we can anticipate that our children will build upon our achievements. Our experiences and expectations are far removed from the realities of many of the asylum-seeking and refugee children in the UK – the subject of this book.

Our research interests in the experiences of children whose families are seeking asylum and refuge in the UK began at different points. Our academic perspectives are different. Mano has a history of research on childhood and in social policy which gave her access to a wide range of settings across the UK where asylum-seeking families lived. The testimonies she collected from individual children and their parents provided a unique source of data. The Research Consortium on the Education of Asylum-seeking and Refugee Children – which included the General

Teaching Council (GTC), the National Union of Teachers and the Refugee Council, and which was set up by Madeleine and Halleli – gave them access to the perspectives of NGOs, teacher unions and the teaching profession. In 2005 Madeleine and Mano were funded by the Faculty of Education in the University of Cambridge to conduct a study on the relations between asylum-seeking and refugee students and their 'hosts'. By 2006, we were finally in a position to consider collaborating on a book.

No book is easy to write but this book has been particularly challenging and we would like to thank in particular those who have helped us bring together our ideas, given us the benefit of their experiences and insights and advised us on the relevance of particular literatures, policies, and fields of research. We are grateful to the late Carol Adams, Leslie Saunders and Shiraz Chakera at the GTC, which contributed funds and support to the policy project conducted by Halleli and Madeleine and published the first report of our research; to Nora McKenna, then Educational Advisor at the Refugee Council, and Samidha Garg, Principal Officer (Race Equality) for the National Union of Teachers, for sharing their knowledge and research findings. Bill Bolloten's advice and insights were particularly appreciated, from his initial involvement on the Advisory Committee of Mano's 'Extraordinary Childhoods' project and later studies, right through to the production of this book. His expertise is especially valued since he plays such an exceptional role in supporting schools and authorities in this field. We would also like to express our gratitude to Simon Blackburn at the University of Cambridge, UK, for his advice on the philosophy of compassion, and to Yossi Yonah at Ben-Gurion University in Israel for reading and commenting on early versions of our attempt to make sense of the politics of compassion. Special thanks are due to Alan Prout, University of Warwick, and Priscilla Alderson and Peter Moss at the Institute of Education, London, for their assistance in developing our thinking on refugee children and the diversity of childhoods, and to two graduate students who helped us; Thomas Meyer for his essay on compassion and to Hagar Bakun-Mazor for the tedious job of sorting out the bibliography for us.

Over the last few years we have gained considerably from our discussions in various academic conferences, seminars and from the comments given to us by anonymous referees to our articles in the *International Journal of Inclusive Education* and *Educational Review*. We would like to thank especially Jo Boyden and Jason Hart at the Centre for Refugee Studies, University of Oxford, for inviting us to present our research and for Jo Boyden's and Caroline Lanskey's insightful responses to our publications and talks respectively.

The research findings on which this book is based draw upon the trust and goodwill given to us by those whom we interviewed. The local authority officers, government officials and inspectors responsible for the education of asylum-seeking and refugee children spoke to us openly despite the risks associated with making public their views. Our first policy project would have not been possible without the cooperation of the officers in the three LEAs we visited. We are grateful for their time and their willingness to share their expertise with us. Our research in schools was greatly assisted by the three headteachers who supported our project and by a group of exceptional individual teachers who had responsibility for organising the support services for asylum-seeking and refugee students. Because of confidentiality we cannot name them but this does not mean that we have not recognised the help they gave us in encouraging students to participate in our study and give us the benefit of their knowledge and experience. Talking to asylum-seeking and refugee students and their classmates was a moving experience not least because in many cases the discussion was the first that they had had about the topic and their involvement in public discussions meant that they were brave enough to talk about the issues in public. We are enormously grateful for their honesty and trust. We hope that we have captured and interpreted the sentiments of all the people we spoke to well.

Writing a book on such a topic takes its toll on those nearest to us. We acknowledge the patience that has been required of our families and close friends when supporting us. They recognised that the research and the book were important to us politically and personally. Very special thanks go to Yona, Arie and Shira Pinson, Robin Young, Kathryn and Adam Arnot Drummond and Anthony Candappa-Rees.

Tables

Abbreviations

ASR – asylum-seeking and refugee
BIA – Border and Immigration Agency
BNA – British Nationality Act
BNP – British National Party
DCSF – Department for Children, Schools and Families
DfES – Department for Education and Skills
EAL – English as an Additional Language
ECM – *Every Child Matters*
EDP – Education Development Plan
EEA – European Economic Area
ELR – Exceptional Leave to Remain
EMAG – Ethnic Minority Achievement Grant
EMAS – Ethnic Minority Achievement Service
ESOL – English for Speakers of Other Languages
EU – European Union
EWO – Education Welfare Officer
GLA – Greater London Authority
GTC – General Teaching Council
GCSE – General Certificate of Secondary Education
HMIP – HM Inspector of Prisons
ICAR – Information Centre about Asylum and Refugees
IND – Immigration and Nationality Directorate
INSET – In-Service Training
LEA – Local Education Authority
MRCF – Migration and Refugee Communities Forum
NASS – National Asylum Support Service
NCADC – National Coalition of Anti-Deportation Campaigns
NF – National Front
NHS – National Health Service
NRIF – National Refugee Integration Forum
NUT – National Union of Teachers
OAU – Organization of African Unity
Ofsted – Office for Standards in Education
PGCE – Post Graduate Certificate in Education
PLASC – Pupil Level Annual School Census
QCA – Qualifications and Curriculum Authority

SAD – Schools against Deportations
SATs – Standard Assessment Tests
SEN – Special Education Needs
UKBA – UK Border Agency
UNCRC – UN Convention on the Rights of the Child
UNHCR – United Nations High Commissioner for Refugees
UNICEF – United Nation Children's Fund
UNDP – United Nations Development Fund
UNJDL – United Nations Rules for the Protection of Juveniles
        Deprived of their Liberty
VCG – Vulnerable Children Grant

1
Introduction

Refugees and asylum-seekers have come to represent the Achilles' heel of liberal democratic states (Turton, 2003). The response of governments to their presence, and especially the level of compassion they attract, is an important indicator of their engagement with the perceived threat of globalisation to national sovereignty. The increasing numbers of asylum-seekers and refugees in the last two decades, the sense of crisis associated with them, and the ways in which their rights are defined and addressed are all important reasons for looking at forced migration as a separate category for social research (Loizos, 2000). Refugees and asylum-seekers today are often seen as aliens, strangers and the ultimate Others in society, and as such expose inconsistencies in the various ideologies that underlie the modern liberal democratic nation-state.

Fundamentally, therefore, the main logic behind conceptualising forced migration separately from other types of migration is that forced migration is a study about *us*. It requires us to rethink issues of membership, citizenship and democratic liberalism – to ask what our responsibility is and what our moral commitments are to the stranger on our doorstep (Turton, 2002). Using the same analogy, as the absolute stranger, the child whose family is seeking asylum can tell us something about how we define education and its role in society. Throughout the book we have adopted the commonly used terms asylum-seeking and refugee children (ASR for short) although, being children, unless unaccompanied, their legal status and any application for asylum are dependent on their parents. By exploring the educational responses to the presence of ASR children in our schools, we can learn more about the social and political values of our education system and the ways in which its principles of inclusivity and cohesion operate in the context of globalising forces.

The prime aim of this book is to offer a sociological perspective into the morality which lies behind the education of ASR children. This book raises the question of how the national civic project represented by a state education system addresses the education of the ASR child – the 'non-citizen' child who has lost the protection which their citizenship status in their home country gave them and has not achieved it in the next. It explores, in this case, how the UK government defines its responsibilities towards such children. Central to our analysis are the ways in which the arrival of the ASR child challenge the depth of commitment to human rights and to the principles of social inclusion.

Children and the contradictory logics of globalisation

With the Enlightenment, children in Western societies came to be perceived as innocent beings, potential victims who need adult protection to maintain their wellbeing (Burman, 1994; Giner, 2006, 2007). The emergence of the global children's rights movement challenged this construction of childhood by replacing the image of children as weak, dependent and incomplete beings with a recognition of the child as an active participant in society (Prout, 2005). This latter notion was enshrined in the United Nations Convention on the Rights of the Child (UNCRC, 1989) and shaped four 'general principles' or basic values about what should constitute the treatment of children and their participation in society. These principles recognise the child's need for adult support as well as children's position as social actors in their own right. These principles concern the child's *right to life* (Article 6), including the survival and development of the child 'to the maximum extent possible' (Article 6, 2); the *best interests of the child* (Article 3) which could over-ride the interests of parents or the state; *respecting the views of the child* (Article 12) including the child's right to be heard; and that *no child should suffer discrimination* (Article 2), stipulating equality of rights for *all* children (Hammarberg, 1995). Within these general principles, the UNCRC prescribed specific norms, such as the right to respect for private and family life (Articles 9, 16); the right not to be unlawfully detained (Article 37(b)); the right to a standard of living adequate for the child's development (Article 27) and the right to education (Articles 28 and 29). Paradoxically, by virtue of their dependent status, the rights of children theoretically now extend well beyond the human rights of adults. Also, nation-states, as signatories to the UNCRC, are the prime guarantors of children's rights.[1] Today, this global commitment to securing children's rights is considered as a sign of progress (Boyden and Hart, 2007; Burman, 1994).

However, within the contradictory logics of globalisation, children are especially vulnerable. Globalisation is simultaneously the greatest threat and most signifcant opportunity for children in terms of their ability to access the rights of the child under the UNCRC (Brysk, 2004). Children are increasingly subject to mobility and displacement (estimates suggest that there are 10 million refugee minors in the world, many of them unaccompanied) (ibid.). Nonetheless, since the implementation of the UNCRC, they have been one of the main groups to enjoy the effects of this international human rights regime which, in recent years, has been much strengthened by the UN Millennium Development Goals and the increasing pressure put on all governments to deliver equal access to education, and to promote children's health, safety and wellbeing. The particular vulnerabilities of ASR children, whose circumstances might compromise their rights, are recognised in the UNCRC which specifies that they should receive:

> appropriate protection and humanitarian assistance in the enjoyment of applicable rights set forth in the present Convention and in other international human rights or humanitarian instruments to which the said States are Parties. (Article 22, 1)

The UNCRC appears set to ensure that children's rights are independent of their status or circumstances (Boyden and Hart, 2007).

However, the changing contemporary discourse of asylum and the image of the refugee brings with it new challenges. The refugee child carries different contradictions from those of the refugee adult. Within the changing image of asylum, the ASR child is positioned within two contradictory discourses: a political discourse which distinguishes between genuine and 'bogus' asylum-seekers[2] and the discursive idea of childhood vulnerability and the commitment of governments to help protect children's rights (Giner, 2007). In this book, we are especially interested in unpacking these contradictory forces and logics by investigating the education of ASR children in the UK.

Towards a sociology of education and forced migration

The implications of human mobility as well as forced migration on the organisation of states, their membership, institutions of citizenship, sovereignty and economic systems, are all issues that have been explored by political theorists, sociologists and social theorists in the past two decades. However, the impact, meaning and relevance of human movement to education have been largely neglected by educationalists, even those concerned with social justice, critical analysis or ethnic issues in education.

We are entering this field as sociologists of education and childhood. Our main concern is not with immigration policies and asylum discourses *per se*, but with their implications for the education of the ASR child. There is no doubt that there is a gaping hole as far as sociological research into ASR children's education is concerned. Despite great sociological interest in the role of education in relation to social inequality and social exclusion, there is very little interest in the education of one of the most socially and economically deprived and discriminated-against groups in society (Pinson and Arnot, 2007). This is perhaps because the 'asylum crisis' is perceived as an adult problem and as a problem of immigration control which affects specific, often London, locations rather than one which concerns many schools in the country. There has been little attempt to relate ASR students' experiences of schooling to contemporary politics of multiculturalism, 'race' and diversity. Surprisingly given the high level of interest in the relationship between globalisation, citizenship and education, there also appears to have been little attention given to the implications of human mobility and the resulting increased cultural diversity within state education systems in general. Little if any attention has been given to the need to understand the political and social significance of the challenges of educating asylum-seeking children who have no citizenship status or who, as refugees, only enjoy temporary access to social rights (for example, the right to work and access to welfare support) and have yet to gain citizenship status in the receiving country. Nevertheless, as children, they have the universal right to education. All this begs the question whether the lives and education of ASR children are invisible as far as the sociology of education is concerned.

In contrast, there is a small volume of literature which is available on the education of ASR children in the UK that has contributed to raising the awareness of teachers, schools and policy-makers.[3] Thanks to researchers and organisations that are often outside mainstream sociological discourse, the specific educational needs of ASR children have been identified. Although embodying some evidence-based research, this field is mostly shaped by practitioner discourses which attempt to describe what constitutes 'good educational practice'. In Jacobson and Landau's (2003) view, such advocacy research could do with more theoretical sophistication and methodological rigour. Nevertheless this material is particularly valuable for schools working with ASR children.

The most substantial account of this embryonic academic line of research is Jill Rutter's book *Refugee Children in the UK* (2006). She focuses on the history of education and asylum-seeking in the UK and offers the ecological model as a basis for good practice for the integration of these children. In the UK, this approach relates well to the recent government initiative *Every Child Matters* (ECM) (DfES, 2003a) which emphasises the need for a multi-agency approach to provision for vulnerable populations. However, such a model is not sufficient in our view to tackle the often oppressive and destructive ways in which not only the needs but also the rights of such children are constructed within the state. In other words, while useful as a tool for examining good educational practice, this conceptual framework is unlikely to offer a sufficiently strong sociological platform from which to engage critically with the impact of forced migration on national educational systems, nor the complex politics which surround the education of these children.

This book therefore explores from a sociological perspective how UK government responses to immigration and asylum affect not just the education of ASR children but the politics of schooling more generally. It investigates how these changes in the politics of immigration are expressed, experienced and dealt with through the state education system. Schools in the UK have to respond to the relatively high numbers of pupils who have been forced to migrate often from different and distant parts of the world, with many having experienced the ultimate trauma of watching members of their family being killed, abused or abducted. Often ASR children have passed through many countries on the way to the UK. Many are unaccompanied, some are trafficked, most experience considerable trauma and have shown extraordinary courage. They come on occasion from countries with which the UK has no historical connection or affinity, with languages and schooling experiences (if any) very different from students in local schools in the UK. Many have different religions; some have dreams about what the UK represents in terms of safety, freedom and a good life. Their legal status is often transitory, temporary and they experience fear that they may not be able to remain in the UK. Some are looking for parents; some find themselves living in care, perhaps with foster parents nearest the port of entry. Others, the lucky ones, live in their own communities, not having been dispersed by the British government to other places. The diversity of national origin and social background of such ASR children adds to the complexity and heterogeneity of British schools.

From a sociological perspective, what is important is to understand how the presence of migrant children and families with these different immigration and citizenship statuses and particularly those who have not been given the right to remain in the UK relate to the politics of state education. Historically, modern education systems were projects of state formation and the expansion of education is usually associated with the development of a universal welfare state and the social rights of the citizen. This book is interested, therefore, in how one national education system addresses not only the growing cultural diversity of its catchments, and the temporary nature of students' presence in some instances, but also the diversity in status and access to civic and social rights of these pupils. We are particularly interested in how the tension between the universal rights of the child and immigration control is negotiated and how different discourses of asylum-seeking and rights are articulated within the British education system.

Current characteristics of human mobility, and especially forced migration, raise new challenges for a national school system. To name just a few: a) accommodating the asylum-seeking child in a state education system which is designed to educate future citizens, when this child is often neither 'a citizen to be', nor a citizen in the making; b) dealing with ASR children who are often in transit either within the country or moving across countries searching for refuge; c) catering for the needs of pupils who do not speak the national language, have no historic connection with the host country, have different educational experiences (if at all) and who often have multiple needs associated with the conditions of their migration, including trauma; and d) dealing with greater ethnic diversity.

The arrival of ASR children has major implications for the education system both in terms of funding and resources. Also challenging is the implication of their presence for different, and often contradictory, educational agendas such as the promotion of an inclusive ethos, cultural diversity and social justice, at the same time as promoting academic standards and performance in a competitive school environment. To a great extent, the presence of these children and their complex needs puts to the test school ethos and teachers' professional experience, knowledge and ethics as well as the values of both teachers and children. ASR children often act as a litmus test for those agendas and values. Ultimately educational responses to ASR children – the ways in which their needs and rights are perceived, the support we offer them in the UK, and the way teachers and schools define their responsibility towards them – are integral to the promotion of social justice.

The prominence of the asylum debate therefore is as much a moral as it is a political issue. Refugees once invoked compassion (Bauman, 2004). In their suffering and need for protection, they called up benevolence and caring in the host. The scale and the salience of the asylum-seeking debate in public discourses now put that tradition of compassionate reaction to the test. It raises the moral question of whether societies should or could be compassionate towards the full range and numbers of forced migrants in today's world.

Consequently, the notion of *compassion* is a valuable yardstick with which to assess the ways in which central and local government in the UK have responded to the presence of asylum-seekers and refugees and to explore whether the ethos and practice of schools, teachers and students encourage such emotions and moral values. We also consider whether ASR students are encouraged to belong – either to the school community or to British society. The notion of *belonging*, our second yardstick, frames what is British and what it means to 'be British'. Our research investigated in what ways young people feel that ASR children can belong, what the conditions of belonging are and whether teachers and schools ensure that ASR students feel they are valued at a time when the government continually redefines the politics associated with belonging from which asylum-seekers and refugees are excluded.

The structure of the book

This book is organised into 11 chapters. We begin, in Chapter 2, with the context in which the reality of forced migration confronts notions of national sovereignty, citizenship rights and human rights and in turn, engenders new discourses of asylum. Chapter 3 describes how we conceptualised our research and conducted a series of exploratory projects on the ways in which central and local government, schools, teachers and students in the UK engaged with the presence of ASR children in schools. In Chapter 4 we discuss government immigration and asylum policy focusing particularly on dispersal, detention and deportation and the implications for ASR children's education. The impact of such policies on national educational policies and the responses of local authorities to the presence of ASR students are explored in Chapter 5. We demonstrate the ways in which ASR students are located within existing policy frameworks and funding lines and the different conceptualisations which English LEAs use to address their needs. Of special interest is one type of LEA policy response which we refer to as the *holistic* approach.

In Chapter 6 we learn from empirical data how such child-centred holistic approaches reposition the ASR child, from a migrant to that of

a 'learner citizen' and thus equivalent to any other child. This pedagogic approach is explored in more depth in Chapter 7 where we draw
on teachers' interviews from three case study schools. Our findings
reveal some of the complexities, tensions and opportunities schools identify when helping ASR students feel that they are valued and belong.
The voices of ASR students and of other students, explored in Chapters 8
and 9, offer a powerful indictment of the moral ethos of the school
over and above the realities of an aggressive immigration policy that
seeks to exclude them. However, our data also suggest that ASR students often experience exclusive youth cultures within these inclusive
schools and that the interface with other students is affected by ill-
defined but important notions of Britishness and belonging. Our research
suggests that not only are schools, teachers and students repositioned
vis-à-vis the state by UK immigration and asylum policy but, on occasion,
this repositioning can lead to direct confrontation with government
actions. In Chapter 10, we consider evidence of teachers and students
becoming actively involved in critical discussions about human rights
and in public anti-deportation campaigns to prevent the detention
and forced removal of their students and friends. In our conclusion in
Chapter 11, we reflect on the lessons learnt from our research and discuss
what we have understood about the education of ASR children. We relo-
cate schooling in the context of state boundary-making activity, sovereignty and economic changes in the global area, the development of
human rights internationally and highlight the importance of compassionate responses to asylum-seekers and refugees. We conclude by
thinking critically about what a compassionate education might entail,
especially if schools are to engage in teaching about the structural deter-
minants of asylum and ASR children are to given the right to participate
in determining their own futures.

2
Globalisation and Forced Migration: Challenging National Institutions

> Refugees are stateless ... They are outcasts and outlaws of a novel kind, the products of globalisation ... Refugees are human waste, with no useful function to play in the land of their arrival ... from their present place, the dumping site, there is no return and no road forward ... The act of assigning to waste puts an end to differences, individualities, idiosyncrasies ... All measures have been taken to assure the permanence of their exclusion. (Bauman, 2004: 76–8)

Bauman (2004) argues that refugees, being the 'human waste' of globalisation, are stripped of all other identities but one – that of being stateless and statusless. While this position, as outcasts, makes them highly visible as the 'Other in our midst', all other aspects of their being and individuality are erased. Refugees are physically and symbolically 'out of place' (Turton, 2002); they are often described as one of globalisation's 'discontents'.[1] In the current complexity of global human mobility, asylum-seekers and refugees have become one of the most visible and politically sensitive aspects of this reality (Jordan and Düvell, 2002; Richmond, 1994).

The end of the Cold War, the outbreak of many ethnic and civil conflicts at the end of the 20th century, and unequal economic globalisation, have contributed to a rapid increase in the number of forced migrants (Gibney, 2004; Roberts, 1998). Recent waves of refugees have responded not merely to violent conflicts but also to 'the uneven distribution of security and welfare across states' (Gibney, 2004: 5). According to the UNCHR the number of forced migrants worldwide rose dramatically after the end of the Cold War, reaching its peak in the mid-1990s with 18.2 million refugees. The resolution of several armed conflicts in the following decade, and stricter immigration and asylum policies implemented by many Western states, have since contributed to a decrease in the number of refugees and asylum-seekers.[2]

By the end of 2007 UNCHR had dealt with 31.7 million people of whom 11.4 million were refugees and 634,000 were asylum-seekers – the majority of whom came from Afghanistan, Iraq, Sudan, Somalia, Burundi and the Democratic Republic of Congo (UNCHR, 2008). In contrast to the popular belief that Western developed countries are 'flooded' by refugees, UNCHR's statistics suggests that between 83 per cent to 90 per cent of the entire refugee and asylum-seeking population fled to neighbouring countries and settled within their region of origin (UNCHR, 2008).

In the past three decades, this global movement of refugees and asylum-seekers has been accompanied by the growing unwillingness of states to grant asylum (Marfleet, 2006; Roberts, 1998). Since the 1980s, immigration in general and refugee flows in particular have provoked extensive activity in Western states (Turton, 2002). Western states have struggled with the question of what constitutes their responsibility towards asylum-seekers. They have had to decide whom to admit, based on what grounds and how ethically and politically they could defend their responses to this mass movement of people.[3] Today, the image of the asylum-seeker and refugee, more than any other stranger or alien, exposes major tensions underlying the nation-state as a political community and as the universal principle of political organisation. Therefore, the significance of asylum-seeking in public debates and the hostile representations of asylum-seekers, in particular, cannot be attributed merely to the actual numbers of asylum-seekers and refugees. The topic provokes such strong public responses because it stirs a debate about the physical and symbolic boundaries of the nation-state, its identity and the legitimacy of preserving this concept in an age characterised by the global fluidity of migration. In the context of liberal democratic states, as we argue below, the topic creates major tensions within the logic of political and human rights.

Given this social and political importance, it is surprising that there is a lack of sociological research on forced migration (Castles, 2003; O'Neill and Spybey, 2003) and how it affects Western societies. The paucity of research into the impact of such globalising social change on national institutions, such as education, could perhaps be attributed to the difficulty of agreeing on the meanings and characteristics of forced migration and what distinguishes it from other movements of people across borders.[4] In the age of globalisation and growing human mobility, the distinction between asylum-seekers and other migrants (especially economic migrants) is becoming not only highly politicised but also blurred (Castles, 2003; Castles and Loughna, 2002).

This definitional debate shapes international attempts to try and assist refugees in the aftermath of the Second World War; the 1951 UN Refugee Convention, for example, attempted to offer a universal legal definition of who is a refugee, their rights and the obligation of states towards them. This Convention was intended to address the post-war reality in Europe when millions of people were displaced and, up to the Amendment to this Convention in 1967, the definition of a refugee was aimed solely at those who fled their country as a result of events in Europe (Gibney, 2004; Suhrke and Zolberg, 2002). The Convention defined refugees only as those who are persecuted personally, as individuals, and did not encompass those who are persecuted and displaced because they belong to a certain group (Boyle et al., 1998; Turton, 2002). It also leant heavily towards the view that (in order to qualify as a refugee) a person had to have faced political persecution rather than persecution based on ethnicity or religion (Boyle et al., 1998). In retrospect, although attempting to universalise the definition of refugee, the 1951 UN Refugee Convention offered a Euro-centric definition which suited the Cold War reality in Europe.

In 1969 the Organization of African Unity (OAU) offered an alternative definition more suitable for non-European contexts. It expanded the definition of refugee to include those who are persecuted as a result of their group affiliation. The range of recognised causes for forced migration and displacement there included the experience of violence, war, natural disasters and plagues (Boyle et al., 1998; Gibney, 2004).[5]

Two central concerns remain at the heart of these contemporary political, international and academic debates. First, there remains a concern about what should be considered genuine and legitimate causes of forced migration. Should the definition of forced migration include only those who flee wars and violent conflicts, or should economic and political instabilities and environmental disasters also be considered as valid causes of forced rather than economic migration? Today, since many asylum-seekers have a range of different reasons for moving across national borders (Castles, 2003), governments are urged to take the broadest definition possible and provide refugee status to all those who cannot enjoy state protection, regardless of the reasons for the need for that protection or the reasons for the failure of their state to provide it (see Gibney, 2004). The second major point of dispute is whether the movement of people across regions is perceived as voluntary or involuntary. The assumption underlying this debate is the common belief that forced migrants are only those who had no choice but to flee.

This debate about the definition of forced migration should be understood as part of a certain political, social and economic context – that of a perceived 'asylum crisis' (Gibney, 2004) in Western European and other income-rich host countries such as Australia and the USA. In the context of this 'crisis', the distinctions between what are valid and invalid causes for forced migration and the question of a person's choice can be understood to be discursively constructed – particular 'regimes of truth' are put into the public domain about the nature and reasons for so many asylum-seekers requiring refuge in richer nations. Not only do such debates discursively construct differences between the categories associated with forced migration but they also, as we shall see, determine who is deserving of sanctuary and protection. These debates also seek to determine those migrants for whom Western liberal democracies have a moral responsibility to protect and those who are assigned to Bauman's (2004) category of 'human waste' for whom there is no such responsibility. This distinction between 'the deserving' and 'the undeserving' which we explore in the book represents a certain type of state politics – as such it affects the sorts of educational provision considered appropriate for these different categories of migrant.

In effect, these hotly contested discursive debates about the 'asylum crisis' are central to other challenges that modern nation-states face in the age of globalisation and are critical to the processes by which in the modern world, nation-states define their identities and a certain politics of belonging. The significant numbers of asylum-seekers and refugees arriving at the borders of Western democracies require receiving societies to address issues of membership, rights and belonging (Barlo and Morrison, 2005; Turton, 2003). Governments are forced to rethink their moral obligation to what Benhabib (2004) called the 'non-citizen' – those without the legal status to claim citizenship but who nevertheless seek state protection in the 'host' society. Marfleet (2006) suggests that, although the idea of asylum is ancient, the 'refugee' is a modern concept which is embedded in the idea of rights and the sovereign nation-state. Therefore the ways in which we define forced migration, refugee and asylum-seeking communities and individuals are part of what has been called the 'politics of belonging' in Western nation states (Crowley, 1999; Yuval-Davis et al., 2006). Below we take time to explore what that means in practice in terms of the rights of the citizen and those 'non-citizens' for whom citizenship is either lost, in transition to becoming something else, or denied.

The economics and politics of forced migration

Educational systems today are caught up in the maelstrom of globalisation – the massively increased movement of capital, trades, information, values and, perhaps most visibly, the movement of people. Human mobility in past decades has significantly changed in terms of its scope, pace, composition and direction, as a result of other forms of movement, especially economic movement of capital, goods and trades, as well as the development of transportation and communication (Graham, 2000; Jordan and Düvell, 2002). However, despite the relationships between these diverse forms of movements, they entail different logics and invoke different state reactions.

The economic movement of capital and the border crossing of business and trade, for example, are welcomed and encouraged under the logic of global free markets and the spread of capitalism. Those focusing on the flows of economic capital from a neo-liberal perspective see globalisation as a positive integrative force, arguing that the intensification of economic and cultural interdependency has the potential to contribute to international political solidarity (Brah et al., 1999). However, when looking at the scope and makeup of human mobility which often reflects the growing economic disparities between states (Graham, 2000) a different picture emerges – that of a 'world of increasingly uneven development' (Marfleet, 2006: 23). This uneven development is also reflected in the different logics that Western governments employ in their reaction to different types of human mobility. The border crossing of people is addressed using a different logic – one that relates to national politics, belonging and membership (Jordan and Düvell, 2002; von Bredow, 1998). As Bauman (1998: 9) argues, one of the main tensions around globalisation is that 'power in the form of capital, and particularly financial capital, flows while politics remains tied to the ground bearing all the constraints imposed by its local character'.

In this context, so called 'host' societies view the movement of people overtly or not, according to the migrants' assumed economic contribution or liability. For instance, the 'highly skilled migrant' schemes in the UK and Canada are designed to encourage the immigration and reception of people with capital or skills needed by the local labour market. While European Union (EU) countries have introduced stricter immigration control measures to prevent the entry of some migrants – especially asylum-seekers – the formation of a regional market in the EU has led to the opening of borders and the free movement of citizens of the member states (Carter, 2001). Global capitalism is prepared to integrate or include some people while others, most notably refugees, are seen as an economic burden. The processes of economic inclusion, therefore, can be especially exclusive. Bauman (1998: 9) argues that the tension between these economic and political logics means that human mobility has 'become the most powerful and most coveted stratifying factor'. Richmond (1994) takes this argument a step further when he represents current systems of immigration control in the developed world as part of a global apartheid system dividing those with and those without political rights.

Of central importance to education is the fact that globalisation, and especially global migration, in the 20th century disrupts modern regimes of rights upon which notions of national citizenship are based. Global migration has meant that nation-states have become more ethnically, racially and culturally diverse and that millions of people today hold dual citizenship or reside in a country to which they do not fully belong. There is therefore even greater disparity within a state demographic in terms of types of civic status and of access to the right of residence and employment. Castles and Davidson (2000) claim that this increasing cultural and social diversity within a nation not only exposes the myth of national homogeneity but also undermines the idea of cultural belonging as necessarily linked to political membership (citizenship). They suggest that globalisation breaks the territorial link and nexus between political power and place – a link which represented one of the most important foundations for the modern nation-state and of citizenship.

The institution of citizenship today and therefore the education of the citizen are more likely to be defined by contemporary tensions between inclusion and exclusion rather than by simple definitions of national membership. As Benhabib (2004) points out, in this new context, the concept of citizenship which traditionally meant unity in terms of the rights of residence, subjection to the same administrative regime, democratic participation and cultural membership, is disaggregated. As a result, the boundaries of national civic communities and regimes of rights are changing and modern links between nationality and citizenship are uncoupled. Importantly, there is a growing separation between the traditions of citizenship and human rights, and their different logics – that of *nationhood* and *personhood*. Consequently, modern states today have to face the decision about whether an individual's social rights should continue to be distributed according to *citizenship* or *personhood* (Benhabib, 2004).

Since citizenship rights are distributed to members of a specific political community by virtue of their belonging to that community (Brysk and Shafir, 2004), social and political solidarity is encouraged through these rights and through the education system no less over and above social inequalities. In contrast, human rights derive from an entirely different logic. Drawing their meaning from the philosophy of natural law and perceived as universal by nature, human rights are 'anchored in a person by virtue of his or her humanity and not by virtue of his or her status in the body politic' (Shafir, 2004: 13). Moreover, human rights are intended to protect individuals against the arbitrariness of government or other political entities. They are not designed to equalise or regulate access to power or to create a sense of community as do citizenship rights (Shafir, 2004). Human rights therefore have more to do with personhood as described by Benhabib than with nationhood.

However the new opportunities for human rights are not enjoyed by all. Despite the internationalisation of human rights (Brysk and Shafir, 2004), their enforcement remains largely national. Nation-states remain the prime institution that ratify international human rights conventions, and sign up to deliver and administer human rights (in ways that often restrict and set conditions on the delivery of such rights). This creates a fundamental paradox since 'individuals do not enjoy rights by virtue of their humanity, but by virtue of their membership in the major political institution of the day – a particular, territorial based nation-state' (Shafir, 2004: 23).

Especially in the context of the EU, access to the supra-national sphere and to the rights attached to it is based on the precondition of national membership. In this context Morris (2003) takes the view that the language of human rights is not necessarily an indication of the emergence of 'universal personhood', but rather a complex inclusion/exclusion regulatory mechanism used to distinguish between different types of migrants which she terms *civic stratification* (Morris, 2003: 79). Civic stratification operates as a system of inequality which, in the case of the EU, is reflected in the differential access to rights of national citizens, EU citizens and non-EU citizens. This opens 'up the possibility that delivery of social rights can be harnessed as a vehicle of control and as a means of monitoring those "lawfully present"' (Morris, 2003: 80). Although social rights in the context of the EU have become more relevant than national political rights, and even though such social rights can transcend state boundaries, they are still maintained by the nation-state. As a result there is even more stratification in access to citizenship rights (Dell'Olio, 2005). Arguably this stratification in access to rights and the control nation-states have over the distribution of human rights strengthen the notion of being a citizen which then becomes an even more important element in gaining rights (Bhabha, 1999; Dell'Olio, 2002).

The different logics of immigration control

Of significance too for state-provided educational institutions is the fact that while nation-states lose sovereignty in global economic and technological domains, their sovereignty 'is nonetheless vigorously asserted and national borders, while more porous, are still there to keep out aliens and intruders' (Benhabib, 2004: 6). Human mobility, and especially the extent to which non-citizens enjoy access to rights, are both an indication of the materialisation of transnational spaces, as well as a space for nation-states to exercise their sovereignty. Immigration policy is one area in which nation-states still exercise their power – it offers the chance to continue with boundary-making activities such as administering the right to access the soil and the right to belong.

It is generally agreed that liberal democracies have a right, as part of their sovereignty, to grant entry to some and exclude others and that the sovereignty of a state takes precedence over the right of individuals to immigrate (Whitaker, 1998). The presence of refugees and asylum-seekers therefore symbolically represents the limits of state sovereignty and power. Whether the decision is to keep the door open or closed in the face of increasing numbers of refugees, the presence and pressure represented by the movement of refugees globally reflects, by and large, the incapacity of nation-states to exercise fully their power of sovereignty within a globalising world (Muller, 2004). As Whitaker (1998: 416) argues, the problem lies in the fact that '[r]efugees have claims upon the host country that arise from outside the host country's jurisdiction'. But the tension between the sovereignty of the nation-state and human movement is not just a matter of a policy. A liberal democracy faces a moral challenge since the presence of asylum-seekers and refugees raises the question of fairness, especially in relation to human rights.

The immigration policies of affluent nations are now publically judged by the strength of their commitment to the human rights of others (Carter, 2001). Thus, more than for any other type of migration, the presence of those who seek protection in liberal democratic states raises the moral and ethical questions underlying the tension between sovereignty and human rights (Gibney, 2004; Weiner, 1995), including the moral appropriateness of applying compassion. Liberal democracies and their educational systems become embroiled in this ethical question since they have to balance their legal and ethical responsibility to protect those in need with their legal and moral responsibility to their citizenry to protect the community's resources and limit the access of 'aliens' to it (Gibney, 2004). They also have to both protect the interests of the nation-state and demonstrate their commitment to universal human rights (Benhabib, 2004; Weiner, 1995).

The privileging by immigration control policies of the logic of state sovereignty (often over and above the commitment to universal human rights) is legitimated today by the way in which immigration in general and asylum-seeking in particular are represented by Western societies. Various arguments are put forward in favour of restricting immigration: economic concerns; concerns about possible integration of minority groups; potential internal security threats; and threats to the existing social, cultural and political order (Collinson, 1993). Stalker (2002: 163) pointedly argues that 'there are two main conflicting factors when it comes to accepting refugees'. The main reason given for accepting refugees is 'responding to the humanitarian impulse' to create a safe haven for those who have a 'well founded fear of persecution'. However, '[t]he primary reason for trying to limit the flows of refugees is usually economic, since refugees can be seen as a drain on publicly funded welfare service ...' (ibid.).

There is a widespread assumption that citizen and migrants' rights are juxtaposed and their protection and distribution is a zero-sum game (Gigauri, 2006). In recent years, numbers of those seeking asylum in Western states have risen, and the compassionate reaction towards them has been replaced by images of 'bogus asylum-seekers' and 'scroungers'. The current 'politics of belonging', represented often in the degree of openness to migration, is determined by the needs of the labour market and the extent to which we believe that a particular migrant group can be integrated into 'our' society (Barlo and Morrison, 2005; Marfleet, 2006; Stalker, 2002). The supposed economic value of an individual (or a group) and the extent to which they 'fit' the mainstream neo-liberal profile of a well-educated, mobile consumer is intimately linked to the judgement about whether or not they pose a threat to 'our' society or values (Geddes, 2005; Yuval-Davis et al., 2006). Today, those who are defined as 'strangers', as unwanted, are also those who are unable to partake in the consumerist game (Bauman, 1997: 14).

In this context, those who are most vulnerable are in effect the *'non-citizens'*. Non-citizens are transient people who are neither strangers nor insiders (Benhabib, 2004), living in what Agamben describes as a state of 'bare life' (Agamben, 1998, quoted in Yuval-Davis, 2008: 106). This non-status of refugees and asylum-seekers today reflects the moral values of society:

> ... the refugee has come to symbolise 'the Other', who is displaced, has no rights and whose life is in danger. The way refugees are treated is thus indicative of a system's approach to inclusivity and belonging. (Yuval-Davis, 2008: 105)

As part of the moral debate about immigration and the tension between human rights and the sovereignty of the nation-state, Western states start asking why should 'we' provide for 'them'? To a large extent the economic discourse is used to justify and strengthen the legitimacy of restricting immigration in the name of social stability and preserving the national identity and character of the state. In the context of these tensions, between nationhood and personhood, between sovereignty and human rights regimes and between economic and political-ethical considerations, refugees are left most vulnerable.

As we shall see, because of the conflict between sovereignty and protecting the nation's economic interests on the one hand, and the commitment to human rights and the protection of those who are persecuted on the other, many liberal democracies have decided to shift the weight from immigration policy – controlling the right of asylum-seekers and refugees to enter the country – to social policy – which controls their access to rights once admitted. To a large extent, immigration policies then can be divided into policies dealing with control of entry and those designed to address absorption and integration and to regulate access to rights (Hammer, 2000; Weiner, 1995).

Trying to capture this complexity in immigration policy, especially when it extends into social policy, Hammer (2000) suggests that we now need to understand the difference between *non-citizens, denizens* and *citizens* and recognise that there are now three gates of entry that correspond with these statuses. The first gate is the *regulation of immigration* (entry), through which non-citizens are permitted or denied entry; the second gate – *the regulation of access to social rights* – is used to determine the status of denizens; and the third gate is the *regulation of naturalization through which one can obtain the status of citizen*. These three gates of entry and especially the growing restrictions of access to rights of different non-citizen groups in Western European countries could be seen as an indication of the power of citizenship to define what constitutes 'belonging', despite and over and above the weakening of the nation-state as a result of globalisation.

Contemporary images of the refugee and asylum-seeker

More than half a century ago, Hannah Arendt observed that the problem associated with those who are in permanent alienage status – today namely asylum-seekers – lies not with the loss of home but with the impossibility of finding a new one:

> Suddenly, there was no place on earth where migrants could go without the severest restrictions, no country where they would be assimilated, no territory where they could found a new community of their own ... it was a problem of not a space but of political organization. (Arendt, 1958: 293–6; quoted in Xenos, 1996: 243)

Today, most developed countries still honour their moral obligation to promote human rights by allowing asylum-seekers to claim asylum. However, at the same time, they vigorously act to reduce the numbers of those receiving the status of refugee (those allowed to settle and find a home at least temporarily) and use access to social rights as a mechanism of deterrence and exclusion from full membership. This has major implications, as we shall see, for the education of ASR children. To borrow Hammer's (2000) distinction, it is possible to think of the ways in which the UK for example has tried to make the transition from the first to the second gate much more difficult – to control fully the numbers of people entering the state through asylum-seeking procedures. This change in the focus of UK immigration policy makes Arendt's observation more accurate than ever. It is not the right of asylum that is being challenged through immigration policies, but rather the right of (certain) individuals and groups to claim it (Barlo and Morrison, 2005).

Consequently, the issue of asylum-seeking has become a matter of public debate (Gibney, 2001). Contemporary discourses concerning the refugee are powerful and complex (O'Neill and Spybey, 2003) and are significant for schools, particularly those in which there is a large number of asylum-seeking or refugee families. There are powerful negative images that shape national and local hostility often carried through the media which encourage governments to take a tough stance over immigration. These often racialised images represent refugees, irrespective of their histories, as 'scroungers and criminals' and as 'terrorists'. Below we briefly explore each in turn.

From 'scroungers' to 'criminals'

Asylum-seekers and refugees have increasingly been represented as a threat to the welfare state, to the economy (Geddes, 2005), and as 'scroungers' and 'baggers' (Sivanandan, 2001) searching for ways to enjoy the wealth of income-rich states. The main assumption underlying this image is that asylum-seekers are in fact economic migrants, looking for better lives rather than safety (Marfleet, 2006). Thus they are nothing but bogus asylum-seekers (until proven otherwise) who are abusing the system (Jordan and Düvell, 2002) and hence not only illegal immigrants but also those most likely to be involved with fraudulent activity (Essed and Wesenbeek, 2004). 'At best, the redefined refugee is a maker of false or unfounded claims that must be unmasked through effective bureaucratic scrutiny. At worst, the refugee is criminalized or politicized as a threat to order' (Whitaker, 1998: 414).

The refugee movement, since it is seen as a threat to order, is today increasingly associated with criminality (Marfleet, 2006). This discourse leads to public pressures on governments to act to prevent 'unlawful' asylum-seekers entering the country, and to make the host country less hospitable for them (mainly by restricting their access to welfare and social rights) with the hope that this will deter 'bogus' asylum-seekers. The image of the bogus asylum-seeker as a mere economic migrant seeking a way to a better life through fraudulence has also a direct effect, as we will later see, on the levels of compassion offered to them once in the country.

Floods of asylum-seekers, security and terrorism

> [T]abloids are quick to link and blend the two warnings into an asylum/terrorist hysteria ... The novel fear of the terrorists merged and cemented with the already well-entrenched but constantly in need of new food, hatred of 'spongers', killing two birds with one stone and arming the ongoing crusade against 'welfare scroungers' with a new, indomitable weapon of mass intimidation (Bauman, 2004: 54).

More than any other type of human movement, the irregularity and unpredictability of forced migration have come to symbolise the deficiency of the sovereign power of the state and the permeability of its boundaries (Moran, 2005). Refugees have become the scapegoat of our fears of insecurity in the new unstable global order. Today's common image of *waves* of refugees allegedly *'swamping'* Western states represents this sense of threat and insecurity. The 9/11 events have intensified the sense of insecurity generating a political view of asylum-seeking that draws heavily on discourses of threat and fear to the extent that the labels 'asylum-seeker' and 'refugee' have become identified with terrorism (Muller, 2004).

The new 'Others': racialised discourse

The non-entry policy towards asylum-seekers adopted by Western European nations in the past two decades has much to do with changes to the makeup of the refugee population (Chimni, 1998). Against the backdrop of increasing numbers of asylum-seekers and refugees from developing countries, a new myth has emerged portraying such refugees as fundamentally different from their European counterparts. This belief suggests that, while European refugees satisfy the criteria of political persecution, refugees from the developing world are allegedly just economic migrants. 'By producing the image of a "normal" refugee – White, male, anticommunist – a clear message was sent ... that asylum-seekers were here for no good reason, that they abuse hospitality, and that their numbers are too large' (Chimni, 1998: 357).

Critics argue that the rather generous post-war policy towards asylum-seekers was a Cold War luxury reserved for White European refugees, whereas today the White and wealthy countries seek to protect themselves from what is seen as a threat to their lifestyle and their identity (Richmond, 1994). Therefore, refugees and asylum-seekers find themselves increasingly a target of racism (Marfleet, 2006) – and even *the* main group to suffer from blunt racism in Western countries today. It is possible that racial discourse and the different racial characteristics of contemporary asylum-seekers define the politics of belonging in the UK. This politics of belonging acts as one of the most powerful exclusionary mechanisms towards asylum-seekers, especially when it comes to denying them access to social rights and opportunities to rebuild their lives.

Maintaining such a racialised politics of belonging arguably is only possible when the other emerging images of asylum-seekers (that of 'scroungers' and 'terrorists') justify the withdrawal of Western states from humanitarian discourses and from what otherwise might have been simply racist immigration policies. These different discursive frameworks not only changed the meanings and feelings towards refugees and asylum-seekers but they also created a distinction between, on the one hand, 'normal' or 'genuine' asylum-seekers who still might attract compassion and, on the other hand, those who are bogus, criminal, terrorist and ultimately 'Others' who do not deserve and are unlikely to receive the same reaction. In other words, these discursive shifts influence the access of different individuals and groups to the 'normal' and 'genuine' image of the refugee who is still considered deserving of compassion and access to rights.

In the next chapter we describe the ways in which we conceptualise compassion and belonging – two yardsticks which we used to assess central and local government policy approaches to asylum-seeking and the education of the ASR child. We describe how we designed and conducted empirical research on these sensitive topics within local authorities and with teachers and students in a sample of secondary schools.

3
Researching Compassion and Belonging in the Educational System

One of the challenges, both methodologically and theoretically, when studying forced migration (in educational contexts or others) is how to define the subjects of the research. There is a lack of clarity regarding the definitions of the different types of forced migrant that are often used interchangeably (Phillimore and Goodson, 2008). The most commonly used categories in the UK are *refugees* and *asylum-seekers*, which represent different legal statuses. According to British immigration law, asylum-seekers are those who have applied for asylum, while refugees are those who have proved to be genuine asylum-seekers and have been granted the status of refugees. Refugees are given temporary permission to reside and work in the UK. After five years they are able to apply for indefinite leave to remain (permanent residency) and a year after that they can apply for British citizenship.[1] In contrast, the concepts of 'non-citizen' and 'citizen'[2] are analytical categories which are useful to social scientists when focusing attention on the relationship between different groups of migrants *vis-à-vis* the state, especially in terms of their access to rights, inclusion, belonging and security.[3] We use the term 'citizen' child here to refer to a heterogenous group of young people who have citizen status. The majority are of British descent and have British citizenship but the group also includes naturalised British citizens, EU citizens and those with citizenship in their own country who are temporarily resident in the UK. What they have in common are the rights of citizenship within a nation-state. In contrast, the 'non-citizen' child refers to those children who, having fled, have lost their rights in their own country and have not gained citizenship in the 'host' society. Both asylum-seeking and refugee children are included in this latter category.

The key distinction between these two categories of 'citizen' and 'non-citizen' children are their differences with respect to their right to be children – their right to a 'normal' childhood. The 'citizen' children have an entitlement to health care and education. They may not be fully fledged citizens until they become adults, but they are citizens 'in the making' (Rose, 1990). They are expected to be involved, to be consulted, and to be encouraged to develop their own sense of agency. Their preparation for citizenship is encouraged by the government. The entitlement of the 'citizen' child to education is justified within the logic of citizenship and membership.

In contrast, 'non-citizen' children and their families represent the realities of forced migration of people as a result of war, violence and political conflict. They seek sanctuary in the UK, often on the basis of their country's membership of the Commonwealth, a colonial British past, or diasporic communities. As asylum-seekers, they ask for temporary shelter within the UK; as refugees, they seek the right to build a new life in the country. Yet once here, they are entitled to health care and education under a different logic – that of personhood and more specifically the logic of children's rights. By virtue of being a child and not by virtue of being a citizen, they gain access to certain limited rights which are seen as attached to them as children, including the right to education.

There are various ways in which the significance of this distinction between two groups of young people can be researched. On the whole, social scientific research has employed a macro perspective focusing in particular on the impact of forced migration and diversity of citizenship status on national policies. Yet human mobility and forced migration often have a great effect not just at the level of government but also on local communities. Castles argues that there are contradictions between the logic of central state immigration policy, which is designed to control immigrants, and the approach taken by local government, which is more concerned with the social costs of immigration. He argues therefore that: 'Local dimensions of migration need to be treated as central issues in research and political action' (1998: 182). Similarly, Humpage and Marston's (2006) study of the integration of refugees in Australia found differences in their experiences of recognition and integration at the level of the central state and local communities. These authors suggest that, whereas national immigration policy in the Australian case marginalised and excluded refugees, they nevertheless gained a sense of local belonging. Recent policy reports into the education of ASR children in the UK (such as Mott, 2000; Reakes and Powell, 2004;

Remsbery, 2003) as well as our own research (Arnot and Pinson, 2005) hint at the importance of sociological research into this tension between central and local state.

A sociological imagination is needed to address the complex diversity of civic status which can now be found in our communities and schools. Within educational institutions, the political responses to forced global migration are being played out but not always in the ways intended by central government.

The politics of compassion and belonging

Our research set out to explore these complexities. The approach we have taken involved, as we mentioned earlier, the use of two conceptual lenses, those of *compassion* and *belonging*. We employ these concepts as yardsticks with which to assess the different experiences, practices and understandings developed by central government, local education authorities, schools and teachers in relation to the education of ASR children, their rights and needs and the responsibility of 'others' for their welfare. The integration of these children into mainstream education, the ways in which they are included, the extent to which they are allowed to feel they belong and the degree to which they are treated with compassion are indicators of the degree of commitment on the part of the state education system to its expressed principles of promoting social inclusion, cultural diversity and equality in education. Below we describe the ways in which we conceptualised compassion and belonging when exploring how ASR students are encountered and engaged with in schools.

Conceptualising the politics of compassion

The first yardstick we used to assess the educational policies and practices associated with ASR students was the concept of *compassion* – a concept that has been associated with asylum since 'ancient times'. Historically, a variety of religious traditions endorsed the notion of refuge as implying a moral obligation to offer protection to those seeking asylum. In the Judaeo-Christian tradition, for example, the notion of 'cities of refuge' is referred to. In the Old Testament, the book of Joshua 20 describes them thus:

> [2] Speak to the children of Israel, saying, Appoint out for you cities of refuge, whereof I spake unto you by the hand of Moses:

[3] That the slayer that killeth any person unawares and unwittingly may flee thither: and they shall be your refuge from the avenger of blood.

[4] And when he that doth flee unto one of those cities shall stand at the entering of the gate of the city, and shall declare his cause in the ears of the elders of that city, they shall take him into the city unto them, and give him a place, that he may dwell among them. [...]

[9] These were the cities appointed for all the children of Israel, and for the stranger that sojourneth among them (King James Authorized version)

The notion of compassion entails a diversity of meaning. In our research we wanted to consider not just whether the image and presence of the refugee evokes a compassionate reaction but also to consider the kind of compassion that is expressed and in what ways it might be connected to the politics of national belonging within immigration policy. From a sociological point of view, we needed to consider social and moral reactions to the presence of ASR children in a range of different contexts and among a range of different groups within the education system. But we also had to consider whether compassion could take different forms and, if so, how might such a variety of moral and emotional responses within education affect the ways in which ASR students in schools experience their 'host' society.

In our research, we were particularly interested in thinking about what Williams (2008) recently called the 'moral psychology of social justice'. From his perspective:

Compassion is that disposition, or way-of-being that is most fundamentally other-regarding – always interpersonal [...] It *expands* the boundaries of the self rather than tightening or strengthening them. (Williams, 2008: 7)

Western philosophers (from ancient to modern) have actively engaged in a long-standing debate about the nature of compassion as an emotion, and as a moral and political construct – its meaning, significance and substance.[4] They have occupied themselves since ancient times with exploring the extent to which compassion should be seen as part of moral judgement, and whether it is a natural disposition, a natural human trait, or one that should be cultivated. The relevance of emotions, including compassion, to moral philosophy and whether or not compassion is fundamental to morality is hotly disputed.[5]

Nussbaum's (2001) comprehensive account of these Western philosophical debates provided us with excellent indicators of how we might distinguish different types of compassion. For example, drawing on Aristotle, Nussbaum outlined three key cognitive judgements that have been considered necessary for developing compassionate emotions:

1. An appraisal of the 'size' of suffering of another – making a judgement that the suffering is serious;
2. The belief that the person does not deserve the suffering, that it is not his/her fault or that the suffering is disproportionate in relation to the blame; and,
3. The judgement of one's own vulnerability and possibility of being in the other's position.

Western philosophers who argue for the role of emotion in morality address the nature of such judgements by considering the likely *source* of such compassion. For David Hume (1748[1975]), for example, compassion (he used the term 'benevolence') and sympathy are two intertwined concepts which are central elements of human nature that steer moral conduct. Benevolence is described as our natural desire, as human beings, for the general welfare of others. Hume wrote that 'there is some benevolence, however small, infused in our bosom: some spark of friendship for human kind' (1748[1975]: 271–2) and that this sentiment alone can provide the basis for morals, confronting self-love. It is, however, through our own suffering and the desire to relieve it that we seek to relieve the suffering of others. Sympathy produces a copy or reflection of another person's suffering for us to experience. The sympathy we feel towards the other was what Hume saw as the mechanism that allows the action – benevolence or being compassionate. In other words, there are no purely altruistic acts of compassion. Benevolence and acts of compassion cannot be detached from our own self-interest. In that, he suggested that the source of compassion is in *me* and not in the *other*.

Rousseau's discussion of the nature of compassion in *Emile* (1762[1974]) is particularly relevant to any analysis of the role of education as a moral institution. Rousseau argued that compassion, or what he called *'pitié'*, is not only important for the moral conduct of the individual but it also plays a central role in *social morality*. He saw the young Emile's astonishment at the pain of another as one of the essential foundations of society. The ability to be overwhelmed by the suffering of others was an important part of the moral foundation of any society.[6] Since compassion leads us to recognise our own vulnerability as human beings and our shared humanity with others, it leads us (in turn) to question our fortunate position.[7] Rousseau's notion of compassion therefore is different from that of Hume since he argued that the sources of compassion are not merely in *me* but also in the sense of community or shared humanity:

> the suffering of another will arouse my concern only insofar as I acknowledge some degree of community between us ... what unites all sentient beings in commune is a shared vulnerability to suffering. (Rousseau 1762[1974], quoted in Williams, 2008: 12)

It was also important for us to note that Rousseau gave different meanings to the notion of community. In some of his writings, he stressed the idea of shared humanity as the basis for the sense of community. However, his notion of community also included what we might identify today as a national community. In this context, different social markers (such as 'race', ethnicity, gender and class) might act as barriers to compassion. In that respect, Rousseau's discussion moved us closer to our own sociological concern with the politics of belonging.

Another influence on our thinking through the relationship of self and Other is to be found in the work of Schopenhauer (1837[1995]) who saw compassion as a *union* between the self and the Other, as a pure concern for the wellbeing of the Other which is detached from internal motivations.[8] Influenced by if not indebted to Buddhism, Schopenhauer asserted in *On the Basis of Morality* that only actions stemming from compassion, those of pure justice and philanthropy, have true moral worth (1837[1995]: 138–9). The compassionate individual who identifies himself or herself completely with another is able as a result to remove the barriers between the 'I' and 'non-I'. This identification is not empirical but happens at a metaphysical level. For the compassionate individual, the others are not non-I but 'I once more [...] he [sic] feels himself intimately akin to all beings, takes an immediate interest in their weal and woe' (1837[1995]: 211).

Given this as a proposition, Schopenhauer himself was pessimistic and held a rather negative view of human nature. Not only did he suggest that the majority of human actions are the result of egoism, but he also believed that the amount of compassion that each person possesses is finite and unchanging (1837[1995]: 76–9). Some persons have bountiful amounts of compassion, and others have almost none. Putting aside this rather negative view of people, Schopenhauer's theory raised some important questions for us. For example, what happens when the perceived 'non-I' is very different from the 'I' and when the person's suffering and presence are threatening to the 'I' (as, for example, in how the presence of asylum-seekers is often perceived by the 'host' society). In other words what happens when there is a conflict over resources between the 'I' and the 'non-I' and when the 'I' 'and 'non-I' belong to distinct and different groups?

Nussbaum's (1998) critique of the Christian tradition also alerted us to a key distinction between *agency* and *victimhood*. In Christian traditions, compassion is understood as expressing pity towards the vulnerable. Christian thinkers who understand pity as a central part of Christian life argue 'that these emotions are appropriate expressions of and responses to our vulnerable and imperfect earthly condition' (Nussbaum, 1998). Criticising the expression of compassion as pity, Nussbaum (2001) argues that the existence of agency makes disaster and the suffering of the Other in our eyes even more tragic. Moral social judgements of compassion, therefore, she adds, need to be based on a notion that the Other who suffers has agency and is only a temporary a victim of circumstances.

The social conditions for compassion: equality, respect and justice

These philosophical debates, particularly the arguments of Nussbaum and Schopenhauer, were important stepping stones for our research in schools and our interpretation of our data not least because of the distinctions they make between pity, victimhood and agency, and between the 'I' and the 'not-I'. We needed, however, to go further and think sociologically about the social and educational conditions for encouraging compassion. Moving Schopenhauer's (1837[1995]) argument from the individual level to the social, it is conceivable that a society, as a collective, develops compassion towards another group – a group of *Others*. When the boundaries of 'us' are extended, we are able to conceive the wellbeing of the *Others* (other groups or societies) as part of our own collective wellbeing and see their suffering as our own.

Similarly the relationship between compassion and rights was important for our understanding of the politics of compassion. Having compassion, according to Simone Weil, is taking the other person's rights to our heart. Weil points out that rights are often used as 'a barrier which insulates and isolates others from us' (Weil quoted in Teuber, 1982: 235). Here compassion, she argues, requires that we see rights as a means designed to secure and protect. Therefore, in order to act with compassion it is necessary, not merely to respect the rights of another, but also to look 'behind' these rights to the interests his/her rights are designed to secure and protect (Teuber, 1982). In other words compassion calls for a *needs-based equity*. Through Weil's writings, the three elements of *equality, morality* and *emotions* are starting to merge.

For example, Weil argues that equality involves respect for the whole person. It is the public expression of love. Friendship and love, she writes, 'make equalities and do not search for them' (Weil, 1970). Compassion then can be seen as a kind of friendship without intimacy (ibid.). Weil claims, in ways not dissimilar to Rousseau, that compassion allows us to put ourselves in someone else's place, to look at them as equals, and hence to be concerned about their rights. Thus equality can be understood not just as a principle for organising society but as a moral virtue (Teuber, 1982). Thus, for Weil, the concepts of equality and compassion are uniquely bound together along with our regard for other human beings – primarily our love and friendly regard for others naturally builds equal relationships. Here compassion is seeing someone from the point of view of what *matters for him/her*. This notion is closely embedded in her definition of equality as reading people without reading them off and allowing their reality to emerge.

> A respect for persons in their concrete specificity, urges us to regard each person on his or her own terms [...] The compassionate individual looks upon his[her] view and opinions of others as provisional [...] Compassion involves seeing someone other than ourselves for the being he[she] is [...] and regardless of whether his[her] actions fit into our expectations. (Teuber, 1982: 227, our additions)

Being compassionate in this sense allows us to see the Other, even a distant Other, from the 'inside' and take the issue of their rights to our hearts, seeing it as our own concern (Teuber, 1982). Weil believes that it is especially important to cultivate compassion, especially for persons in situations significantly different from our own. One way of cultivating such compassion is, as Nussbaum (2001) suggests, to develop the ability not only to judge the suffering of another as serious and unfair but also as mattering to our own scheme of goals – in other words being able to see the suffering of the Other as contradicting one's own goals, or seeing the interests behind the Other's pursuit of rights and protection as part of those goals.

Conceptualising the politics of belonging

As we saw in Chapter 2, our study also needed to operationalise in the empirical sense the concept of 'belonging', particularly the 'politics of belonging' – a relatively new analytical (sociological) concept (Croucher, 2004) which so far has received little empirical attention in social research (Crowley, 1999). To a great extent the use of 'belonging' emerged as part of the dissatisfaction with the usefulness and adequacy of 'identity' and 'citizenship' (or 'membership'). Croucher (2004) suggests that the power of 'belonging' lies in the fact that it captures the affective dimension of identity and membership which other concepts neglect. It is different from citizenship or formal membership since it involves a consideration of reciprocal relations *between* group members and *between* an individual and a group (Crowley, 1999: 19). The notion of belonging refers to who belongs and how belonging is determined, but it is more than that. It also captures the emotive aspect: whether individuals *feel* that they belong, whether they develop an attachment or commitment to a certain group. 'Belonging is about emotional attachment, about feeling "at home" and … about feeling "safe"' (Yuval-Davis et al., 2006: 2). Moreover, belonging is something you achieve or become (Bell, 1999; Croucher, 2004).

The notion of a 'politics of belonging' is 'an attempt to give a "thicker" account of the political and social dynamics of integration' (Crowley, 1999: 22). The aim is not asking merely *who* belongs – rather it is about the discursive processes within which people achieve the affective dimension of belonging and are able to perform it (Bell, 1999). It also means asking who has the power to articulate what it means to belong (Crowley, 1999) and who is allowed to perform it. Not surprisingly, the politics of belonging take place in different contexts and at different levels. It can refer to the process in which individuals as well as societies negotiate belonging (Croucher, 2004). As Crowley (1999) points out, when used in the context of national polities, the politics of belonging can represent 'the dirty work of boundary maintenance'.[9] In a globalising age characterised by human mobility, immigration policies become a powerful site for the politics of belonging.

Yuval-Davis et al. (2006) suggest that we need to consider three different contexts in which such boundary-maintenance work is conducted: the temporal, the spatial and the intersectional. In other words, different groups of people are subject to different politics of belonging according to place and time; and in the same temporal and spatial contexts, various groups might be subject to different politics of belonging (depending on their positionality in terms of ethnicity, 'race', religion, class, gender and immigration status). This is especially evident today in relation to asylum-seekers and refugees and the reception they receive from Western democratic states. The politics of belonging reflect the need of the state to define its boundaries, its political identity, and its commitment to tolerance and equality (as we discussed in Chapter 2).

In our study, we use the concept of the politics of belonging to examine the different and contradicting logics behind immigration control policies and the changing discourses of asylum-seeking in the UK. Our interest focuses on the seemingly contradictory activities and policies which contribute to the discursive construction of belonging at national, local and institutional levels. We were made aware that the various agencies of the state can employ different politics of belonging towards the same group and at different junctures (Humpage and Marston, 2006). This understanding of the complexity of assessing government policy on civic belonging and membership was valuable in thinking about how to research the education of ASR children.

How to research forced migration

Here we describe our various interlinked research projects on the politics of ASR education. The book draws on the findings of a number of exploratory, empirical studies conducted by the three authors. The first study, entitled *The Education of Asylum Seeker and Refugee Children: A Study of LEA and School Values, Policies and Practices* (Arnot and Pinson, 2005),[10] was a policy project that sought to map the approaches and support systems developed by central government (the Home Office and DfES) and LEAs in response to ASR children's needs and rights. We also draw on a second project entitled *Schooling, Security, and Belonging: The Relations Between Asylum-Seeking and 'Host' Students In Secondary School.*[11] This qualitative project focused on teachers' values and compassion for and reaction to ASR children and explored the sense of belonging and security of 'citizen' and ASR secondary school students. We also drew upon supportive material from two empirical studies on the experiences of ASR children in the UK: the *'Extraordinary Childhoods'* study conducted by Mano Candappa and Itohan Egharevba (2000),[12] and a study of education and schooling for ASR students in Scotland (Candappa et al., 2007).[13] Finally, public testimonies of named teachers and schools posted on anti-deportation websites were also drawn upon in order to uncover the range of political engagements of teachers and schools with government immigration policy.

Combining several research projects has become rather common in the field of refugee studies as well as in research into the education of ASR children, despite the methodological and analytical challenges it carries. Phillimore and Goodson (2008) explain that the scarcity of data, the difficulty of obtaining data, and the fact that it is a relatively underdeveloped area both methodologically and theoretically, calls for such flexibility. Though drawing on different sources of data, all the different projects have a common thread providing the book with methodological and theoretical coherence – that thread is our concern with the ways in which the presence of the ASR child influences the education system and exposes the educational values of the state and its institutions.

In 2003 we set up the *Consortium for Research on the Education of Asylum-Seeking and Refugee Children* under the umbrella of the General Teaching Council (GTC) and later to be joined by the National Union of Teachers (NUT) and the Refugee Council. This consortium funded the first project by Arnot and Pinson (2005). It was clear that there were no central official public data on ASR children, information about their admission to schools or their academic attainment. In other words, ASR children were statistically invisible.[14] The first challenge was to consider how best to research the educational experiences of the undocumented, the statistically invisible, and the hidden. Furthermore, there was no central policy addressing what should be the standard of education provided for these children or how it should be provided. The first task, therefore, was a national 'mapping exercise' that aimed to grasp the national, local and institutional picture. This mapping exercise had two aims: 1) to gain better knowledge and information about the types of experience LEAs and schools provided for ASR children, and 2) to build the necessary body of information for our partners, the GTC, the NUT and the Refugee Council, to generate 'good' practice, and for ourselves to provide the base for further research.

We designed a two-phase policy study which first focused on the ways in which central and local government and various ministries addressed the arrival and settlement of ASR families and the education of their children. This phase included a telephone survey of 58 English LEAs, using mostly open-ended questions[15] to discover the nature of their policy and funding strategies, their methods of data collection and monitoring practices, and the forms of support they offered such children. The telephone survey was followed by case studies of three LEAs with a strong inclusive ethos.

Building on this experience and Candappa's previous (2000 and 2007) research, the second project, *Schooling, Security, and Belonging*, went deeper into the nature of ASR students' school experience – in particular teachers' views of such students and the ways in which 'citizen' students perceived and related to ASR students in their school community. Focusing this time on case studies in three secondary schools with a strong inclusive ethos, we sought to explore the ways in which the presence of ASR in these schools affects the worlds of teachers and 'citizen' children and how the schools' ethos, policies and values influence the experiences of ASR students and their relationship with teachers and 'citizen' students. Here we were searching for ways that would allow us to unpack the complex values, experiences and relationships within schools. We used the second project to develop appropriate research tools to explore both compassion and belonging.

The sampling challenge

We grappled with a number of sampling challenges: one of which was the problem of finding the relevant sites in which ASR students were located, the most appropriate people to talk to, and the best schools in which to explore such issues. We also faced the challenge of how to capture the diversity of ASR experiences and relationships with teachers and other students. Our aim in the first project was to capture the different local experiences, practices and policy approaches. We employed a 'purposeful sample' (Patton, 2002) of local educational authorities in England. The sample included 58 local authorities in a range of different rural and urban localities. We purposely included a high number of LEAs in dispersal areas and London boroughs since we believed that, in these locations, there would be more activity around the presence of ASR students. The sample included 35 rural and urban LEAs that were defined by the Home Office as 'dispersal areas', 12 LEAs in non-dispersal areas and 13 London boroughs – most of which hosted large numbers of asylum-seekers and refugees. Numbers of ASR students in these 58 LEAs varied from as little as 10 to over 5,000 in some London boroughs, where some LEAs had more than a decade of experience with ASR students and some had been dealing with ASR students for only a year.[16]

Another methodological challenge was identifying the informants from whom we would learn about the local authority approach to ASR pupils. Our strategy involved asking each of the 58 LEAs to identify the officer responsible for ASR students in the LEA. When a contact person was hard to identify, we approached the EMAS (Ethnic Minority Achievement Service) or EAL (English as Additional Language) units and asked them to identify the officer responsible for this area. The 58 LEA officers that were interviewed for our survey had different roles and ranks within the LEA.[17]

The second stage of this project, *A Study of LEA and School Values, Policies and Practices*, developed the analysis through three LEA case studies. In both projects, we decided to focus on cases (LEAs and schools respectively) that had an inclusive ethos. They would be most likely, we felt, to be trying to promote a more explicit commitment to children's rights and social belonging. Drawing on the analysis of the telephone survey, three LEAs were identified in 2004 as employing a holistic approach in very different settings – Cheston, a northern urban LEA in a dispersal area with a group of some 300 ASR students; Greenshire, a rural LEA in a non-dispersal area that also had approximately 300 ASR students; and Horton, a London borough, with 5,500 ASR students.

In each of the three case study LEAs, we collected relevant policy documents, interviewed one member of the senior management of the LEA and all key officers working directly with ASR students (between three and six officers in each LEA). Our strategy was similar to the principle that guided us in tracing key informants in the first survey phase. We asked each LEA to nominate a primary and secondary school that exemplified the ethos and approach to ASR students adopted by the LEA. Our school sample therefore reflected in some ways what was seen as 'good practice' within the maintained sector in those localities – however, because of this they cannot be considered to be representative or to reflect the work of all schools in these authorities. We conducted interviews with headteachers, deputy heads and support teachers in these schools trying to find out how they conceptualised and addressed the needs of ASR students and the politics around the presence of such students in the locality.[18]

The *Schooling, Security, and Belonging* project focused on three secondary schools with contrasting demographics, which were known to their LEAs for their inclusive practice. The project investigated teachers' values and practices in supporting ASR students, and the latter's experiences and their relationships with 'citizen' students. It was important to sample case studies with different school populations. A maximum variation sample meant that we needed to include schools where ASR students would find themselves in very different social environments. We selected *Fairfield School*, an ethnically mixed school which had over 40 per cent Pakistani, Bengali, Black African, Indian and African-Caribbean population and small numbers (approximately 30 a year) of ASR students. *City School*, a typical inner-city multi-ethnic, multi-faith London school in which in 2003 asylum-seekers and refugees constituted 10 per cent of its 1,343 students, was our second school case study. This school had a strong history of work on anti-racism, anti-bullying and other equality policies. Fairfield and City schools were located in LEAs which the first project found had multi-agency inclusive (holistic) approaches. Fairfield was first visited as part of the first project in Greenshire. We also wanted a school that represented a different demographic, a predominantly White school with manageable geographical proximity. Since such an LEA was not found in the first project we drew on Candappa's previous research to ask another LEA to recommend an appropriate school; *Fordham School* was identified as having both an inclusive ethos and ASR students. Fordham, a large, predominantly White school, without a strong history of anti-racist or multicultural work, had small numbers (under 10) of unaccompanied ASR students. We considered it particularly important to find such a school in order to understand how inclusive approaches might emerge when there has been no previous extensive experience of ethnic minorities, where ASR students are much more visible, and hence might suffer from greater hostility, and where schools, as we know from other projects (Ofsted, 2003a), have much greater difficulty dealing with the presence of ASR students.

In each school, individual semi-structured in-depth interviews were conducted with four or five key members of teaching or support staff who worked in close proximity with ASR students, or had an overview of the school policy in relation to them (for example, the headteacher, assistant head, citizenship or religious education teachers, EAL and EMA support teachers, or pastoral care staff). However, we were aware that a different image might have emerged had we interviewed other teachers who would not necessarily know who were ASR students or who might be less sympathetic to their needs as a distinct group, having had that much less contact with them. The individual interviews with the Head and staff focused on the sorts of values ascribed to in relation to ASR students and families, and whether the school was considered a safe place in which ASR students felt they belonged, and in which they could prosper academically. Teachers were asked directly about compassion. They were asked to describe their understanding of compassion, the obstacles to compassion, and whether and how they would actively encourage compassion towards ASR students in their classes. Below we describe some of the issues we faced as researchers.

Sampling invisible and visible students

The ways in which a sample of ASR students is obtained and interviewed raises a number of methodological and ethical concerns. ASR students are often a 'hidden' or 'invisible' population; schools do not necessarily collect data on students' immigration status (often preferring not to), and parents are not obliged to disclose such information. For research purposes we therefore could not readily identify ASR students – sampling was heavily dependent on the level of knowledge in the school. Phillimore and Goodson (2008) observe that researchers seeking to sample asylum-seekers and refugees often had to rely heavily on community organisations. This raises the question of whether in this way they can identify the best cases related to their research questions for qualitative research, or to obtain a representative sample if using quantitative methods. Our success in obtaining a diverse sample of Year 7 to Year 13 male and female ASR students in terms of their ethnicity, religion and educational experiences, was in great measure due to the support of participating schools. The difficulty we faced here was that schools may have chosen ASR and 'citizen' students whose views illustrated the school's approach.

We were very much aware of the issue of exposing students publicly as asylum-seekers or creating anxiety in relation to their legal status. Since these students cannot be called out easily and often wish not to be labelled, sampling raises ethical questions about the role of the research in their lives. We overcame the problem of 'making them visible' by interviewing a range of pupils: ASR, minority ethnic and White British. For that purpose we also avoided a design that included mixed discussion groups of ASR and 'citizen' students that might have revealed their legal status. We were conscious of the fact that bringing ASR students into a group discussion (even if comprising only ASR students) could put pressure on them to talk about their experiences in front of their peers (for the first time perhaps). We addressed this difficulty by not asking them directly during the focus group discussion about their asylum experience but rather we phrased questions in a more general way, allowing them to bring out their personal histories if they wished to. In the event, we found the ASR students selected for interview chose what to say about themselves and while some kept their silence, others had no hesitation in discussing issues surrounding security and belonging.

Our sample contained considerable diversity of experience that in the space of the project we could not explore in depth. For example, some of the ASR students were refugees, others asylum-seekers; some were unaccompanied, while others were living with various relatives. Some had been in the UK for some time, others were newly arrived. We were keen to hear a diverse range of voices so the ASR students who participated in the individual interviews and group discussions came from a wide range of countries (for example, the Congo, Somalia,

Lebanon, Afghanistan, Croatia, Nigeria and Iran). However, one of the criteria we had to use was that they were able to communicate in English. This, of course, also tipped our sample towards the more 'integrated' student.

When sampling 'citizen' students in the same year groups as the ASR students, we were also aware that we needed thoughtful students who could engage with the issues of the research, and as a result we probably did not access the full range of student voices in the community. Those students who agreed to participate in individual and group interviews tended to be self-selecting and reflective on issues around asylum and migration, and on how ASR students are viewed among their peers and wider community. Our sample contained British students with a range of hyphenated identities. While a few were White British, many of the minority ethnic British students had other cultural–national origins, including Pakistani, Italian, Spanish, Irish, Moroccan and Nigerian. Describing such students just as British would ignore many students' own migrant family histories which might have also affected their views on asylum and the compassion needed to address the stranger. Our research strategy was therefore not to focus on their national identity and identification but on their citizenship status.

Ethics and language

There are many other methodological and ethical issues in conducting research with young people (Alderson and Morrow, 2004). Our concern was that we engaged with students as social actors, influencing as well as being influenced by the world they live in (Prout, 2002). We needed to recognise that they were active participants in the research. Our objective was to uncover the world of the school and peer relations from the perspectives of young people, and to give them a voice in our understanding of their worlds. At the same time we were aware of the 'ethical asymmetry' (Christensen and Prout, 2002) in power relations within research, especially with young people, which needed to be reduced as far as possible. We therefore paid special attention to empowering students within the research process: we sought their consent to participate through a colourful leaflet which explained the research objectives in young-person-friendly language, and how their participation in the research could help improve schools for all students. We gave students the option of discussing the project further with the researcher prior to consenting, if they so wished. At the interview the young person's right not to reply to a question(s) if they so wished, and to withdraw from the interview and the research at any time, was explained; and, as with all other interviewees, we requested young people's consent to have the interview recorded. Privacy and confidentiality were also issues of particular concern; students were assured of this, and to protect their identities, and as discussed with them, their names and those of their schools were anonymised. To mark our appreciation of their participation in the study in a way that could contribute to their school record, participating students were presented with an individually signed Certificate of Achievement from the University of Cambridge. In short, we endeavoured to ensure that respect was integral to the design and conduct of the study.

Our research aimed to uncover the types and forms of expression of compassion and belonging. These concepts immediately raised specific methodological and language issues. We had to be careful in designing our instruments that the language we used was accessible to students and relevant to their lives. At the same time we were discussing complex issues such as rights, migration, justice and belonging. We were concerned with the question of how to retain depth and complexity while using everyday language. To overcome this difficulty in the individual 'citizen' student interviews and group discussions, we used scenarios based on the real-life experiences of refugee children drawn from Candappa and Egharevba's (2000) research as a way of teasing out students' initial reactions to the notion of asylum. This method proved to be useful and generated rich and complex discussion with young people, especially in relation to the concept of Britishness and to students' understanding of what it would mean to belong.

The issue of language became more pressing when interviewing asylum-seeking children. Many of these students were new to the UK and did not have the language levels to engage fully with in-depth interviews. In our interviews we used simple concepts such as 'home' to trigger a discussion about a complex notion such as 'belonging', and in general we used simple language, with concrete examples if the language in the interview schedules was proving difficult. We were very aware that probing experiences of forced migration might lead to a reawakening of painful memories. Therefore we made a decision not to probe deeply. Over and above the student's right to request that the interview be temporarily halted or terminated, we were alert to signs that the young person did not wish to continue a particular line of discussion. We asked about migration experience, about moving between countries and about being new to school, but not directly about what it felt like to be an asylum-seeker or refugee or how their legal status affected their lives. We mostly felt there was a lot about them we did not know. Phillimore and

Goodson (2008) also point out that since ASR students often feel dis-empowered both by their state of origin and the host state, in order to investigate their experience in a way that will not disempower them or 'force' them to present an image they think is expected of them, trust between them and the researcher is crucial. We were aware that research with vulnerable groups requires a rapport and trust between interviewer and interviewee, which needed to be built into the research process. Yet, although time was given in the interview to build up a rapport with the interviewee, we often felt that more time to build trust was needed. Our findings reflect the level of trust we achieved rather than the depth of young peoples' experiences – they can only be read as indicative of patterns which would need much more in-depth research.

Reflections

This chapter has laid out a difficult research terrain. Our theoretical goals were challenging and in conducting this research we were mindful of the need to ensure that at each level of the educational system we identified the discursive work that frames ASR education. Our research is exploratory in the sense of attempting to define a sociological approach that is focused on the moral conditions underlying educational policy-making.

The starting point for our account is the political context in which schools operate. We begin by taking a critical look at the messages which schools receive from central government about the most appropriate approach to responding to the issue of asylum. The political messages create the conditions under which schools are resourced and advised. The messages given by the UK government, as we shall see, are contradictory and open to the criticism that they bear little relation to the historic connection of asylum to compassionate values. As well, the notion of belonging that they create raises the question as to whether, from the UK government's point of view, schools should even consider it appropriate to try and integrate the asylum-seeking child.

4
The Asylum-seeking Child as Migrant: Government Strategies

> [A]sylum has been an active area of government policy... but one
> where policy has had the effect of generating social exclusion, rather
> than preventing or ameliorating it. (Burchardt, 2005, p. 210)

The education of asylum-seeking children in the UK has been substantially influenced by the country's immigration and asylum policy
developed by the Home Office. The extensive state activity in the past
two decades in the area of asylum and immigration has, in effect,
co-opted other arms of the state (the educational system being one) into
immigration enforcement (Cohen, 2002: 538). Changes in immigration
policy have far-reaching effects on the lives, education and wellbeing of
asylum-seeking children resident in the UK and also, as we shall show
in later chapters, on the work of teachers and the ways in which schools
and students engage with the issue of asylum emotionally, morally and
politically.

Our aim in this chapter is to describe the ways in which ASR children
are constructed and located within immigration policy and treated by
central government. We consider, on the one hand, the politics of compassion and belonging which are constructed through contemporary
immigration and asylum policies, and on the other, the ways in which
young asylum-seekers fit into these politics. We explore the UK response
to the 'stranger at the gate' and the 'stranger within', the construction of
different categories of migrant and the consequences for ASR children
who find themselves caught up in the processes of dispersal, detention
and deportation.

Granting asylum: a matter of pride or a threat?

For many centuries, Britain has had a proud reputation as a country
where people fleeing harsh treatment from their political or religious

views can find safe refuge and build a new life. (Home Office, 2005a: 12)

Even prior to the 1951 UN Refugee Convention the UK prided itself on being open to receiving refugees. Both Conservative and Labour governments in the post-war period strengthened this image of Britain's ethical position in global affairs (Joppke, 1999; Pirouet, 2001). Even, or perhaps especially, today – when there is extensive state activity around issues of asylum (aimed at reducing the numbers of those applying for asylum and those granted the right to stay in the UK) – this long-standing commitment to those fleeing persecution is publicly emphasised. In the introduction to a Home Office report Des Browne MP wrote: 'The fact that Britain has always extended a hand to refugees from persecution around the world is one of the proudest elements of our tradition' (Home Office, 2004c: 3). The 'moral duty to protect those genuinely fleeing death or persecution' (Charles Clarke, Home Office, 2005a: 7) was seen, as the then Prime Minister Tony Blair argued, as integral to what it means to be 'British':

> I believe the people of this country understand all this. It is in their nature to be moderate and tolerant. They have, over many decades, welcomed those who desperately need a safe haven. This generosity and tolerance helps explain why race relations here have in general, been a quite success story. (Home Office, 2005a: 5)

However, 'being tolerant' means being compassionate only towards those who are seen as 'desperately' in need of 'our' help where a person's suffering is understood to be 'real', 'grave' and, most importantly, 'unfair'. At the heart of such compassionate reactions lie powerful notions about what Britishness is rather than any necessary understanding of the needs of the Other. In fact, the refugee as Other who should be helped by a compassionate Britain is somewhat hidden in these statements. Welcoming refugees seems to have more to do with the country's self-interest in maintaining its image as a tolerant society than with social morality. Also, as Gibney (2004) argues, such tolerance towards asylum-seekers was associated with the period between 1900 and the 1970s when there were relatively low numbers of refugees and, importantly, when those seeking asylum came from Europe and were predominantly White. At that time, not only was the suffering of refugees seen as genuine, but the perceived similarity between 'us' and 'them' also contributed to their positive reception.

In contrast Joppke (1999: 128) notes that when asylum-seekers started to come in large numbers from Asia and Africa, expressions of compassion were sacrificed to a different political logic – 'in the age of mass asylum-seeking, that tradition [of welcoming them] fell victim to the zero-immigration imperative'.[1] At the official level Britain never withdrew its public moral commitment to protect those in need. What changed was the discursive representation of the refugee and the ways in which the government judged who was a genuine asylum-seeker, and therefore deserving of such protection.

As in other Western countries, the image of asylum-seekers in Britain has changed greatly over the past two decades. Some scholars identify the arrival of Tamil refugees in 1987 as the turning point in a shift in British public opinion and government immigration policy (Joppke, 1999; Parekh, 2000; Pirouet, 2001). The Tamils were not only more visible than European refugees, and different from 'us', but they also arrived in larger numbers and in groups rather than as individuals (Pirouet, 2001). With the arrival of the Tamils, and more profoundly during the 1990s when the volume of those seeking asylum in Britain increased significantly and their national origins diversified even further, the term 'refugee' arguably lost both its humanitarian as well as its legal technical meaning (Kundnani, 2001). Asylum-seekers came to signify not just an Other but an unwanted, more dangerous 'alien' (Cohen, 2006; O'Neill and Harindranath, 2006). At their most dangerous, asylum-seekers create an impression, in Bauman's words, that:

> There are always too many of *them*. 'Them' are the fellows of whom there should be fewer – or better still none at all. And there are never enough of us. 'Us' are the folks of whom there should be more. (Bauman, 2004: 34)

Recognition of this danger can be found, according to Gedalof (2004), even in the title of the White Paper *Secure Borders, Safe Haven*, since it suggests that first 'we' need to secure 'our' identity, 'our' borders, before we can let 'them' in. Government regularly uses such phrases as: 'those coming into *our* country' (Home Office, 2002: 4, emphasis added), or 'around 191,000 of *them* came here ...' (ibid.: 40 emphasis added). Shire (2008: 9) adds that the image of asylum-seekers swamping the island is also racialised. The underpinning of that discussion, the alien wedge notion, is still there – the notion of being invaded by hordes of people coming over here to 'rip off' and 'swamp us'. The recent concept of 'immigrant', Shire (ibid.) argues, has replaced the once 'non-White' Commonwealth subject, returning 'to a kind of Powellism[2] in the British social, cultural and political landscape, but with a twist'. By the turn of the 21st century, asylum-seekers had become the new aliens who posed a threat to social stability, not least because of their non-Whiteness (a racialised image of those most needing protection and shelter). They became a legitimate scapegoat for normally taboo racial sentiments in the UK (Kundnani, 2001; Lynn and Lea, 2003; Sales, 2005). Further, the image of the asylum-seeker as non-assimilable, as a threat to social cohesion, gave legitimacy to policies of control and exclusion (Malloch and Stanley, 2005) and to a politics of belonging that reaffirm so-called 'British values' (Yuval-Davis, 2005). Similarly Kundnani (2001: 52) concludes that:

> [T]he image of asylum seekers is defined not by what they are, but simply by the fact that they are 'not one of us', and are, therefore, a threat to 'our way of life'. The emphasis is not on who is to be excluded but on what is to be protected.

The threat to Britain's traditional values and even the loss of the country's image as a safe haven for refugees was blamed now not on these processes of Othering but on 'bogus' asylum-seekers who exploited Britain's traditional hospitality:

> [T]raditional tolerance is under threat. It is under threat from those who come and live here illegally by breaking rules and abusing our hospitality. (Prime Minister Blair's Foreword, Home Office, 2005a: 5)

As we shall see, one of the ways the Home Office and the Labour government in the last decade justify the focus of immigration control on asylum-seekers is by portraying asylum-seekers as 'bogus, unlawful refugees', 'illegal immigrants' and 'criminals' seeking better lives rather than sanctuary (Cohen, 2006; Kundnani, 2001). The White Paper *Secure Borders, Safe Haven* (Home Office, 2002) was found to have 219 instances of words associated with criminal activities attached to asylum-seekers, such as illegal, crime, abuse, fraud, offenders, terrorists and violence (Summers, 2004).[3] In recent years Home Office publications have added to this pathological criminalised view of ASR families and individuals by placing terms such as 'illegal immigrants' and 'asylum-seekers' in contiguity and often using them interchangeably. It is not insignificant that in the introduction to *Secure Borders, Safe Haven*, David Blunkett, then Home Secretary, referred to the need to address criminal activities such as trafficking in the same breath as he mentions targets in relation to asylum policy:

> We will need to be tough in tackling, Europe wide, the people traffickers ... It requires us to tackle illegal working ... and dealing with gangmasters and corrupt businesses ... We need radical changes to our asylum system to ensure its effectiveness, fairness ... (Home Office, 2002: 6)

This inferred illegality of asylum-seekers was also given official recognition in the Home Office asylum and immigration five-year strategy *Controlling our Borders*, 'since the late 1980s there has been significant abuse of the asylum system by those who are economic migrants but claimed to be persecuted' (Home Office, 2005a: 17).

The politics of compassion emerging from this narrative are clear. If asylum-seekers are potentially no more than illegal bogus refugees whose suffering is neither real nor grave, then they are not in need of protection and the UK government and the country itself have no moral obligation to show compassion towards them. This criminalisation discourse intensified and was aggravated by the violent events of 9/11 and 7/7, with asylum-seekers now additionally portrayed as potential terrorists and as threats to security (Malloch and Stanley, 2005; Sales, 2005; Yuval-Davis, 2005).[4] Summing up government and public discourse on asylum in this period, Pirouet (2001: 3) asks whether

> the British people are being robbed of a cause for pride with regard to those who seek refuge here? Is what is happening really the fault of 'bogus' asylum seekers who have abused our hospitality, or has the welcome worn thin?

However, there are other consequences, not least the ways in which asylum-seekers and refugees are talked about in public and particularly in the mass media – a civic context which can directly affect the work of the school. The ways in which media politics takes up the issue strongly influences government concerns about the hostility of the electorate to more immigration. The media has played to common-sense populist notions of Britishness and fears about asylum-seekers and immigrants generally. The tabloid press in particular allows the racialised voice of, for example, the BNP to be heard, while at the same time implying that the arrival of new asylum-seekers will reduce, if not wipe out, working-class opportunities in schools, jobs, housing and even medical treatment. Asylum-seekers also tended to be blamed for a variety of social problems in Britain – from a high crime rate, through terrorism, to the state of the housing and job markets (Greenslade, 2005). Given this powerful role, it is worth taking account of the findings of media researchers who have focused attention on the exceptionally hostile press given to asylum-seekers and refugees.

Media politics

Greenslade (2005: 3), for example, supports the widely held view that the media 'has done little, if anything, to inform the public about the complexity of asylum and immigration issues or to engender *any sense of compassion* ...' (our emphasis). In the past decade, the media has played a pivotal role in the criminalisation of asylum-seekers, strengthening the thesis that the majority of asylum-seekers do not deserve compassion and steering hostility towards them. Research conducted by the Information Centre about Asylum and Refugees (ICAR) (2004) suggests that, in the past decade, the media has become obsessively occupied with the growing numbers of asylum-seekers. The media often uses alarmist language such as 'millions', 'thousands and thousands' and 'massive' (IRR, 2000; Malloch and Stanley, 2005) which fosters the image of Britain being 'swamped' and 'flooded' with asylum-seekers.

In 2003, ICAR monitored 17 newspapers in the span of two months and found that: 'This two-month sample of newspapers yielded so many articles on asylum that it was difficult to devise a monitoring scheme which was broad enough ...'(ICAR, 2004: 19). Within this period, the *Daily Mail* and *The Sun* ran stories on asylum up to six and seven days a week, sometimes with several per day. Greenslade (2005) reported that in 2003–4, the *Daily Mail* and the *Daily Express* had become obsessed with asylum issues and ran more articles than any other newspapers, frequently dedicating the front page to negative stories on asylum-seekers, fostering a false sense of crisis. Research reported by the Migrant and Refugee Communities Forum (MRCF, 2007) found that, between January 2000 and January 2006, *The Sun, Daily Mail, Daily Express, Daily Star* and their Sunday editions published 8,163 articles on refugees and asylum-seekers (almost five articles per day).

Media reports of asylum-seeker and immigration statistics, especially in the British tabloids, have often been found to be inaccurate, exaggerated and unsourced (Buchanan et al., 2003; Greenslade, 2005; ICAR, 2004; MRCF, 2007). Such coverage also often fails to distinguish between different types of migrants, especially between economic migrants and asylum-seekers, in a way that gives the false impression that the majority of migrants entering the UK are in fact asylum-seekers (Buchanan et al., 2003). The report 'What's the Story?' (Buchanan et al., 2003), which analysed British media coverage of asylum issues over a 12-week period in 2002, found that 51 different labels were used by the media to describe asylum-seekers – the majority of which were derogatory, provocative and often meaningless (for example, the use of labels such as 'illegal refugees'). The ICAR (2004: 35) study also found out that the most commonly used terms in tabloid headlines about asylum-seekers were 'arrested', 'jailed' and 'guilty'. Words frequently used were 'bogus', 'false', 'illegal', 'failed', 'rejected'. Other widely used terms in newspapers were 'scrounger, sponger, fraudster, robbing the system', 'burden/strain on resources', 'illegal working, cheap labour, cash in hand, black economy', 'criminal', 'criminal violent', 'arrested, jailed, guilty', 'mob, horde, riot, rampage, disorder', 'a threat, a worry, and to be feared'. In contrast, the words 'genuine', 'real', 'successful' did not appear even once in headlines in the two-month period.

An awareness by the Labour government of the political role of such media labelling and the power of mobilising negative public opinion on asylum-seekers may have led it to adopt stricter rather than more humane responses and measures in relation to asylum applicants (Statham, 2003). Kundnani (2001) describes how recent official and public discourse operates as a vicious circle when it comes to asylum-seekers. Suspicions are raised by the media or by the government about the sincerity of asylum-seekers' claims; this has the effect of driving the Home Office to introduce more obstacles in the way of those wishing to gain refugee status; as a result fewer asylum applications pass as genuine; which in turn proves the popular view that the majority are bogus and justifies ever more draconian measures. The result of this government–media interface is that asylum-seekers find it more and more difficult to prove that their claim is genuine, to gain protection and to receive a compassionate or welcoming response.

Indeed, the main concern of the Home Office in the past decade has been to reduce the numbers of asylum-seekers,[5] to decrease the number of applicants granted refuge and to increase the numbers of swift and successful removals of 'failed' asylum-seekers.[6] The Home Office makes considerable effort to advertise any drop in asylum numbers as a success. For example, the summary of the Home Office Annual Asylum Statistical Report in 2004 stated that, while the numbers of asylum-seekers in Europe fell by 19 per cent during 2003, in the UK they fell by 42 per cent (Home Office, 2004a). There is a machismo in immigration controls that manifests itself in comments such as those by Charles Clarke, when introducing the five-year asylum and immigration plan:

> We have made major progress in the last few years. We have strength-ened our borders by operating our own controls [...] We have tight-ened the asylum system against abuse, reducing applications by 67% from their peak. We have doubled the number of removals ... since 1997 (Home Office, 2005a: 7).

In order to meet these political goals, recent immigration and asylum policies have tightened control over UK borders and the conditions of entry into the country. New visa restrictions have been introduced, travelling without documentation has been made a criminal offence, practices such as designating certain countries as 'safe', or so-called 'safe third countries' were designed to prevent potential asylum-seekers from applying for refuge in Britain in the first place, and more 'effective' and speedy processes of asylum decision were developed with the purpose of deterring unfounded applications. In April 2008 a new unified border agency was established – the UK Border Agency (UKBA) – which brought together the work of the Border and Immigration Agency (BIA), UK Visa Services and customs detection work at the border by Revenue and Customs (HMRC), with the purpose of tightening border controls. 'The agency has been structured to further strengthen our protection against crime and terrorism while encouraging the flows of people and trade on which our future as a global hub depends' (Home Office, 2008: 49).

These discursive shifts in the labelling and image of asylum-seekers were likely to have had an effect on ASR youth and the schools which had taken them in. The new political and moral terrain within which schools and local education authorities have had to operate has become increasingly fraught, not least because of the turn of government towards reducing the welfare of asylum-seeking families. Below we describe first how the UK government confronts asylum seekers on arrival – 'the stranger at the gate' – and secondly how it has transformed the concept of compassion associated with asylum into an exclusionary set of policies aimed at the 'stranger within'.

The stranger at the gate

For many years, Britain refrained from developing an asylum policy that was different from its immigration policy (Gibney, 2004). However, by the 1980s the attention of immigration policy had shifted from

Commonwealth non-White immigrants to refugees and asylum-seekers[7] (Bloch, 1999; Cohen, 2003; Gibney, 2004). The first direct asylum policy (which was also designed to allow for a future common European policy) was the Asylum and Immigration Appeals Act 1993. Its main outcome was a reduction in the number of asylum-seekers receiving refugee status. In the years that followed, asylum became a salient issue in immigration policy (Bacon, 2005; Crawley, 2005) and a range of legislation has represented the official reaction to the entry of asylum-seekers. More immigration and asylum legislation was introduced in 1996 and 1999. The White Paper *Secure Borders, Safe Haven* (2002) was followed by yet more immigration legislation in 2002, 2004, 2006 and, most recently, the *Borders, Citizenship and Immigration Act 2009*. Despite such legislation, since the 1990s there has been a growth in the number of asylum applications. From a steady intake in the 1980s of few thousand a year (Smith and Jenkins, 2003), in 2002 the number of asylum applications reached its peak of 103,000 applications (including dependents). This increase was accompanied by a sense of crisis. According to a Populus poll for *The Times* conducted in February 2003, nine out of 10 voters believed that the number of asylum-seekers in the UK was a serious problem, with 39 per cent of the public regarding it as the most serious 'problem' facing British society.

To a large extent, the 'asylum crisis' and the image of Britain being 'flooded' by 'hordes' of asylum-seekers was fuelled by Home Office declarations and by the sheer volume of legislation it passed on asylum. For example, in a Departmental Report, Sir John Gieve, the then Permanent Secretary, stated: 'Our biggest immediate challenges remain the area of asylum' (Home Office, 2003: 21). Yet Joppke (1999: 130) argued that: 'Reviewing British asylum policy, one is struck by its inclination to make maximal fuss over minimal numbers.' Indeed, according to the UNHCR (2008) and in contrast to popular belief, in 2007 the UK was only fifth on the list of Western destinations for new asylum-seekers, receiving only 5.1 per cent of individual asylum claims worldwide.[8] Interestingly, research on recent patterns and trends of immigration initiated by the Home Office itself (Dobson et al., 2001: xviii) suggested that, during the 1990s, when the number of asylum applications reached its peak, the overall number of foreign citizens as a proportion of the total population was lower in comparison to other European countries. Moreover, these flows included a relatively high proportion of immigrants from high-income countries and only between one-sixth and one-third were asylum-seekers.

Although there are no official figures on how many asylum-seeking and refugee children there are currently in the UK, there are some indications to be found in official statistics. For example, among the 28,300 applications made in the UK in 2007, apparently some 3,535 were unaccompanied children under 17 and of the 4,870 applications with dependents, 80 per cent were children under 18 (Home Office, 2008). Unfortunately, and indeed significantly, there are no accurate national and local demographic data on the numbers of asylum-seeking and refugee children attending British schools. However, Rutter (2006) estimates that, in 2005, there were at least 60,000 refugee and asylum-seeking children of compulsory school age residing in the UK.

Immigration and asylum legislation in the past decade had the explicit aim of ensuring that control over migration was more effective and that entry was more difficult. What is important for our purposes is to note that with each piece of immigration legislation, the UK government has not only tightened controls over those entering the UK, but added more restrictions to the entitlements of asylum-seekers and their access to various social services – a policy that has directly affected all ASR children in the country. Indeed, one of the major trends in the six pieces of asylum legislation in the past 10 years[9] has been that the weight has shifted from controlling the entrance to the first gate (entering the soil) to monitoring those who gained entrance (the second gate). The changes in the image of asylum-seekers, their criminalisation, as well as concerns about the security and social cohesion of British society, have all contributed to a politics of belonging which is not only concerned with who and how many enter the country, but also with their entitlements and integration once inside. This concern is heavily embedded in the discursive construction of the deserving/wanted and the undeserving/unwanted categories that were used publicly to discriminate between different types of migrant (Sales, 2005).

The stranger within: the deserving and the undeserving

In the past, moving through the second gate, the gate to what Hammer (2000) described as *denizenship*, was less problematic (see Chapter 2), and in fact once an immigrant had legally obtained entry through the first gate, he or she was entitled to the majority of rights a citizen enjoys. However, by the beginning of the 21st century, asylum-seeking families were to find that access to social and welfare rights (including education) had become much less attainable. As Sales (2005: 448) commented: 'The boundaries of exclusion are thus shifted and made more impenetrable.' During the 1990s, the UK government had begun to remove those asylum-seekers and other people subject to immigration control from the welfare state (Cohen, 2002; Sales, 2005). For example, the Asylum and Immigration Act 1996 minimised the role of local authorities in relation to asylum-seekers; Section 9 introduced restrictions to asylum-seekers' access to local authority housing and linked the receiving of state benefits, including child benefits, to a person's immigration status (Cohen, 2002; Dell'Olio, 2002; Pirouet, 2001).

The Immigration and Asylum Act 1999 further removed asylum-seekers from the provisions of the welfare state and from the responsibility of local authorities (Cohen, 2002; Sales, 2002) by placing responsibility for them with the newly created National Asylum Support Service (NASS). NASS's responsibility is to provide those asylum-seekers waiting for a decision (subject to their application being filed in reasonable time after their arrival in the UK), with accommodation in dispersal areas and with subsistence payments. These payments stand at the rate of 70 per cent of benefits for adults and 100 per cent for children (NASS, 2004b). The 1999 Act also forbade asylum-seekers from working and removed their rights to all social benefits including those granted on the basis of the Children Act 1989 (Cohen, 2002) (except in the case of unaccompanied minors, who were protected under this Act).

Serious concern was expressed about this aggressive exclusion of asylum-seekers from welfare support and its ramifications for asylum-seeking children and their wellbeing. Voluntary organisations such as the Refugee Council, Save the Children, UNICEF and the Children's Society, as well as researchers in the field (Rutter and Stanton, 2001; Rutter, 2006), warned that such restrictions would have far-reaching effects on asylum-seeking children and especially on levels of child poverty in this group. By introducing these restrictions and removing asylum-seeking families from the welfare state, the government has been heavily criticised by children's advocates for adopting a position in which the asylum-seeker child is defined not as a child whose welfare is important but rather as a migrant at the mercy of state immigration policy (Crawley, 2006).

With 2002 and 2004 immigration and asylum legislation, the situation for asylum-seekers worsened – bearing little relation to either compassion or charity. Wolton (2006: 459) argues that 'what is significant here is that forcing asylum seekers to beg for charity appears to be government policy'. Section 55 of the 2002 legislation only permitted welfare support to destitute asylum-seekers who applied 'as soon as is reasonably practical' (Wolton, 2006). The government claims that the measure was necessary in order to prevent welfare rights being given to those who lived illegally in Britain. However, in practice NASS refuses support for those who cannot prove that they entered the country no more than 72 hours before making the application. The effect is to force asylum-seekers to live in great poverty and to beg for charity (Goodwing-Gill, 2004; Wolton, 2006). Section 9 of the Asylum and Immigration Act 2004 additionally allows the Home Office to withdraw support from families with children whose application has failed. Blunkett, as Home Secretary, even threatened not only to remove support but also to place those children whose families no longer receive support in care (Lewis and Neal, 2005).

The new hurdles put before asylum-seekers in accessing different services and resources were justified by the argument that these measures will deter 'unlawful' asylum-seekers and 'bogus' refugees from arriving in the UK. The assumption was that the British welfare system acted as a 'pull factor' to asylum-seekers (Wolton, 2006). *Secure Borders, Safe Haven* stated that 'one of the key drivers for more people coming to the UK is our strong economic position [...] Our strong labour market acts as a magnet for those seeking better jobs and lives for themselves and their families' (Home Office, 2002: 24). In the introduction to *Secure Borders, Safe Haven,* David Blunkett, then Home Secretary, explains: 'There is nothing more controversial, and yet more natural, than men and women from across the world seeking a better life for themselves and their families' (ibid.: 5). The White Paper then lists the measures that the Home Office intended to take in order to prevent economic migrants disguising themselves as asylum-seekers:

> In order to manage entry into the UK better, we are developing legal, sensible and controlled routes for economic migration; ensuring that our asylum system is fair but robust and credible; and taking the powers that we need to tackle the criminals who abuse our borders and exploit desperate people. (ibid.: 23)

These practices were to pass on a clear message: 'if people want to come to the UK for economic reasons, they must apply under the economic routes available to them' (ibid.: 48).[10]

The use of welfare as a tool of immigration control for asylum-seekers reinforces their image as a potential economic burden on British society (Sales, 2002). In the past two decades asylum-seekers have increasingly been associated with negative economic impact (Gibney, 2004). Indeed, Sivanandan (2001: 89) argues that 'Britain is putting its economic interests before those of the politically persecuted'. The dominance of the logic of the market, or what Cohen (2003) refers to as 'economic nationalism' is used to differentiate between 'wanted' migrants (who presumably can contribute to the UK economy) and asylum-seekers who in this discursive framework have come to represent the economically 'unwanted' migrants.[11] This distinction, as we shall see, has considerable consequences for the sorts of government support that asylum-seeking and refugee children receive socially and educationally.

'A bare life'?

More and more people who some years ago would have been entitled to the rights and protection of the status of a refugee today have no legal means to obtain it, ... who exist in a state of *'bare life'* (Yuval-Davis, 2008: 106–7, our emphasis).

Asylum-seeking children and their families find themselves excluded by state dividing practices that now clearly distinguish between those who are considered 'deserving' and 'undeserving' of welfare support. Immigration policy in the past decade has separated out asylum-seekers from recognised 'genuine' refugees under the assumption that the majority of asylum-seekers are 'bogus' and therefore 'undeserving'. Charles Clarke expressed this clearly:

We will continue to welcome *genuine* refugees respecting our obligation under the 1951 Geneva Convention [...] We will continue to root out abuse of the system by rigorously implementing the measures we have taken to ensure that we distinguish between genuine refugees and those who are looking to come here to work or claim benefits, and by further strengthening our borders and removing those whose claims fail. (Home Office, 2005a: 7–8, our emphasis)

Of educational significance is the fact that the Home Office in recent years has applied this differentiating principle to its integration policies.[12] *Secure Borders, Safe Haven* declares that '... we help those who have a right to remain here to rebuild their lives and to fulfil their potential as full members of society' (Home Office, 2002: 70). Two years later, the Consultation Paper *Integration Matters: A National Strategy for Refugee Integration* (Home Office, 2005c) confirmed that the concept of integration was only to apply to those who had been granted refugee status:

This integration strategy does not cover asylum-seekers. [...] While the Government does accept that the experience of asylum-seekers before they are recognised as refugees will affect their later integration in a number of ways, it believes that integration in the full sense of the word can take place only when a person has been confirmed as a refugee and can make plans on the basis of a long-term future in the UK. (Home Office, 2005c: 10)

To meet this end, the National Refugee Integration Forum (NRIF) was set up in 2002, representing a new partnership between the Home Office, DfES, the Department of Health, the NHS and representatives of local government and the voluntary sector. The aim of the forum was to advance refugee integration, especially in the fields of education, health and other social services – in other words, '... to help all refugees develop their potential and to contribute to the cultural and economic life of the country as equal members of society...' (Home Office, 2002: 70–1).

Since 2005, NRIF has completed some significant work in setting out the indicators for successful integration for refugees. However, its brief confirmed the discursive construction of the refugee as a separate category from asylum-seekers, and the different levels of moral commitment of Britain applicable to these two types of migrants. The decision to include only refugees in integration programmes symbolically deepened the exclusion from which asylum-seekers already suffered. In effect the message to schools from the Home Office was that only some of their students needed be integrated, to be prepared for a national model of democratic citizenship or for membership of a local community. It would not be surprising if this policy led to confused local authority and school responses.

The Home Office recognised the potential long-term problems associated with this policy, especially when the waiting period for an application being approved could be long. Des Browne MP, in the foreword to *Integration Matters* (Home Office, 2005c: 3), explained what appears to be a circular political logic thus:

A number of respondents have urged us to acknowledge that 'integration begins on day one': in other words, that the integration needs of asylum seekers as well as refugees are important. I want to be clear about the government's view on this important point. No one can sensibly deny that much valuable integration activity occurs among asylum seekers ... But asylum seekers are not allowed to work; and some two thirds of them will not in the end be given the right to remain in the United Kingdom. So this strategy is founded on the belief that integration can only begin *in its fullest sense* when an asylum seeker becomes a refugee.

Indeed the decision to focus on refugees only is also explained by their ability to partake in the labour market. Düvell and Jordan (2003: 302) commented on the significance of this logic, arguing that: 'The New Labour government has announced its commitment to a new version of social justice, based on social inclusion through labour market participation.' In effect, the UK government has shifted its integration policy away from an ethos of rights and duties and into line with the dominant neo-liberal economic discourse. Participating in the labour market and, even more so, contributing to the UK economy and its prosperity (a duty of a citizen in a consumer society) was now represented as one, if not the most, important indicator of successful refugee integration. This shift is clearly represented in *Integration Matters: A National Strategy for Refugee Integration*:

> In order to achieve their full potential, refugees face the challenges of communicating effectively in the host community's language and of gaining employment appropriate to their abilities and skills. The solutions lie in provision of opportunities for language training, [and] early contact with JobCentre Plus. (Home Office, 2005c: 6)

The majority of the integration programmes are geared towards assisting refugees to enter employment. From a school perspective,

> the education system serves as a significant marker of integration, and also as a major means towards this goal [integration]. Education creates significant opportunities for employment, for wider social connections and for language learning. (Home Office, 2004a: 16)

Significantly, the new integration agenda focuses less on issues of British citizenship and far more on measures of academic achievement such as: five or more GCSEs; two or more A-levels; rates of admission to university; and the number of refugees completing vocational qualifications (Home Office, 2004a: 16).

This social exclusion of asylum-seeking youth and their families and the economic approach to the 'genuine' refugee which makes more reference to their contribution to the economy than to claims of compassion and social justice define the parameters for educational policymakers. The effect has been to use an immigration approach for the education of asylum-seeking children that leaves them effectively not only out in the cold but also potentially severely damages their wellbeing, and denies them their rights as children. In the final theme of the chapter, we focus on the consequences of this aspect of government immigration policy on asylum-seeking children and their families.

Marginalisation of the education of asylum-seeking children

As we have seen, the negative effects of immigration legislation on asylum-seeking children are to be found in the fact that it treats them first and foremost as asylum-seekers rather than as children (Crawley and Lester, 2005; Giner, 2006, 2007). The UK government has repeatedly excluded asylum-seeking children from its own provisions. Central government made the education needs and often the rights of asylum-seeking children irrelevant to their approach to immigration and even integration. As we have already noted (Chapter 1), under the UNCRC all children have rights as children; they should all enjoy minimum standards of care and provision, including the right to education and the right to be consulted, regardless of their status. The UK government ratified the UNCRC in 1991, and successive governments have stressed their commitment to children's welfare and rights, including through legislation such as the Children Acts 1989 and 2004, and the *Every Child Matters* agenda. However, the government's stance on immigration exemplifies the ambivalence towards the needs of asylum-seeking children and the subordination of their needs to that of immigration control.

When ratifying the UNCRC the UK government entered the maximum three reservations permitted, one notably that it would apply the Convention insofar as it coincided with immigration and nationality legislation.[13] In practice, this reservation meant that asylum-seeking children did not have to be fully protected (Giner, 2007; Pirouet, 2001), and could legitimately suffer discrimination:

> This reservation clearly discriminates against refugee children [...] It is clear that refugee children can never be entitled to the same rights as other children in the UK until withdrawal of the ... reservation. (Candappa, 2002: 224–5)

In the face of repeated criticism from a number of influential bodies such as the UK Joint Parliamentary Committee on Human Rights and the Council of Europe's Human Rights Commissioner, as well as campaigns by children's charities and children's rights activists, the UK government agreed in 2008 to remove this particular obstacle to the implementation of the UNCRC. However, some argue (Aynsley-Green, 2006; Crawley, 2006; The Joint Chief Inspectors, 2005) that the initial reservation protected the exclusion of the Immigration and Nationality Directorate (IND) and NASS from Section 11 of the Children Act 2004[14] and legitimated the lack of national statistics on asylum-seeking children.

Every Child Matters (ECM) and the Children Act 2004, *inter alia*, stressed the responsibility of different state agencies for the safeguarding of all children. Pertinently, the drive behind ECM was the case of serious neglect and murder of an immigrant child (Victoria Climbié, by her private foster carers) which came to represent the failure of the state to protect a vulnerable child.[15] Three measures were identified which would help achieve such goals: 1) a list of agencies accountable for the safeguarding of all children was to be constructed (Section 11); 2) a multi-agency approach was to be encouraged; and 3) frameworks for information-sharing between agencies were to be created. The exclusion of immigration agencies from this section of the legislation meant that the wellbeing of asylum-seeking children could be compromised and overridden in, for example, immigration practice such as detention (which runs contrary to Articles of the UNCRC), during deportation, or in interviews with immigration authorities.[16] This exclusion symbolically supports the precedence which immigration control had over the best interests of the asylum-seeking child.

Margaret Hodge, who was at the time Children's Minister, made it clear that such safeguarding notions did not or should not apply to asylum-seeking children:

> [W]hen we consider this issue [the safeguarding and wellbeing of asylum-seeking children], we had to be absolutely clear that the primacy in this issue has to be the immigration control and immigration policy. If we had given, for example, the duty to co-operate and duty to safeguard to the Immigration Service, I think that we would have opened a loophole which would have enabled asylum-seeking families and unaccompanied asylum children to use those particular duties to override the immigration controls and the asylum-seeking controls. (House of Commons Education and Skills Committee, 2005: Ev.180)

The arguably unjustifiable exclusion of immigration authorities such as the IND from safeguarding responsibilities laid down in the Children

Act 2004 effectively meant that children currently in the UK were to be divided into two tiers. According to Bill Bolloten, a leading refugee education consultant, there seemed to be 'one tier for children for whom their best interests are the paramount consideration, and another for those whose best interests are a secondary consideration'.[17] Charities, NGOs, children and asylum advocates were outraged at these injustices perpetrated on asylum-seeking children. Nowhere are these injustices more strongly displayed than in government policies of dispersal, detention and deportation of asylum-seeking children.

The use of these three practices of immigration control – *dispersal, detention* and *deportation* – have become a normalised way of managing asylum-seekers (Bloch and Schuster, 2005). Each contributes (in different ways) to the marginalisation of asylum-seeking children and could also have considerable implications for the schooling, wellbeing and achievement of such students and for the LEAs, schools and teachers who are working with them. Below we describe how these policies are likely to affect ASR children.

Dispersal as a form of social exclusion

Dispersal policy was first introduced by the Immigration and Asylum Act 1999, and was purportedly meant to avoid 'swamping' and its associated racial tensions (particularly White backlash) by reducing the cluster areas, mainly in Greater London and to some extent in the South East of England. By 2000, asylum-seekers were dispersed to the nine regions of England, to Scotland, Wales and Northern Ireland. Certain assumptions were embedded in this programme. The first was premised on a 'good race relations thesis' and a government-held view that there was a limit to the tolerance that should be expected from indigenous communities (Gedalof, 2004). It was believed that avoiding cluster areas and spreading asylum-seekers across the country would render them less visible and would therefore contribute to better race relations. Secondly, sharing the economic burden of catering for the needs of asylum-seekers was another assumption (Bloch and Schuster, 2005). However, as Bloch and Schuster (2005: 507) point out, the effect in reality was that '... asylum seekers have found themselves in areas outside urban centres where they lack support services and that are ethnically homogenous ... where they become targets for abuse and violence'.

The Immigration and Asylum Act 1999 linked dispersal with access to welfare services and benefits. In other words, full benefits were granted only to those who accepted accommodation in dispersal areas, or to those the Home Office decided not to disperse, such as unaccompanied minors or those in 'exceptional circumstances'. Asylum-seekers who are dispersed have no choice as to where they are going to be housed. A request to receive housing and not to be dispersed is very unlikely to be authorised. The lack of compassion associated with the dispersal policy is captured by this NASS Policy Bulletin:

> An asylum-seeker may request to be allocated accommodation in London or the South East because they have relatives there [...] But in the absence of exceptional circumstances, dispersal will generally be appropriate. For, example, if a person asked to be housed in London because they have an adult son there, then this would not normally be entertained. Asylum-seekers may ask to be accommodated in London or Kent because the area has an ethnic community there, which does not exist in the dispersal area ... this would not normally be accepted as sufficient reason to depart from the dispersal policy. (NASS, 2004a)

Family or community networks which might have assisted distressed, or even traumatised, asylum-seeking youth are not recognised as sufficient reason for a family not to be dispersed. As a result, asylum-seekers are often housed away from their prospective communities in predominantly White English areas where housing is available and which, in many cases, are also socially and economically deprived areas (Bloch and Schuster, 2005). Tying access to benefits and social rights with access to accommodation turned dispersal into yet another form of exclusion, taking from asylum-seekers the right to choose where to live and often removing them from social and familial networks. Indeed suffering from hostility in the areas to which they were dispersed, and being disconnected from their natural social networks, many asylum-seekers decided to opt out from the dispersal programme, and to choose their place of residence while often living in poverty (Bloch and Schuster, 2005; Kundnani, 2001).

Dispersal as a policy shapes the schooling of those dispersed but also those youth whose parents chose to opt out. The policy has a negative impact not least because in its implementation the government failed to present dispersal as a process that could enrich local communities and failed to consult them (IRR, 2000). From an educational perspective, dispersal as a temporary 'integration' strategy for asylum-seeking students was and is extremely problematic both to schools and the dispersed child. The findings from our study of local education authorities (Arnot and Pinson, 2005), as well as the findings of other studies of local government approaches (Ofsted, 2003b; Remsbery, 2003), suggest that, often, insufficient notice of the arrival of asylum-seekers was given to LEAs. It was not clear whether LEAs or schools had any say in the process of dispersal, especially with respect to whether there was sufficient educational support for such children. Asylum-seekers with families were dispersed to areas where there may not have been any school placement for the children, where the schools may not have had adequate resources and funding to meet their educational needs and where schools may have had very little experience of non-White students, those with English as an Additional Language (EAL) needs, or new arrivals who appeared at unusual times in the school year. The school community may be predominantly White, often putting the children at greater risk of being racially bullied. According to one English former school inspector, 'in reality what happened, the driver was the accommodation and the one aspect that wasn't really looked at [was] education'. In contrast, LEAs and schools in a non-dispersal area, especially in London, had to face the challenge of helping children whose families chose not to be dispersed and, as a result, suffered from considerable poverty.

Finally, given the knowledge educationalists now have about the important role of social capital in shaping educational outcomes, it is not without significance morally that asylum-seeking students (if dispersed) are removed from the precise community contexts which might have assisted their schooling.[18] Central and local educational policy-makers have had to cope with the after-effects of dispersal, not least the fragmentation of asylum-seeking families, the loss of social capital associated with community networking and help and the lack of involvement in planning decisions among asylum-seeking communities and parents in relation to the child's education.

Detention: the erosion of human rights

Unlike its legitimation of dispersal policy, the UK government has made little attempt to associate compassion with its policy of detaining asylum-seeking children and their families in prison-like centres or even to use the rhetoric of 'in their best interests'. If there is any evidence of the erosion of the ethos of human rights today it is, according to Silove et al. (2001), the expansion of the practice of detention of children as well as adults in the UK.

The power of immigration officers to detain those arriving to the UK, including asylum-seekers, was first introduced in the Immigration Act 1971. It was designed to allow short periods of detention before removal at the port of entry of those who were refused entry. Until the 1990s, asylum-seekers were very rarely detained and by and large detention was seen as an extreme and exceptional measure.[19] However, by the 1990s and especially under the Labour government, detention of asylum-seekers was normalised and used more frequently (Bloch and Schuster, 2005).

The Labour government's approach, articulated in *Secure Borders, Safe Haven* (2002) is that 'detention has a key role to play in the removal of failed asylum seekers and other immigration offenders [...] Detention remains an unfortunate but essential element in the effective enforcement of immigration control' (Home Office, 2002: 66). The decision to call these camps 'removal centres' confirmed their role in the control and deportation of asylum-seekers who had lost their case to remain in the UK. However, *de facto*, today many adult and child asylum-seekers are detained even when their applications are still pending and they have entered the country legally. They are detained for longer periods (often for over two months) although around 10 per cent find themselves in detention for longer than six months (see Wolton, 2006).

Increasing the rates of removal to such centres is also represented as presenting a deterrent for 'bogus' asylum-seekers. However, it is those asylum-seekers who have fled their country quickly, without carrying proper documentation, who find it harder to prove they are genuine refugees and hence find themselves in detention (Silove et al., 2001). Those criticising detention policy therefore argue that there is no evidence to support the claim that detention deters people from arriving in the UK or that it is necessary in order to ensure that asylum-seekers will comply with asylum procedures (Bacon, 2005). Detention quite clearly succeeds in separating and excluding asylum-seeking children from mainstream education and their families from society.

Today the UK detains more asylum-seekers, for longer periods and without judicial procedures, than any of its European counterparts (Bacon, 2005; Bloch and Schuster, 2005; Malloch and Stanley, 2005; Silove et al., 2001). The number of detention places has expanded since 2002 by 40 per cent and a large number of asylum-seekers are routinely detained. According to Bacon (2005), in 1993 the British government only had the capacity to detain 250 asylum-seekers – however, by 2005 it had the capacity to detain 2,644 asylum-seekers including[20] 456 family detention spaces at Yarl's Wood in Bedfordshire, Oakington in Cambridgeshire, Dungavel in Lanarkshire and Tinsley House near Gatwick airport.

Detention is criticised heavily for breaching human rights, for its ineffectiveness, its arbitrary character, its conditions of detention and the risk in which it puts particular groups of detainees such as those who have already suffered torture (Malloch and Stanley, 2005). While in detention, many asylum-seekers do not have access to suitable health care, social and legal services, and education. Regardless of whether they have committed an offence, they are kept in prison-like conditions and subjected to prison-like discipline (Silove et al., 2001). Criticisms of the UK practice of detention is shared not only by refugee advocates and researchers but also by mainstream organisations and agencies that might have accepted the logic of detention if they did not have substantial criticisms of its implementation.[21]

Since October 2001 restrictions on the detention of families have been lifted, allowing the government to detain families not just immediately prior to their removal from the country but for longer periods. As a result, families now can be detained at any stage and for unlimited time, just like single adults (Bloch and Schuster, 2005; Crawley, 2005). These intentions were repeated in the 2002 White Paper *Secure Borders, Safe Haven*: '... families can in some instances give rise to the same problems of non-compliance and thus the need to detain' (Home Office, 2002: 67). The Children's Commissioner for England, Sir Al Anysley-Green, critically observed:

> [T]he detention of families was not reserved for use as a genuine 'last resort' as required by the United Nations Convention on the Rights of the Child (UNCRC) or 'exceptionally' as required by the United Nations Rules for the Protection of Juveniles Deprived of their Liberty (UNJDL). Rather, it appeared to be used as routine procedure where a family did not apply for voluntary departure after the failure of their appeal. (11 Million, 2009: 15).

As well, the Home Office does not publish detailed statistics on the number of detainees,[22] their status or the periods of time in which they were detained. They are effectively removed from the public eye. It is therefore not clear just how many children are detained. Crawley and Lester (2005) estimate that around 2,000 children a year are held in the three detention centres for purposes of immigration control. Around half of the children detained with their families are held in Yarl's Wood enclosed within razor-wired walls; others are held in Dungavel House or in Tinsley House. Yarl's Wood, which has 353 places for families, is the main detention centre (HMIP, 2005).

Crawley and Lester found that half the asylum-seeking children were detained for more than 28 days, and that their length of detention varied from seven days to almost nine months. It is government policy not to detain unaccompanied children. However, there is evidence that asylum applicants whose age is disputed might be detained as adults. In fact, age-disputed children comprise a significant portion of children in detention (Crawley and Lester, 2005). Further, while children should not be held at Dungavel or Tinsley for more than three days, there is no limit to how long they can be detained at Yarl's Wood (*Guardian,* 14 April 2009). In 2008, a report from Yarl's Wood (this time from an announced visit by HM Chief Inspector of Prisons) indicated that the average length of stay of children had increased from eight days at the previous inspection to 15 days (HMIP, 2008). An Ofsted Joint Chief Inspectors' report the same year (Ofsted, 2008) indicated that this figure masks longer periods of detention experienced by some children, with greater numbers of children being detained for longer than 28 days, Indeed, Her Majesty's Inspector of Prisons (HMIP) commented:

> The plight of detained children remained of great concern … an immigration removal centre can never be a suitable place for children and we were dismayed to find cases of disabled children being detained and some children spending large amounts of time incarcerated. […] Any period of detention can be detrimental to children and their families, but the impact of lengthy detention is particularly extreme. (HMIP, 2008: 5)

Cole (2003) criticised the logic behind the detention of families, arguing that they are the least likely to abscond and mostly comply with restrictions imposed on them by immigration agencies because they have children. She adds: 'It must, therefore, be assumed … this [detention policy] was intended to demonstrate that *the Government was not going to let even compassion stand in the way of a need to take a tough line with asylum seekers'* (ibid.: 2; our emphasis).

Since the expansion of detention to families, children's rights activists as well as the Children's Commissioner and HMIP have become extremely concerned about the conditions in which children are held and the detrimental effects they might leave with them. In their inspection report, HMIP used strong language to describe the inadequacy of conditions for children:

> [O]ne of our major concerns continues to be the detention of children. […] We continue to find that decisions to detain children are made without taking account of their interests, and that there

are no independent assessments of the welfare needs of detained children. (HMIP, 2005: 7)

The report continues:

In all centres holding children, we found the mechanism for detaining, and reviewing detention, to be poor. [...] *There was little evidence that the welfare of the child was even considered when decisions to detain were made, and no systems existed for the welfare and needs of detained children to be independently assessed.* [...] Centre staff were caring, but in general underqualified. (ibid.: 64, our emphasis)

Crawley and Lester (2005) found from their interviews with 32 child detainees and their parents that children in detention are at risk of health problems and a deterioration in their mental health. Parents reported eating and sleeping difficulties experienced by their children, including persistent illness. Both parents and children were concerned about the disruption of the latter's education. This particularly applied to those parents whose children were detained for long periods.[23] These findings were confirmed by Aynsley-Green's review which also found major health-care shortcomings at the detention centres, including 'inadequacy of clinical care; poor care provided to children and adults with mental health needs ...' (11 Million, 2009: 6). HMIP (2008: 13) added that educational provision for children at Yarl's Wood was 'unsatisfactory overall' and a 'cause for concern'. The quality of their education was described as deficient for all but the youngest children; many could not complete the GCSEs that they had started in mainstream schooling (The Joint Chief Inspectors, 2005). In a recent report on the safeguarding of children, Ofsted (2008) expressed concern about whether the wellbeing of children in detention centres was safeguarded. It argued that immigration authorities did not take into account the educational needs of detained ASR children or their individual special needs in the decision to detain their families. Again these children's educational and other needs were being marginalised in central government decision-making.

As far as Aynsley-Green (2006) was concerned, detaining families with children could be seen as a breach of the rights of the children. The most disturbing aspect of state detention of children is the contradiction between the representation of the child as in need of adult support in the UNCRC and the logic of exclusion that such practice entails. As opposed to dispersal that might have some integrative inclusive logic to it, detention of ASR children represents the morality of social exclusion, separation and eventually ostracism. The justification, according to David Blunkett, speaking on BBC Radio 4's *Today* programme on 24 April 2002 (quoted in Malloch and Stanley, 2005: 58) is that teaching asylum-seeking children separately in accommodation centres is necessary since they are 'swamping' local schools.

Deportation: the ultimate exclusion

Our third and final section on immigration control focuses on measures which have evoked immense criticism – deportation. Here asylum-seeking children are gathered up by the state and deported alone (if age-disputed) or with their family members to another country (whether to their own country where arguably they might be in danger, or to another 'holding' country where they would remain in transit, or to the first EU country of their arrival where the whole immigration process might re-start). In its implementation it could be seen not just to ignore human rights but also as creating the conditions for greater fear and trepidation on the part of asylum-seeking children.

Deportation, the physical exclusion of a person from the territory of the state, is a policy which embodies some of the paradoxes faced by nation-states in the global era. On the one hand, deportation is a mechanism central to the sovereignty of the state and its ability to protect its borders (Gibney and Hansen, 2003). On the other, it can often be seen as breaching basic human rights and as a practice that does not correspond well with a commitment to the ethos of human rights. Yet raising the number of successful removals has become one of the main targets of the UK government in recent years. The rationale offered by the Home Office emphasises the need for deportation in order to secure national borders: 'Swift removal is central to the credibility of our immigration system ...' (Home Office, 2005a: 30). However in reality only a minority of those receiving deportation notices are actually deported and there has been only a marginal increase in the numbers of deportations (Bloch and Schuster, 2005; Gibney and Hansen, 2003). As Gibney and Hansen (2003) point out, deportation is often costly and difficult to implement.

Paradoxically it is easier to deport those who entered the country legally and those who find it harder to disappear under immigration control's radar – mainly families. It is often easier to locate families, and since the introduction of the controversial section 9 to the Asylum and Immigration (Treatment of Claimants, etc.) Act 2004, if asylum-seeking parents do not leave the country voluntarily their children risk being taken into care. This inhuman policy makes it easier to pressure the whole family to leave the UK (Giner, 2006).

Significantly, in the decision to deport families with children, the government's target of successful removal of failed asylum-seekers takes precedence over the educational needs of the asylum-seeking child. The deportation of families and children, especially those who are enrolled into the school system, has been extensively criticised. Most of the opposition to deportation comes from children's rights activists, but also from those who are in direct contact with those families – schools, teachers and local communities – who are directly affected by the removal of the child. In Chapter 10, we discuss deportation further, showing how this practice has mobilised students, teachers, educationalists and local communities politically.

Conclusions

Pirouet (2001: 166), who questioned whether the British people were robbed of their heritage of being a safe haven for refugees, suggested that such an ethos can still be found at the local level, in civil society and communities, and amongst individuals: 'It is among these groups that the people are to be found who strive to keep the UK a welcoming society whose members were once proud to provide a place of refuge for the persecuted.'

The marginalisation of children and children's rights in immigration policy and the exclusive immigration practices implemented by the state place a huge pressure and responsibility on LEAs, schools and teachers. In the next chapter we explore how the DfES, renamed in 2007 the Department for Children, Schools and Families (DCSF), and local authorities responded to immigration and asylum policy and grappled with the needs of new arrivals in the school system.

5
Devolution and Incorporation: Whose Responsibility?

The hostile response of the Home Office and immigration authorities to asylum-seeking communities, families and children leaves educational policy-makers in central or local government in a particularly difficult position. Central government ministries are not necessarily working with the same agenda and, as we shall see, by the turn of the 21st century the key concern for educational officials under a Labour government included raising standards, promoting excellence and encouraging social justice (McKnight et al., 2005). While the government had reshaped the educational agenda to address social exclusion issues – particularly the exclusion of pregnant teenagers, looked-after children, traveller children and the disaffected – its main thrust was to raise access to higher education for working-class youth, improve levels of academic performance in literacy and in the main school subjects at GCSE, and encourage a stronger sense of civic engagement and participation, especially among disaffected youth. These educational priorities and subsequent policy initiatives potentially had much to offer asylum-seeking youth; however, it was never clear that they would be included in any or all of these ambitions.

Drawing on the analysis of policy documents and interviews with central government officials in the spring of 2004, in the first part of this chapter we describe what could be considered a minimal interventionist approach to the education of ASR children in the period between 2000 and 2005. Although estimates suggest that there were some 60,000 ASR students in the school system during that period, the DfES strategy held onto a line that was reminiscent of the policy strategy used by the UK government in relation to racial inequality in the 1970s and 1980s. Kirp (1980) famously called this approach 'doing good by doing little'. To some extent, this approach has shifted as a result of recent developments such as the *Every Child Matters* agenda (2003), the transition from the DfES to the DCSF with its new emphasis on children and families, and the recent cooperation between the DCSF and the QCA, and the DCSF and the Home Office in relation to the education of ASR children.[1]

The DfES (now DCSF) made it clear that the prime responsibility for the education of transitory and often traumatised ASR children resides with local authorities. According to section 14 of the Education Act 1996, local authorities have a legal obligation to provide education for all children aged 5–16[2] and therefore, by implication, legally all asylum-seeking children should have access to education. Also, formally, under the Children Acts of 1989 and 2004, all children are eligible for health care, education and support from children's services, by virtue of being children. This legislation ostensibly confirms that ASR children should be given the same opportunity to benefit from education as any other child in the UK. However, with no specific government policy addressing the educational needs of asylum-seeking students and, as we have seen, with the curtailment of the rights of these families to social and economic benefits and restrictions on support arrangements, it was likely that their chances of making full use of their right of access to education would be seriously jeopardised.

Local government was therefore put in a difficult position since it was held responsible for the educational, social, physical and psychological wellbeing of asylum-seeking youth in its region. At the same time, Home Office decisions to police and pursue such communities and individuals with vigour and aggressive tactics would be visible on the ground. Asylum-seeking students and their families could well be confronted with the harsh treatment associated with dispersal, detention and deportation that we described in the previous chapter.

Many local authorities became hosts to dispersed asylum-seeking families and (undispersed) unaccompanied youth even though some did not necessarily have any experience of or knowledge about how to cater for ethnic diversity, how to address the complex needs of ASR families, and would not necessarily have had procedures in place to prepare schools for the arrival and education of their children. Even those local authorities, particularly urban authorities, who were already familiar with the politics of 'race' and with the demands of holding down social conflict and encouraging community cohesion, would be hard-pressed to know how best to respond to high levels of ASR students in their schools. Gone were the days when LEAs in the UK had sufficient budgets and staff to support vulnerable groups in systematic and coherent ways or prepare school staff for their arrival. The market-isation of education, with its attendant problems, made educational planning difficult.

In the second half of this chapter, using our survey data, we describe the ways in which local educational authorities negotiated their respons-ibilities, the dilemmas they encountered, and how they conceptualised the 'problem' of ASR education. Many LEA policy responses have been shaped directly or indirectly by the context of immigration policy as much as by the level of their own resources.

The policy of inexplicitness – devolving responsibility

ASR students have rarely been identified by central educational policy frameworks as a distinct category with specific educational needs that attract special support and funding arrangements. The DfES/DCSF has not published a policy statement on ASR education, nor has it offered any more than limited support for LEAs and schools coping with ASR students. Some references to ASR students are made in official policy documents such as the *School Admissions Code of Practice* (DfES, 2002d), *Aiming High* (DfES, 2004b) and *Managing Pupil Mobility* (DfES, 2003b). The *Good Practice Guidance on the Education of Asylum Seeking and Refugee Children* (2002b) that Jill Rutter, then Education Advisor for the Refugee Council, was commissioned to write is the main source of advice given to schools and LEAs. In 2004, a new, yet almost identical, version of the 2002 guidance: *Aiming High: Guidance on Supporting the Education of Asylum Seeking and Refugee Children – A Guide to Good Practice* (DfES, 2004b) was published under the 'Aiming High' framework.

The guidance makes clear that LEAs, schools and ASR parents have prime responsibility for fulfilling legal obligations to provide ASR children with access to mainstream education:

> Parents are obliged to ensure that their children receive an educa-tion and LEAs must offer school places in accordance with their published admissions arrangements and must ensure that *all* chil-dren resident in that local authority receive full time education. (DfES, 2002a: 17, our emphasis)

Yet the DfES/DCSF has remained vague as to what LEA responsibilities entail. Despite the declared aim of providing information about what constitutes good local practice, in both the 2002 and 2004 versions of the guidance there is considerable ambiguity about what good practice means. The advice quoted here exemplifies this ambiguity: 'LEAs should ensure that there are *no unreasonable* delays in securing the admission of ASR students to school' (DfES, 2002a: 10, our emphasis). Neither the guidance nor the *School Admissions Code of Practice* (DfES, 2002d) which also addresses the entitlement of asylum-seeking children to receive a school placement as quickly as possible, offer any time framework as to how quickly ASR children should receive their placement and what might be considered an 'unreasonable delay'. The timing of asylum-seeking students' admission into schools – their only legal entitlement – is left to the discretion of LEAs and schools.

The guidance further states that LEAs 'also have a role to play in promoting good educational practice. LEAs are expected ... to respond to the needs of asylum seeking and refugee children' (DfES, 2004b: 4). Yet the notion of 'good educational practice' or what is the standard expected from LEA provision also remains vague. Defining the LEA's duty of providing *certain* support for ASR children without clarifying what 'certain support' might look like leaves a significant space for interpretation.

In 2004, only three officials in the DfES were involved with the education of ASR children, as part of the team promoting the Vulnerable Children policy. The head of the team was responsible for policy and development, another for children in care which included ASR children in care, and a third team member was responsible for unaccompanied ASR children.[3] When asked to define the ways in which they see the role of the team and the DfES, one officer responded[4] that the team's main responsibility was defined as mainly one of publishing and disseminating guidance on good practice to LEAs and schools. However, our telephone survey data suggested that, despite it being available online, many LEAs and schools were not aware of this guidance. Similarly, one Ofsted officer stated in interview: 'When we talked to the schools, the DfES at that time had on their website good practice in supporting asylum-seekers ... [but] Not many schools knew about it.'

Over time, government approaches towards ASR students demonstrated little new thinking. One LEA officer in our survey stated that when coming to address the needs of ASR students she felt that '[w]e were all reinventing the wheel'. Our research in 2004 found that LEAs with developed policies were quick to point out that, like other LEAs, they were the ones informing the DfES rather than the other way around. This relationship was not necessarily problematic for those authorities that had experience of dealing with diverse populations. It was, however, problematic for those local authorities in dispersal areas which had to address the challenge of ASR for the first time. The government's ambivalence towards the education of ASR children meant that a clear comprehensive and arguably moral national education policy towards young asylum-seekers was not developed.

Data monitoring and funding arrangements

The first sign that local authorities are operating within a moral vacuum is indicated by the difficult choices that they have had to make in terms of whether to monitor the presence of such students and their families. Robinson (1990 in Stewart, 2004: 36) argues that the absence of official data on refugees results in the UK government operating within an 'information vacuum' which impacts long-term planning. The 'culture of ignorance' is both a cause and a consequence of the lack of data. The lack of accurate national data on the presence of young asylum-seekers and refugees creates a moral quandary for local communities. Should data be collected on ASR students even though it would expose them to public scrutiny and potential harassment by the state and local communities or should they remain hidden within the general student population?

In 2002 when the DfES was under pressure from those concerned about 'race' inequalities and Black students' underachievement in the UK, it finally made it obligatory for all schools to collect detailed data about the ethnic origin of their students through the Pupil Level Annual School Census (PLASC).[5] When introducing PLASC, DfES recognised that '[t]his information will help authorities to identify barriers to achievement, to establish strategies to raise standards to comply with equal opportunities' (DfES, 2002c: 2). However, only relatively fixed categories, such as language and country of origin, were included in this ethnic database; immigration status was excluded from the list of categories which schools are asked to collect. According to a DfES officer we interviewed, this was a conscious decision that came after some deliberation within the DfES. Pragmatic reasons were given for the absence of ASR status in monitoring of minority ethnic students: the decision was based on a view about the inaccuracy of any data that might be collected – an inaccuracy that has to do with the high level of mobility of such students and the fact that their status was liable to change. Also since ASR students form only small number of most school populations, the DfES felt that asking schools to collect data about students' immigration status was an unnecessary burden.[6] However, without such statistics, ASR students and their needs remain invisible, dependent upon parents and children themselves volunteering to provide such information to schools and local authorities.

While such statistical invisibility could contribute to the integration of ASR students into a school community, reducing any chance of labelling, stigmatisation and bullying, it can also create considerable difficulties for those committed to helping ASR children. In recent years one of the main challenges in terms of meeting the needs of asylum-seeking children is securing their legal right of accessing education. This task is made considerably more difficult if local authorities are not aware of how many such children are in their district and how many attend (or do not attend) mainstream education. Such data would also make it possible to track the progress or achievement of such children locally. As the Children's Legal Centre (2003: 10) points out: 'Knowing how many refugee and asylum-seeking children are in an area is an important part of determining the services that are likely to be needed by them.'

Yet, perhaps the most noticeable consequence of this lack of information about ASR students is the lack of targeted funding arrangements to ensure adequate support systems. The arguments here are circular. A DfES official in an interview argued that the lack of targeted funding justified the lack of information collection. Since there is no specific grant, or special provisions for ASR students, it was argued that there is nothing really to gain from collecting such information. In contrast, Robinson (1999 quoted in Stewart, 2004: 36–8) argues that this lack of data often is the main reason why ASR services receive lower priority in terms of funding. Robinson warns us that when there are no data, poor services might be justified because of ignorance about the presence of ASR students and their families.

The question of dedicating specific funding for ASR students is also a moral question. Underlying this issue is the problem of scarce resources but it is also about what should be the moral obligation of a national state education system to the so-called 'non-citizen' child, and in what ways such young people are helped to mobilise their right to be consulted, protected and to have access to and benefit from education and other sources of support for their wellbeing as children.

DfES/DCSF policy has been to mainstream ASR students within existing funding policies, focusing in particular on minority ethnic students' achievement and the broader social policies associated with supporting vulnerable children. ASR students are included in the Ethnic Minority Achievement Grant (EMAG) and the Vulnerable Children Grant (VCG). The DCSF website states:

> It is Government policy that children from asylum-seeking and refugee background are given the same opportunities as all other

children to access education [...] Schools receive funding for children of asylum-seekers and refugees in the same way as they do for *all other children* on the school roll, through the Education Formula Spending Share. The children of asylum-seekers can also benefit from two grants which are available to all LEAs: the first is the Vulnerable Children Grant. [...] The second is the Ethnic Minority Achievement Grant. (www.dcsf.gov.uk, accessed May 2009, our emphasis).

In this case, the DCSF has ruled in favour of mainstreaming. EMAG, as stated in the DCSF guidelines, is intended to close the gap in the UK between ethnic minorities and the majority of students by raising the achievement of the former. The aims of this grant are twofold: to enable schools and LEAs to narrow the achievement gap; and to meet the cost of additional support for bi-lingual learners. The EMAG grant was devolved to schools based on the number of EAL and ethnic minority students and the number of those receiving free school meals (DfES, 2003a). As EAL students, ASR students might enjoy this grant, but often it does not support them directly and does not cater for other emotional or welfare needs. In addition, these funding arrangements classify all asylum-seeking students as minority ethnic (a euphemism often for Black students), subsuming the diversity of their cultural, religious and national origins and their socio-economic backgrounds. The result is that ASR students are seen as another disadvantaged group and located within the categories associated with lower-achieving students, even though some might have been academically successful students in their own country before fleeing to the UK.

Key to the whole funding approach of central government is that LEAs and schools have discretion on how to use EMAG funds and to decide whether ASR students are beneficiaries. When asked, schools voiced concern about using EMAG as the main source of supporting ASR students since such support could come at the expense of other groups which might take it amiss that money is passed to 'strangers' (Remsbery, 2003; Reakes and Powell, 2004). Similarly, the report *Aiming High* recognised that where EMAG has been used to meet the needs of ASR students, this gave 'less flexibility to focus on raising achievement of British-born minority ethnic students' (DfES, 2004b: 38). Some LEAs and schools which participated in our study raised similar concerns. For example, a headteacher in one of the schools we visited stated:

Obviously support for these children is always an issue. You feel you are pulling the support for one group of children to meet the needs of another group and you know the thinner you spread it, the less impact it has. (Cheston – dispersal area)

There are issues, too, around student numbers. EMAG is devolved to schools and LEAs once a year based on PLASC which means that, even where data about the ethnicity and EAL needs of ASR students are being collected, the grant does not cater for the majority of those students who arrived mid-term (Rutter, 2001a). EMAG started as EAL support for students originally from the Commonwealth, and it has been progressively reduced over the years. In contrast, the numbers of asylum-seeking students has increased and EMAG arrangements have not increased accordingly.[7] Rutter suggests, and the findings of our project confirm, that the reception given to asylum-seekers and refugees is a 'matter of educational debate': 'In England, the failure of ... EMAG to deliver support to refugee children, particularly those outside London, is a key component of this debate' (Rutter, 2001a: 29). Mott's (2000) survey data found that, while the majority of EMAG is devolved to schools, many LEAs felt that the needs of ASR students would have been better addressed by having a central support system. Existing funding arrangements for supporting refugee and asylum-seeking students were often described by LEAs as 'limited', 'inflexible' and 'inadequate', especially when considering their complex needs.[8]

The second funding stream in which ASR students are placed is the Vulnerable Children Grant (VCG). The *Vulnerable Children Grant – Guidance for Financial Year 2004–2005* describes its purposes thus: 'To support attendance, integration or reintegration into school ... and to provide additional educational support to enable vulnerable children to achieve their potential' (DfES, 2004c). In contrast to EMAG, the intention was that the VCG grant would cover some aspects of pastoral and academic support for vulnerable groups of students. The VCG therefore allows LEAs more flexibility and is said to encourage a more holistic child-centred approach to address the needs of different groups of vulnerable children (Kendall et al., 2004). ASR students are listed as one of the seven groups who might benefit from this grant.[9] Funding is provided for LEAs based on the number of students out of school, the number of students receiving free school meals and the number of gypsy/traveller students. However, only students of asylum-seeking families who have been dispersed and therefore receive Income Support can receive free school meals. Once more, since the devolution of this grant is not based on the total numbers of ASR students, not all will necessarily enjoy its benefits.

Like EMAG, the Vulnerable Children Grant has been represented as a solution to the problem of catering for asylum-seeking students; however, there also continue to be similar concerns about its impact:

> DfES is arguing now that ... [ASR student need] has been incorporated into the Vulnerable Children Grant, but, you know, how much of it is being recognised within that pot, there is a whole range of groups of pupils including Gypsy pupils, you know again, there is a limit to how far this particular fund will go. So it ... only gave marginal relief in that sense to some of the schools. (Interview with a former Ofsted inspector)

When the DfES commissioned an evaluation of the implementation of the VCG, its authors found that, despite the flexibility of the grant, LEAs tended to use it to facilitate and maintain existing strategic approaches and support services (Kendall et al., 2004). Therefore, the three main groups that benefited from this grant tended to be 'looked after' children, children with medical needs and gypsy/traveller children. However, the evaluation also noted the improved ability of LEAs to provide holistic support across vulnerable groups and that some had used the fund to develop work with unaccompanied asylum-seeking students (including work on mental health issues) and to fund college places for asylum-seeking students arriving late in Key Stage 4. One could argue that the existing funding arrangements (EMAG and VCG) allowed the school system to meet the needs of ASR students through mainstream arrangements without having to face the backlash of a hostile tabloid media which regularly accuses asylum-seekers of draining 'our' resources, including educational ones. At the same time we have to ask whether such funding is sufficient to support the successful integration of ASR students in to the ethos of the school and its learning culture.

Integration through achievement

In line with a neo-liberal marketisation agenda and the Home Office indicators of successful integration for refugees, the main prism through which the DfES/DCSF defines the results of good practice in relation to refugee students has been that of academic achievement (despite the failure to provide statistical evidence of that achievement). Asked what are the main concerns and challenges in relation to the integration of ASR students, one central government official listed the following: integrating students who arrive in school just before an examination period (especially Year 11); helping students acquire sufficient English in order to achieve; and ·developing a mechanism to overcome language barriers that will allow identifying gifted and SEN asylum-seeking students. The guidance given to LEAs and schools by central government therefore emphasises the need to ensure the educational achievement of ASR students and learning is defined as the main path to integration. For example, induction into a welcoming environment is defined as important if such students are to 'become *effective learners*' (DfES, 2002a: 17). Schools and LEAs are alerted to the importance of working with asylum-seeking students' families and communities: 'Establishing strong links with parents is an essential part of raising the *educational achievement* of asylum-seeker and refugee pupils' (ibid.: 29, our emphasis).

In the context of a competitive school market, Gillborn and Youdell (2001) found shifts in the priorities of teachers towards the high-achieving student (who brings in high reputation, increased enrolment and hence income) and the would-be-achieving students (who are expected to demand a good deal of the teachers' time). ASR students could so easily fall into the category of students who are considered as 'not suitable cases for treatment', not needing to be helped to achieve their potential since their achievements are seen to be of no reputational or financial consequence (Gillborn and Youdell call this categorisation *educational triage*).[10]

In addition in this competitive situation, ASR children might even be regarded by schools as a potential threat to school standards and record of achievement (McDonald, 1998). Aware of this danger, refugee advocates fought for the right of schools to be given the option of excluding ASR students (if they had been less than two years in the country) or any student with English as additional language from the school's examination results. The argument put forward was that without this option ASR students might find that they are located in lower-achieving schools. The decision not to count such students in school league tables might have a positive effect and even encourage schools to accept and welcome them[11] – a view supported by the ASR Student Officer at Horton:

> The other thing I think that's helped is not having to include new arrivals in the league tables because all our schools obviously are very, very worried about their results and their position in the league tables and I think that the fact that we don't have to include the new arrivals means that they are welcomed into schools where perhaps they wouldn't be if it was thought that they would be included.

However, there are potentially negative implications of the decision to omit ASR students from performance results. It might send the message that LEAs and schools have limited responsibility towards these children and that they are not entitled to the same opportunity as other students. Such concerns were articulated by some LEA officers who took part in this study, as the example below shows:

> So if we are going to take out those who have been in the school less than two full years, do we ever make a report on how those youngsters have actually performed compared to other similar youngsters elsewhere? [...] and I think that's one of the difficulties, that there isn't actually any good government data on performance of refugees and asylum-seekers. (Head of Inclusion, Horton)

There is also the risk that, by excluding asylum-seeking students from school performance results, the impression is given that such students are only temporarily in the country and therefore have less status in the school and that their integration is only perceived by schools to be relevant once they cease seeking asylum.

In sum, the DfES/DCSF policy approach to the education of ASR students veers between the decision to keep such children out of the public eye, and removing them from the achievement agenda at the same time as encouraging their achievement. The morality of this approach lies in the desire, if it is genuine, to protect such children from social conflict, but arguably by using invisibility and marginalisation as the means of protection, they may yet be protecting the government more than the children.

A reactive stance and the policy void

A third feature of the DfES approach to ASR education was, as one official argued, its reactive rather than proactive nature. In principle the DfES has not initiated any intervention on behalf of ASR children, seeing its role as responding to individual requests made by LEAs, parents or ministerial appeals. Monitoring the implementation of its guidance and developing new policies have not been seen as part of its role. In contrast one government body has taken a more proactive approach. In 2001, Ofsted set up a two-year research project on the impact of ASR students' arrival on schools; this was followed by a report entitled *The Education of Asylum-seeker Pupils* (Ofsted, 2003a). As one Ofsted inspector we interviewed commented,

> the other aspect that generated the Report is that, at that time, the Home Office was implementing a dispersal programme [...] We also

wanted to look at LEAs that haven't got this long established tradition, who were part of the dispersal areas. We wanted to see how
they *are* coping, how they are getting up to speed.

It is not clear whether Ofsted wished to help schools promote inclusion or
help government become aware of the impact of its immigration policy, or
both. Whatever the reason, Ofsted publicly argued that its evaluation
project was part of the inclusion and race equality agendas.[12] Thus:

> It is very much part of the inclusion agenda in terms of what we
> are looking at. So it wasn't a one-off exercise: it was very much
> part of looking at issues of race equality, issues to do with inclusion,
> very much current in education, part of the inspection framework.
> (Interview with an Ofsted inspector)

The report highlighted key difficulties that schools were experiencing in
dispersal areas because of the way in which the policy was implemented.
These included a lack of expertise among teachers with pupils new to
English; a lack of basic knowledge about linguistic, cultural and educational experiences of dispersed asylum-seeking pupils; and no training
to help identify pupils who might have suffered severe distress and
trauma. As the report noted: 'The impact on LEAs and schools of the
location of the housing in the dispersal areas was rarely thought through
fully by the various agencies' (Ofsted, 2003a: 7). Despite this, however,

> many asylum-seeker pupils made good progress in relatively short
> periods of time and almost all made at least satisfactory progress.
> The combination of their determination to succeed and the strong
> support of their parents provided a potent recipe for success (Ofsted,
> 2003a: 6).

As we have already argued, forced migration can have a great effect
on areas other than government education policy. The tensions inherent in immigration and asylum policies between different regimes of
rights are also negotiated and experienced at the local level. Local government and community response to the presence of asylum-seekers
and refugees are most likely to be different from government and
national discourses (Castles, 1998; Humpage and Marston, 2006).
Joppke (1999) reminds us that, in the 1970s, when so-called 'racial
inexplicitness' (Kirp, 1980) was the norm for government policy
towards the integration of immigrant and ethnic minorities, racial

equality was dealt with more explicitly and sometimes even radically at the local level. Local authorities took the lead on race relations, collected data on ethnic minorities and developed their own affirmative-action programmes and anti-racist and inclusive practices across and within schools. Joppke (1999: 238) concludes:

> [L]ocal immigrant integration is ... the result of statecraft. In Britain, local governments are 'key agents of the welfare state' [...] To the degree that immigrant integration was welfare state integration, its natural site was local government.

Cohen (2002) also argues that local authorities in Britain have a history of adopting a more proactive, radical line in relation to immigration issues than central government. A report published by the Great London Authority (GLA) (ICAR, 2004: 1), for example, stated:

> London has for centuries been a city of immigration, and a very striking feature of this in recent years has been the arrival of asylum-seekers and refugees from all parts of the world. Asylum-seekers have a legal right to seek asylum in the UK [...] Furthermore, there is a responsibility to safeguard the welfare of asylum-seekers and refugees who have a legal right to be in the UK and are likely to have suffered victimisation already in their country of origin.

Put sociologically, the GLA drew on a different 'politics of belonging' than the one constructed by central government. Underlying this different approach is arguably a different and more compassionate reaction than that of the Home Office towards those seeking asylum. This sense of compassion which sees the Other as having rights is closer to what Weil (1970) described as compassion in relation to concepts of social justice. It encouraged the GLA to define its responsibility towards those seeking asylum in a way that countered both government and public discourses. Such compassion, however, did not necessarily remove the dilemmas that local authorities faced in providing necessary and sufficient support services for ASR students.

Local dilemmas

The educational service at local level, as in many other societies, struggles with the pressures of exclusionary immigration policy, hostile media and the need to identify a compassionate stance towards ASR students that adequately reflects the educational goals of social inclusion and educational achievement. Discursively, local authorities are positioned as arbiters of community values and social cohesion. On the shoulders of local authority politicians and officers rests the responsibility of ensuring that all ASR children receive their entitlement to education but also find sufficient support to survive in a competitive educational environment and, on occasion, in a milieu of tense community relations. The rest of this chapter focuses on how LEAs negotiate this role in relation to ASR students.

Our attention was drawn particularly to a number of different political and moral dilemmas which LEA officers face: how to define ASR children; how best to cater for their needs; and what level of support service and funding priority should be made available to them. Like the DfES/DCSF, local authorities also have to decide whether data on ASR students should be collected – in other words, whether to *keep them invisible* or *make them visible*. Secondly, should local authorities develop *targeted policies* and funding for this group of often traumatised children (a particularist approach not dissimilar to that which was used for girls in the 1980s [Arnot, 2009]) or should they use the principle of universalism and *mainstream* such students within existing policy approaches – in other words treat them like everyone else. Thirdly, local education authorities have to decide what it means to *include and integrate* ASR students, especially in light of the Home Office view that the concept of integration should only apply to refugees (see Chapter 4). Put more theoretically, LEAs have had to decide whether they conform to the government's version of a 'politics of belonging' or articulate an alternative politics that prioritises children's rights over and above immigration policy considerations and engages, in a more compassionate way, with their circumstances.

Studies of the education of ASR students in the past decade have all indicated general goodwill at the local level (LEAs and schools).[13] However this goodwill does not express itself in a similar form across the country. Given the political void and tensions created by the central government stance on immigration, it is not surprising that our survey of 58 LEAs revealed considerable diversity in the ways in which ASR students were conceptualised, positioned and their needs addressed within mainstream education. LEAs differed in the decisions they took in terms of supporting ASR students. Below we explore issues to do with making ASR students visible, choosing between mainstreaming or targeting approaches and deciding how support services are to be developed, before focusing in greater depth on the discursive policy frameworks which constructed the asylum-seeking and refugee child as a recognisable subject with needs that could be catered for. The pragmatics of compassion come through such data.

Balancing between visibility and invisibility: data collection strategies

As we have seen, the issue of the visibility or invisibility of ASR students is one that was resolved by central government in favour of the latter approach. At the local level visibility carries great social risks for asylum-seeking families, in particular of making ASR students visible in highly emotionally charged environments experiencing community conflict. In some areas of the country the BNP is active in raising local concern about the alleged criminality of ASR families, there has been a rise in Islamaphobia since 9/11 and, even more directly, parents are worried about choosing schools whose students may include former child soldiers, trafficked girls and otherwise traumatised youth. On the other hand, as we saw earlier, without information what could the local authority seriously offer to protect such children's lives and well-being?

Four different strategies of LEA data collection were identified in our survey. Each could be seen as part of a continuum from visibility to invisibility. The most popular decision amongst our LEA sample appeared to be that of making ASR students visible in order to monitor and to cater for their needs. This *'monitoring strategy'* (adopted by 45 per cent of our LEA sample) involved actively collecting data. LEAs which invested substantial amounts of resources and efforts to monitor these children described their decision to single them out in terms of trying to gain an understanding of ASR students' special needs. Some LEAs made great efforts not only to ensure that ASR students had access to education but also to care for those who were not 'in the system'.

In contrast to the DfES/DCSF, LEAs employing this approach created a specific category for ASR students on the local authority database or a separate database which was updated regularly. They either relied on one partial source of data (such as NASS) or created a network of information that usually included NASS, housing providers, social services, schools and voluntary organisations. An example of this approach could be found in Greenshire where the ASR officer commented:

> ... the main thing was that we didn't have any data about asylum-seekers and refugees in school and that's sort of become apparent that you need to know about these students in order to identify their needs or pinpoint what school needs more help and things like that

[...] if you think about it data collection and updating the information because you get it referred to us and you need to check out if people are still at school or if they are gone because there are highly mobile groups but just to have a relatively accurate picture. I have to tell you that there is a slight increase [in the] number of students that we have in Greenshire, which is totally contrary to the experience of social services in Greenshire because their numbers are dropping and that's what the government says as well because the big statistics for the first three months came out a couple of days ago ... that number is dropping but we don't experience this and that is an interesting issue I think because we are not a dispersal area and still we have quite a lot of students and families ...

This officer saw the collection of detailed ASR data as important, not just because of the need to find out about such children and cater for their needs but also in order to counter the government's 'reduce the numbers' policy. If the government has an interest in making ASR students invisible, this officer pointed out, it runs the risk that ASR students will be 'missed out'. On purpose or not, this LEA decision to make ASR visible acts as a means of countering the politics of immigration.

Quite a few of the LEA officers we interviewed felt that the task of maintaining an accurate database was extremely difficult. As one commented, 'it is hard to maintain and very frustrating'. Because of the mobile nature of this population, the data were either inaccurate and/or quickly out of date. Among those who held a separate database, the decision to use different sources, rather than one source, and to cross-reference different sources of information was often derived from the experience (especially in dispersal areas) that data provided by NASS are not useful for a range of reasons. Remarks such as 'NASS does not inform us quickly enough' or 'NASS information is inaccurate' were repeated by LEAs. For example, the LEA officer in Cheston responsible for data collection explained: 'When I get the papers from NASS with the ages, etc., the children are, it gives me the language which isn't always correct and the country which isn't always correct either.'

Almost a quarter of the LEAs in our sample (24 per cent) adopted what we called the *partial monitoring strategy*, where LEAs actively collect data on a yearly basis rather than on a more regular basis. The ASR data were collected by schools mainly upon admission. As a result, children who were not offered a school place could be lost. Another difficulty was that these locally derived strategies did not involve collecting information from schools more than once a year – meaning that the process did not record pupil mobility and mid-term school admissions. Those LEAs less actively involved on a regular basis with data collection, often because of a lack of resources, nevertheless saw great importance in making this category of student visible so as to be able to plan suitable forms of support.

At the other end of the continuum, we found what we called a *deductive strategy*. This was described by 17 per cent of our LEA sample. LEAs adopting this strategy made a conscious decision to collect data but without making ASR children visible by asking them directly to describe themselves as such. These authorities found alternative ways of monitoring ASR students. They did not have a specific category for ASR students on their database, but they deduced their numbers from cross-referencing other databases such as EAL, new arrivals and PLASC. Officers in these LEAs appeared to be particularly concerned about the sensitivity of the issue and the dilemma of catering for these students' needs without stigmatising them as 'problems', especially in light of hostile public and media discourses. For example, one London borough officer argued that the borough 'did not see the status of asylum as relevant' and feared that the term 'asylum-seeker' was now part of 'scare terminology'. Similarly officers in another London borough claimed that it would be a 'bad practice' to ask someone for their citizenship status. The difficulty they faced was how to create a safe form of visibility. As a result they played down the issue, highlighting instead aspects relating to minority ethnic and EAL provision.[14] However, they made a strong effort to deduce as much information as possible about ASR children because of the importance of having this information in order to meet their needs and help them integrate into the school system.

The tensions in the political climate around immigration which we described earlier shaped the following two comments from advisory support teachers in Greenshire who talked about the visibility–invisibility dilemma thus:

> They may have particular needs that are not being addressed simply because you want to treat them the same as everyone else. So you can understand that [data collection] as an instinct but it's not necessarily the best professional response because you really need to know a fair bit about any child to see how you respond to them. (Advisory support teacher, Greenshire)

> There are some schools now where there's almost a sense of we don't want to identify these students as asylum-seeking because it identifies

them as a slightly different group, different to others and I think there's some confusion in their minds between the agenda for inclusion and the need to be aware of the differences. (Senior advisory support teacher, Greenshire).

Officers we spoke to in the eight LEAs (some 14 per cent of the sample) which did not collect any specific information about ASR students explained their decision as having been shaped largely by pragmatic reasons. Having very low numbers of ASR students could not justify such an elaborate exercise – a reason used mainly by LEAs in non-dispersal rural areas. Others claimed, following DfES/DCSF logic, that this was too transient a population to monitor. Others suggested that, from a service provider and funding perspective, asylum-seeking and refugee status was not a relevant category. For example, one LEA officer from a dispersal area with high numbers of ASR students (at least according to the dispersal statistics) explained that, although they collected extensive data on minority ethnic students and new arrivals, they did not have a separate category for ASR students, since:

> It is not relevant for the school practice to know whether someone is an asylum-seeker. From the school's point of view it does not serve any purpose to ask about asylum status, it doesn't attract additional funding.[15]

This officer highlighted a second policy dilemma related to the decision about data collection – whether to mainstream or to develop targeted policies and funding arrangements for such children. The dilemma of universalism versus particularism is one which has shaped many of the debates in the UK about egalitarianism in the post-war period. It addresses the dangers of moving from the universalism of the welfare state to one of targeted specific policy strategies appropriate to different types of disadvantaged groups. Below we examine how, in 2004, the LEAs in our study addressed this problem – one which goes deep into the heart of whether it is more compassionate to separate ASR children from mainstream provision or to ensure that they receive the same opportunities as all other children.[16]

Mainstreaming or targeting policies

Not surprisingly, we found that most local authorities in our sample directed schools to mainstream ASR students into existing policy frameworks, where applicable. Where ASR students were seen to have more than the usual range of needs, the case for new separate policy development was stronger.

The DfES/DCSF does not mandate local authorities to provide a specific policy for supporting ASR students. It recommends, however, that LEAs develop an appropriate policy or include reference to the education of this group *either* under its Education Development Plan (EDP) or in relation to other policies: 'To ensure that the education needs of these children are properly taken into account, LEAs are encouraged to develop local policies and procedures ...' (DfES, 2002a: 10).

When we asked LEA officers whether they had developed a policy for the education of ASR students in their local schools, four types of LEA policy responses were identified. The ways in which LEAs addressed this mainstreaming-targeting dilemma were as follows:

- 15.5 per cent referred to their general policy in relation to vulnerable groups, but had no specific policy or specific reference in existing policies to ASR students.
- 15.5 per cent of LEAs in the survey had developed examples of 'good practice' in relation to ASR students rather than a specific policy.
- 28 per cent of LEAs reported identifying ASR students as a specific category within a broader policy (for example, EMA and EAL).
- 41 per cent of the LEA sample had developed a targeted policy for ASR education.

The first group of nine LEAs (15.5 per cent) saw ASR students as no different from other groups of students which existing educational policies already addressed. The second group of nine authorities (15.5 per cent), like the DfES, saw their role as the dissemination of good practice and basic information on ASR students' needs to their schools. The third group of 16 (28 per cent) of LEA respondents, as suggested by the DfES guidelines, *specifically* referred to ASR students within their broader policy approaches (such as EMA, EAL and EDP).

All these models confirmed that the LEAs wished to see asylum-seeking students as no different from others, and all these LEAs chose to mainstream ASR students. One LEA in a dispersal area with a relatively developed support system felt that schools were overwhelmed with policies, so preferred to integrate policy aspects regarding ASR students into already existing (compulsory) policies such as EMA or Race Equality. They feared that another policy document for overburdened schools might create an antagonistic response within the community.

Officers in some of the LEAs we researched claimed that they preferred to focus on 'doing' rather than writing policy statements. For instance, one LEA officer explained: 'We are good at issues of support but not on the paper side of it; we deal with support not with creating policies.' A few authorities referred to the problem of resources and funding as the reason why they had no specific policy for asylum-seeking students' education while another explained that they were in the process of putting together a policy, but since they did not have a designated officer, and the responsibility for ASR students resided with the EMAS officer, they were unable to make progress. The lack of a specific policy on ASR students' education therefore did not necessarily mean a lack of awareness on the part of the authority or schools, nor did it indicate poor provision or services.

When compared with the results of earlier studies of LEA provision (Mott, 2000), the findings of this study suggest that there has been an increase in the number of LEAs developing a comprehensive focused policy specifically to meet the needs of ASR students. The final group of 24 LEAs (41 per cent) had taken the step of developing specific targeted policies. However, within this group we could identify two types of policies. Nine of them were using a needs-based approach. Their politics were narrowly focused on particular needs rather than general wellbeing. Most of this group had established a separate language policy for such students.

Only 15 of the LEAs that were part of the fourth group had created *separate comprehensive and developed policies* on ASR education. These policies emphasised social inclusion and challenged popular stereotypes. They usually included information about the education, emotional and social needs of ASR students, information about legislation and services, the criteria for good practice and suggestions for the inclusion of these students into mainstream education.

These different policy stances for monitoring the presence of ASR students and locating the policies which apply to their education have consequences for the forms of social and educational support offered to ASR students. Again, the pragmatics appeared to override the politics of compassion, with many attempts made to cater for such students as for any other vulnerable group.

Offering support

The definitional factors used by LEAs shape the ways in which ASR students are positioned within existing policies but does not determine the level and type of support services provided for them. One LEA option for developing such services is to follow the central government policy

approach through funding lines. So, for example, some 22 local education authorities (37 per cent) located responsibility for ASR students
with EMAS officers whose main brief was that of 'raising achievement'.
A small group of LEAs (eight LEAs who made up 14 per cent of our
sample) chose to locate their ASR students with the Race Equality team
and only 7 per cent (four LEAs) located them under the responsibility
of the EAL or New Arrivals team. In contrast, the majority of LEAs
(41 per cent – 24 LEAs) appointed a designated ASR support officer or a
team (four LEAs) who were usually line-managed through EMAS.

Given the attrition of local budgets in the past 20 years, LEA approaches
to organising their services were mostly informed by the availability of
funding. Since the main source from which LEAs have been able to draw
support for ASR children has been EMAG, it is not surprising that the
most frequent arrangement was designating one of the EMAS officers to
support these children, whether in the capacity of a special ASR Student
Support Officer, or as an EMAS officer. Those LEAs which were able to
afford a team or an officer were usually the ones that were able to keep a
significant part of the EMAG money centrally, rather than devolve it to
schools. Some ASR teams managed to secure additional support from the
LEA or successfully bid for external funding. Some LEAs in the survey
reported that they had dedicated the VCG primarily to meet the needs of
asylum-seeking students. On the other hand, LEAs who were unable to
secure funding reported that they struggled to maintain an adequate level
of service that addressed the needs of ASR students.

This was a main problem in dispersal areas and in LEAs with a low
ethnic minority population that had limited access to EMAG. One LEA
officer in a dispersal area argued that the government did not take into
account the fact that they were a dispersal area and so had not diverted
more resources to allow them to meet the needs of these students.
Another LEA in a dispersal area (which originally had only 2 per cent
of ethnic minority students and hence had a very small EMAG) with
high numbers of travellers who also needed to benefit from the VCG,
talked about the difficulty of having very limited resources to draw
upon in supporting ASR students. This evidence suggests that, for
many LEAs, the mainstreaming–targeting dilemma and the decision to
mainstream ASR students was a funding issue rather than a preference
for mainstreaming as the best ethical or professional practice.

While we could not determine whether LEAs offered overall a 'good'
support system for ASR students we were able to glean from our survey
data that LEAs chose a variety of different practices. The survey data
are divided into three different support structures: 1) admission; 2) the

88

Table 5.1 Local authority support services for asylum-seeking and refugee students

	A. Targeted services	B. Partial services	C. Non-specific services
Admission	Very well-rehearsed admission procedure which is facilitated by the ASR officer/team/designated officer and not the LEA's general admission service. Support system might include: home visits; interpreting services; accompanying the child and the family to their first day at school; conducting special assessment that is designed to overcome language barriers; a special welcome kit for the child, the school and information pack for parents. (27 LEAs – 46 per cent)	The team/officer who has the responsibility for asylum-seeking and refugee students can be involved in some aspects of admission, for example home-school liaison, accompanying the child to his/her first day at school or producing materials for parents or schools. (16 LEAs, 28 per cent)	There is no involvement in the admission procedure and there is no special admission procedure for asylum-seeking and refugee children in place. (15 LEAs, 26 per cent)
Training	The LEA provides a wide range of central training INSET training that covers, for example, raising awareness, supporting asylum-seeking and refugee students in classrooms, emotional needs, and so on. (28 LEAs, 49 per cent)	Mainly INSET training or specific reference to asylum-seeking and refugee students in other training such as race equality or EAL training. (17 LEAs, 29 per cent)	No specific training. (13 LEAs, 22 per cent)

Table 5.1 Local authority support services for asylum-seeking and refugee students – *continued*

	A. Targeted services	B. Partial services	C. Non-specific services
Ongoing support	Support covers a range of issues: • EAL support. • After-school activities. • Access into mainstream curriculum. • Special provisions for post-16, or early years. • Supporting refugee communities though supplementary schools. • Psychological support. • Pastoral support. • Raising awareness through citizenship education. • Liaison with other agencies. • Home-school liaison. (23 LEAs, 39.5 per cent)	The support is focused on one or two areas, usually EAL. (30 LEAs, 52 per cent)	No specific provisions for asylum-seeking and refugee students exist. They receive support under EMAS or EAL based on their EAL needs. (5 LEAs, 8.5 per cent)

training of staff; and 3) ongoing support of pupil needs. Table 5.1 indicates the type of local activity associated with the presence of ASR students in a community and the very different approaches to each of the three types of support system.[17]

There was not necessarily any coherence found between the three components of LEA support services. In other words, having highly developed admission procedures and delineated responsibilities did not necessarily imply that the LEA also offered extensive training to teachers and support staff, or that it had a targeted and ongoing support system for ASR students' learning and pastoral needs. However, these support services were indicative of the level of funding available and LEA definitions of what constituted the needs of ASR students, how their rights should be defined and the responsibility of the local community to support them. When we explored these support services and officers' comments about them further we uncovered a range of discursive framings of the ASR student. Through such framings, we started to hear the values which shaped education in the last few years and how the needs of ASR youth, as newcomers and as strangers, were located and made sense of within the existing policy languages and frameworks.

Filling the void: policy discourses

The tendency is to define the educational needs of ASR children using existing policy languages and conceptual frameworks which then define the nature and scope of the 'problem', relevant 'solutions' and the types of support on offer. Rutter (2006), for example, analysed 43 LEA policy texts and interviewed mainly refugee support teachers in 2000-2001. She described six different LEA policy approaches: the *induction approach* which focused on mobility, *the EAL approach* with its emphasis on English language teaching, the *special educational needs* approach which identified emotional and behaviour difficulties of refugee children; the *race equality* approach drawing on equal opportunities; and finally *the ecological resilience approach* which particularly focused on developing refugee children's resilience through a wide range of support services.

On the whole, attention within many of these discursive framings is focused on asylum-seeking or refugee children and their families rather than on the transformation of the school culture and its values. Although such frameworks are notoriously hard to capture empirically since they involve subtle distinctions, our analysis of the 2004 survey data of 58 LEA support service officers and their policy documents (when they were provided) found a similar range of policy approaches to those found by Rutter. These policy approaches employed a conceptual language that drew on particular understandings of 'the problem' and its solution. As conceptual languages, the various approaches were not mutually exclusive; LEAs combined a variety of different discursive frameworks to justify their support services. We uncovered the six discursive frameworks which are described below.

English as an Additional Language (EAL) was by far the most popular discursive framework (22 LEAs). Employing an individualised needs-based approach, this framework identifies ASR students primarily as EAL students. Legitimating the decision, for example, involved collecting data mainly on the languages which the students spoke and their competence in English and focusing the support offered to these pupils on improving their English. This model implied understanding the language needs of young people to be able to access learning but also to integrate socially within the school and community. Rutter also found this to be the dominant local authority approach, although provision of language teaching was not necessarily adequate.

An alternative policy framework highlighted the fact that ASR students were first and foremost 'new arrivals'. A small group of eight LEAs in our study used a *New Arrivals Framework* which had a particular educational focus. Here schools were encouraged to develop strategies for coping with the particular characteristics of ASR students in terms of their being new to the UK education system.[18] LEAs adopting this policy discourse perceived ASR students as those most likely to have experienced an interrupted education (if they had any formal education at all), to be mobile, and to have been admitted to school in mid-term. Implicit in this framework is the assumption that successful integration could be achieved only by early intervention; however it begs the question of how long a child could be considered a ' new arrival' – a stranger – and when he/she would make the transition into being considered part of the community.

The two government funding streams identified earlier – that of the VCG and EMAG – appeared to be less attractive frameworks for our LEA sample. Only two LEAs in our study represented these ASR students as a group of vulnerable children 'at risk' of dropping out of education. Therefore, the support system in these LEAs was mainly organised to ensure the access of ASR pupils to mainstream education and to ensure that they (and their parents) were well informed about their entitlement and the services available to them. The limited use of the *Vulnerable Children* discursive framework is somewhat surprising considering that the VCG, as we have seen, is one of the two main funding sources for supporting

ASR students. Perhaps this finding reflects the inadequacy of the funding arrangements offered to LEAs to support these students.

A small group of LEAs (13) recognised ASR youth primarily as 'minority ethnic' whose needs were assumed to be met through the generic 'raising achievement agenda' and through a school improvement strategy. These LEA teams focused their support services on improving asylum-seeking pupils' ability to learn and achieve academically. Far less attention was given to developing a multicultural approach which could have celebrated the cultural diversity associated with ASR children's country of origin. It could be argued that, by defining these children as minority ethnic students, the racialised experiences of such children and their families in local communities could be reinforced with little space for policy interventions to address racial stereotyping associated with the majority ethnic population.

There were a few (just seven) LEAs in our study which recognised that ASR children could be possible targets of racial harassment and as requiring, therefore, the support of *race equality policies* or *multicultural education*. The main focus of these LEAs was one of raising awareness of the cultural differences and vulnerability of these youth. Considering the hostile media representation of asylum-seekers, the highly racialised public debate around their entitlements and research evidence indicating that asylum-seeking children are often subject to racial harassment (Rutter and Hyder, 1998; Rutter and Stanton, 2001; Stead, Closs and Arshad, 2002), it is somewhat surprising that more LEAs did not refer to the continuing importance of racial inequalities within education or demonstrate an awareness of the racialised context surrounding ASRs in the UK. This limited use of the race equality framework (similarly found by Rutter, 2006) suggests that LEAs and schools may have found it easier to address the needs of ASR pupils within existing frameworks such as the EAL and raising achievement agendas, which are less politically controversial than the race equality model, which would require socially transformative school practices.

One of the strongest indicators that LEAs had started to adopt a different, more integrative approach to ASR education was the fact that some 18 out of the 58 authorities adopted a multi-agency, child-centred policy framework which we called the *holistic approach* (Pinson and Arnot, 2010). This framework, as we have seen, encouraged the development of a separate comprehensive policy for ASR students. It also focused attention on the ethos of schools and the possibilities that schools could, if sufficiently aware, challenge the negative effects of migration and displacement. The focus of this particular discursive framework derives from a humanitarian and humanistic concern for *the child* on the one hand

and the principle of social inclusion through the recognition of difference on the other. This approach, with its emphasis on ASR children as children, with their rights to be treated with respect, ran against the grain of immigration controls and national hostility to asylum-seekers. The marginalisation of immigration discourse about scroungers, illegal immigrants and criminals appeared irrelevant to these LEAs, which were concerned with defining a compassionate and genuinely inclusive school system.

In the next chapter we report on the data from our three LEA case studies in order to reveal some of the assumptions and understandings which underlay this holistic approach to asylum-seeking and refugee children and their education. Our interest in this particular discursive framework is that its concept of 'the whole child' appears to lie at the epicentre of a model of compassion that counters the ethics of UK immigration policy and thus repositions teachers and schools *vis-à-vis* the state.

6
Countering Hostility with Social Inclusion: Local Resistances

While the first gate of entry into the UK is nothing if not hostile, the second gate of entry could be made more conducive to humane values. However, as Chapter 4 demonstrated, the rights of ASR children as children were practically overridden by central government immigration policy; until the removal of the reservation to the UNCRC in 2008, they did not even enjoy the UNCRC's protection and could not expect recognition of their human rights. Although not mentioned specifically in ECM nor enjoying the full protection of the Children Acts 1989 and 2004,[1] (due to the exclusion of immigration agencies up until October 2009 from the obligation to safeguard all children), ASR students nevertheless are considered by some LEAs as not only their responsibility but also part and parcel of their educational mission to promote social inclusion.

We identified in our research a number of local authorities which had adopted a holistic approach[2] towards ASR students which clearly articulated a different political agenda to that represented by immigration policy. The language which officers, headteachers, teachers and other support staff used to speak about ASR students, their understandings of ASR students' predicament, past and present, the empathy they showed towards ASR youth they encountered in their spheres of action, privileged concepts of social inclusion over and above the exclusionary agenda and practices of immigration policy. Many educational officers and teachers spoke about the importance of countering exclusion, using the language and practices associated with child-centred ideologies. On further investigation, it appeared, as we shall see, to be as much about strengthening the inclusive ethos of their schools as it was about ensuring that ASR children received sufficient support to flourish as individuals and to develop their abilities, even if they were only temporarily resident within UK borders. In order to achieve these two agendas together, the ASR child had to be reconfigured back into the vulnerability of childhood to be assured the full support of the educational establishment. The success of social inclusion as an official educational discourse became therefore dependent in part on achieving the safety and happiness of the newly arrived and estranged 'non-citizen' child.

Local diversities but a common approach

We decided to develop in-depth case studies of three such LEAs. Our strategy involved collecting and analysing both descriptively and discursively relevant policy documents, conducting interviews with LEA officers and visiting at least one primary and one secondary school that reflected this seemingly compassionate ethos[3] (for more details see Chapter 3).

The three LEAs which used 'whole child' approaches were located in very different demographic and geographic contexts, with variable numbers of ASR students. Although the three authorities had had different experiences of working with minority ethnic populations and had to deal with different community politics, they all had developed extraordinary levels of support for ASR families. Their common starting point was often a 'needs-based approach' identifying some of the multitude of needs associated with individual ASR youth, and an assumption that many agencies and groups would need to be drawn upon to support them.

Take for example, *Cheston LEA* first – an urban northern LEA in a dispersal area which serves a relatively diverse population with large minority ethnic communities, especially those with an Asian heritage. In 1998–9, for the first time a small group of Kosovan refugees arrived in Cheston. Since 2000–1, significant numbers of asylum-seekers were dispersed to the town. At the time of our study, there were around 850 asylum-seekers and refugees in the county (relatively high numbers for the area) of which about 280 were children of school age who came from some 67 different countries, the main ones being Somalia, the Czech Republic, Iran and Afghanistan. The schools we visited had between 10 and 30 ASR students.

The reaction of the local population and local media in Cheston to ASR families tended to be positive with a very supportive local council. As the Head of EMAG commented:

> We've probably avoided to date and hopefully in the future the issues that have affected other Northern towns and in racial disturbance and

social upheaval terms. Cheston is bigger and perhaps a little bit more cosmopolitan that these towns where there have been problems, but Cheston has not been without its difficulties. There was some damage done to the outside of a mosque two years ago and there are racial disturbances and there is racism that happens in Cheston as it happens elsewhere. But we perhaps avoided some of the worst scenarios, partly by chance perhaps and partly by the nature of the population of Cheston ... by strategy and policy and I think that comes from the Council and the Chief Executive.

Cheston LEA's support for ASR pupils came through EMAS which had designated one of its Deputy Heads as an Asylum-seeker and Refugee Officer. The Deputy Head who had been assigned this responsibility also lead the '[Cheston] Asylum-Seekers Inclusion Consortium'. There was no policy as such for ASR students' education but EMAS provided guidance for schools on late-arrival pupils (mostly focused on ASR students) and information packs for schools about asylum-seekers and refugees. The emphasis in these documents was very clearly focused on the social inclusion of ASR students, facilitating their integration into schools and enabling them to rebuild their lives. The perspective fostered by Cheston was that services such as EAL were there as a means of achieving the inclusion for ASRs rather than as an end in itself. ASR students were also supported under EMA policies such as *Strategy for Supporting EAL Needs and Ethnic Minority Pupils*.

The centralised support services which were targeted at asylum-seeking students and schools were funded mainly by EMAG and also by the VCG (especially in funding school meals and uniforms) as well as external funding obtained through the consortium's bids. Many schools bought services from the LEA which meant the LEA employed and trained support teachers and teaching assistants and ran training and 'raising awareness' sessions for schools, governors, teachers, non-teaching staff, PGCE students and other county services.[4] The LEA ran an extensive induction package that included an in-class teaching assistant for six weeks; it offered classroom resources for EAL students in mainstream classrooms and provided other dual-languages resources. Help was provided to schools in developing programmes for citizenship education and a refugee week was hosted which focused on raising awareness of the school population on issues of asylum-seeking.

The support services helped manage the admission process by considering the different needs of ASR families, such as the need for social networks. As the Asylum-seeker and Refugee Officer commented: 'We try to find them the culturally appropriate place, religious-wise or shared culture within the school.' Support for schools focused on making sure that ASR students had access to the mainstream curriculum. An EMAS teacher in one secondary school commented:

> We're here first and foremost to make sure that all pupils access the curriculum and that their lack of proficiency only becomes a barrier if they haven't got the cognitive ability to access the curriculum.

Other activities involved a special arrangement for post-16 ASR students with the local FE college, a special 'life-skills programme' for late arrivals in Year 11 and after-school activities such as homework clubs for ASR students.

These extensive programmes that focused on the needs of the 'whole child' were not dissimilar from those described by local educational officers and teachers in *Greenshire* – a local education authority in a small shire county in the Midlands. Asylum-seekers first arrived in Greenshire at the end of the 1990s in small numbers. Unlike Cheston, Greenshire was not a dispersal area at the time of study. Asylum-seeking families who had made their own way to the county rather than being directed by NASS settled mainly in towns.

The school we visited in the authority had between 20 and 30 ASR students at any one time. A sudden increase in numbers occurred in 2000 so that by the spring of 2004, there were about 300 known ASR students in schools (a high number for a non-dispersal and non-London LEA), but Greenshire officers estimated that there were another 100 children who were not 'in the system'. ASR families came from, for example, Croatia, Zimbabwe, Lithuania, Kosovo and Somalia. They joined some 16 per cent of the local school population, which was already very ethnically diverse. The local population was predominantly White and in this region, the local media at the time was especially hostile towards asylum-seekers.

When we visited Greenshire authority it had already published a separate policy for the education of ASR students in 2002. The aim of this policy, as stated in its preface, was: '… to raise awareness within the LEA of the needs of refugees and asylum-seekers … [to] provide information and guidance to schools and promote social inclusion'. The policy document gave information about asylum-seekers and refugees in the UK, the LEA and school responsibility towards them and the support system which existed in the county. It defined the responsibility towards ASR pupils in terms of providing school placements as well as ensuring not only that their needs were met but that they were socially included.

In this authority the EMAS team included the Head of Service, a senior advisory support teacher, primary and secondary advisory support teachers, an Asylum-seeker and Refugee Pupil Support Officer and cultural mediators (many of whom were refugees themselves) – all working directly with schools and ASR students and their families. Greenshire EMAS was also part of a multi-agency strategy group which it initiated.

Being a non-dispersal area in which ASRs arrived voluntarily and mostly went unreported, Greenshire had a rather difficult time collecting relevant data; it nevertheless put a lot of effort into maintaining as comprehensive a database as possible after 2001. This was maintained by the Asylum-seeker and Refugee Pupil Support Officer who liaised regularly with other services such as housing, social services and voluntary agencies. The database included information about languages, nationality, school placement, pastoral support and status.

Like Cheston LEA, Greenshire local education authority also operated a targeted system of support for ASR pupils and schools. This included, for example: INSET and central training for teachers which focused on raising awareness; meeting the needs of ASR students; providing schools with translated school letters in different languages; making school uniform grants and free school meals available to those ASR students who were not supported by NASS; and addressing issues relating to trauma and emotional needs through music therapy projects, emotional literacy workshops and more. Advisory support teachers for primary and secondary schools worked closely with mainstream teachers to make the curriculum accessible to ASR students. In addition, Greenshire employed cultural mediators (some of whom were refugees themselves), who saw their role as providing ASR students and parents with the opportunity to share their concerns with someone with whom they shared the same language and culture. The cultural mediators facilitated communication between schools and the families, providing advocacy for the family, in-class support and first-language support for the children.[5]

Action was also taken by schools to raise awareness of refugee issues through the citizenship and religious curricula and to encourage information-sharing about the child's progress across departments. However, during the period of our research, local authority support for ASR students which was delivered through EMAS had to deal with another challenge, moving from client services to prioritising school improvement – a change that was criticised by the EMAS senior advisory support teacher: 'We now find ourselves within a group who do not necessarily have a real understanding ... of how we work, what we do, what our objectives are.'

Greenshire's range and diversity of activity was not unusual for LEAs using a holistic approach to address the needs of ASR students. *Horton Borough*'s (the third case study) profile of work on behalf of the very high numbers of ASR students in its catchment was equally impressive in terms of commitment of time and energy. Horton was the most experienced of our three case study local authorities in supporting the education of this diverse population. The borough had one of the highest percentages of ASR students in London and, at the time of our research, it had over a decade of experience in this area. There were around 5,500 ASR students in its schools – representing 16.9 per cent of its school population. Many ASR students originated from Somalia, the Congo or were Kurdish. Schools in Horton had up to 70 per cent (or more) minority ethnic pupils, with a few dozen languages. The three schools we visited in Horton had between 8 and 30 per cent ASR students. Unlike the officers in Cheston, Horton officers had wide experience of working with new arrivals. There was also a very high level of pupil mobility across schools. As one of the LEA officers stated: 'If you look at the history of [the borough] it's always been continual coming and going of people so it would be very strange if councillors were to do anything but welcome people.'

Horton support for ASR students was provided through EMAS. Here again it was line managed by the Inclusion Strategy Manager and was part of school improvement. Horton had a team comprising two Asylum-seeker and Refugee Pupil Officers, one for primary schools and one for secondary.[6] The Asylum-seeker and Refugee Pupil Support team had recently completed the work on all-embracing LEA guidelines for schools covering admission, through to induction and supporting ASR students' learning and other needs in mainstream education. There was also an Education Welfare Officer (EWO) working in the authority who specialised in ASR students and was also involved in the admission process.

Since the number of ASR students was very high, the team employed a decentralised approach and the local authority asylum team focused primarily on advising and supporting schools in their work through training and developing courses. Most schools used EMAG money to employ an EMAS teacher or a team of teachers that had responsibility for such students. The Horton asylum team also took part in the borough's multi-agency forum that included social services, housing and education.

The asylum team kept a central database. Horton schools collected their own student data upon admission, and there were schools that kept a refugee register and a progress profile for each pupil; this included elements of EAL and academic progress as well as social inclusion and integration factors. However, since Horton considered pupils' status to be a sensitive issue, pupils were not asked to state whether they were asylum-seekers or refugees and the database was mostly *deductive,* using Rutter's framework of cross-referencing information about languages, country of origin and EAL needs. The focus of the database revolved around EAL needs and languages – more pastoral-oriented information was kept by the Education Welfare Officers.

The targeted system of support for ASR students and schools included for example, central and INSET training for teaching staff that covered initial assessment, meeting the needs of these pupils, working with inter-preters, training for administrative staff about how to approach and welcome ASR students, and training for teachers in community sup-plementary schools. The asylum team maintained an active website which included examples of good practice in the borough, information from the DfES, NASS and examples of letters supporting families who were facing deportation. A bulletin was published twice a year which provided information about ASR communities.

Most of Horton Borough support focused on involving ASR parents in, for example: school training on how to encourage ASR parents' involve-ment; weekly surgeries to assist them with the process of admission; and multi-lingual information booklets for parents, including information about the education system and resources available in schools. This information was also available in audio-visual form (cassette and DVD). Of especial note was the directory of services they called Parent Aid which an Asylum-seeker and Refugee Pupil Officer described thus:

> [We] surveyed a number of schools ... and logged every single concern that parents brought to the school and when we actually examined them it covered a huge range of issues, you know, from 'how do I register with a GP' to 'can you help me with the housing department' or 'I need an immigration lawyer', 'I need to get in touch with NASS' and so we built the directory around those con-cerns that we've got, 10 sections ... they're all local contacts.

The imaginative support provided in these three LEAs through limited funding was clearly legitimated and shaped by strong holistic notions of the needs of the ASR student as a child who deserved the best that could be offered not just of schooling but as a new member of the community. As one Greenshire Senior Advisory Support Officer pointed out:

> We were very aware that this [the presence of ASR students in local schools] was not just an educational issue and that we needed to look at this pupil group ... in a very *holistic* way (our emphasis).

Below we describe some of the features of this approach from the perspective of support officers in LEAs and schools. These officers have different professional titles but they all worked closely with ASR students, crossing many boundaries in order to deliver this broader policy approach.

Holistic and multi-agency needs-based approaches

The data we collected through documents and interviews in the three case study LEAs revealed how strongly the authority and its teams had embraced a holistic view of the child's multi-faceted and complex emotional, physical, social and educational needs – an approach which, although often needs-based, appeared to reflect exceptionally strong commitment to notions of caring and compassion for those seeking asylum. For these LEAs, ASR children could not easily be boxed into categories such as 'EAL pupils' or 'newly arrived' pupils or even 'minority ethnic' or 'vulnerable children'. Recognition of the uniqueness of their circumstance made new broader strategies imperative, as the interview extracts below suggest:

> It wasn't the fact that there was a sudden increase in groups of children coming from more disparate ethnic backgrounds or language backgrounds. It was an awareness that some of these children actually brought with them some very distinct needs which we were not necessarily addressing within our normal support mechanisms. (Senior Advisory Support Officer in Greenshire)

> Some of our families have all sorts of issues that affect the children's ability to settle, access the curriculum, that are wider than just learning issues, you know. (Head of EMAS, secondary school, Horton)

Even prior to *Every Child Matters*, the necessity of developing a multi-agency strategy that linked schools strongly to the social services was evident. The ASR child's needs crossed the various professional boundaries for these LEAs, especially Greenshire. As the Head of EMAS there explained:

> If we just concentrate on education we would actually be on a hiding for nothing, in so far as, yes we can provide teachers and schools and instructors [...] But if, for example, they have a theoretically absentee parent ... the child does not have support that they should have. [...] still *our central focus is the child and their education*, but in order for the child to feel secure or safe, and valued, they've actually got to have that parent in some way or shape or form so you have to work alongside health, social services (our emphasis).

Such a holistic multi-agency approach encouraged a deep sense of responsibility towards ASR students, well beyond the legal obligation of the local authority to provide such pupils with an education and even beyond the duty to welcome them and give them additional teaching and classroom support. Schooling was seen as an important factor in creating for those children a 'safe base' and helping them to rebuild their lives. As the Asylum-seeker and Refugee Pupil Support Officer in Cheston stated:

> It's about a lot more than educational support, it's the whole support of starting something new, and in their case [...] It's the new house, the new food, the new clothes, the new sometimes very impoverished lifestyle to what they've left behind. It's the new reduced family if they've lost a parent on the way ... so the induction to the course is about being a carer, a mentor, a teacher, a supporter, it's all those things rolled up into one.

The Asylum-seeker and Refugee Pupil Support Officer in Greenshire described how she liaised with other services:

> I try to liaise with other agencies to try and sort out other needs as well [...] So it's really complex in a sense that you try to sort out that they would go to a GP or find a GP because if something worries them, the education of their children won't necessarily be the highest thing on their agenda.

With the arrival of significant numbers of asylum-seekers and refugees to the county in 2000–1, the Head of EMAS in Greenshire initiated the establishment of a multi-agency strategy group for the education of

ASR students. It met once a term and comprised an educational psychologist, representatives from social services, health and housing departments in the local authority, and other departments such as music therapy, as well as headteachers of schools with high numbers of ASR pupils:

> It is called a strategy group, but it is practitioners who would actually be leading on the appropriate strategies for dealing with particular pupils. So it is a sharing of information, building on people's specialist knowledge and the use of this knowledge collaboratively to be most effective. (Head of EMAS, Greenshire)

The strategy group was also responsible for behind-the-scenes changes at county level:

> [The] county council I think is very supportive [at the moment] for wanting to make provision for asylum-seekers and refugees but not proactive in addressing issues ... there was good planning and multi-agency work particularly between us and social services which the [Head of EMAG] would have initiated and driven. So I suppose the county council and parts of the hierarchy benefit from the fact that [the Head of EMAG] and her colleagues were proactive. (Head of Inclusion, Greenshire)

Greenshire officers saw the role of the support services to be one of raising awareness of asylum issues in the local population countering negative media stereotypes:

> We also have a role of informing a wider audience. So, for example, during refugee week we put displays up within the council area, and within the senior officers' area, because there is a lack of awareness of the issues in this particular field. (Head of EMAS, Greenshire)

To some extent, by informing local communities LEAs challenged the boundaries of the politics of belonging – they saw these ASR students and their families as part of their communities. Below we describe the ways in which officers in Horton, Cheston and Greenshire understood community and parental partnerships, how they constructed new indicators for successful inclusion and integration of ASR students into schools, and how, with these indicators, they challenged dominant performance models of schooling.

Local community and parental partnerhsips

Holistic approaches to the education of ASR students noticeably privilege parental partnerships. Kuhin (1998) and Vincent and Warren (1998), in two different studies, demonstrated the importance of school–parent relationships for the successful integration of ASR pupils, especially to counter the difficulties that some parents might have in understanding the ways in which the British education system works. School–parent relationships are also mentioned as an important factor in raising the achievement of these pupils in the DfES (2002b) *Good Practice Guidance*.[7]

The three LEAs we researched, even though their demographic profiles differed, were similar in terms of their approach to home–school relations. Despite or perhaps because of its ethnic diversity, Horton borough officers attributed great importance to school–parent relationships as critical to the integration of ASR children and seemed particularly to have highly developed practices in this respect. Horton schools were encouraged to invest in these relationships: 'If the parents are included, the children are [included] too' (Head of EMAS, secondary school). An example of this LEA's practice was the partnership established between the London Borough of Horton and the local FE college which provides ESOL courses for refugee parents in schools where 'parents can get accreditation for their own learning as well as helping their children' (Asylum-seeker and Refugee Pupil Support Officer). At the time of the research, 17 schools in the borough were involved in a special school–parent partnership project: 'We're very good in some ways at involving parents because we've actually got a home-school links teacher' (Deputy Headteacher, secondary school, Horton).

The following extracts from interviews with the Heads of EMAS in local primary and secondary schools exemplify the extent of support which schools offered to ASR parents and the partnership they established with them:

> We run ... parent workshops to empower the parents to help their children as well and to understand how the curriculum and the school system works here ... but also to develop their own skills. Like we have an ESL class, we have computer classes [...] We work with the parents on an area of literacy or numeracy to help them to understand the curriculum that their children are doing because, for many of our parents, culturally the system is very different. (Head of EMAS, secondary school, Horton)

The parents' thing, that's one of our big things. We started off a few years ago just running a parents' drop in ... that's developed into quite a solid little club where we now have other activities going on. So there is English language teaching for parents, there is basic adult literacy ... that is organised around the needs of the school [...] It does two things – it helps the parents understand and participate in the education that their child is receiving, but it also helps the parents develop some very early literacy in English [...] It helps the parents get to know each other. (Head of EMAS, primary school, Horton)

Horton LEA policy emphasised the importance of *social capital* for the successful integration of these children into mainstream schooling. The Head of EMAS in the secondary school suggested that one of the aims of the parents' club is that they would have a chance to meet with other parents and find a network of support. ASR parents were made part of the school community and offered not only routes to help them feel they belonged but provided with an experience that constructed them as active parents of their learner child. They wanted to give such parents ways to be empowered and to feel encouraged to rebuild their lives through having a meaningful role in their child's education and in the school community.

In Cheston, since some of the schools were aware of the social isolation that ASR families who have been dispersed might suffer, they made an effort to link new ASR families to existing communities in the county. Considerable benefit for these families was meant to be gained from such links:

[Y]ou may have asylum-seekers who are coming in who don't have a community to support them in the same way and therefore the role of the school is perhaps important. But we always try and liaise, and do liaise with any community. (Headteacher, secondary school, Cheston)

Cheston also understood that developed community links and social networks would contribute in the long term to the integration of the community in the wider society in the county. Thus, despite Home Office strictures that the concept of social integration was only to apply to refugee students and their families, the views expressed by officers and teachers in Cheston were precisely the opposite:

When we see (community activities) beginning to develop we say, Do you need any help? Perhaps you'd like to join in our grant application and maybe put a bit of funding their way or offer them [asylum-seeking students] opportunities for photocopying. However mundane, sometimes this can make an enormous difference [...] You know, it's just making things available but you've got to let it develop how they see it, it's their community. Hopefully they become part of the wide community [in the country] as well. (Asylum-seeker and Refugee Pupil Officer, Cheston)

Out of the three LEAs studied, Cheston had the most developed relationships with local minority ethnic communities in general and refugee communities in particular. The county's Consortium for the Inclusion of Asylum-seekers and Refugees, which was led by the LEA's Asylum-seeker and Refugee Pupil Support Officer, included representatives of some of the refugee communities in the area. Other forms of consultation with refugee communities existed both at county and school level.[8] Otherwise, schools and colleges reported that they often sought the assistance of refugee communities, especially when admitting a new family to the school. For example:

The Somali community is one in particular where we've worked very closely with representatives from the Somali community ... particularly to identify other issues that are affecting those students. It's working like a focus group to some extent. We're getting feedback from them, we're trying to change the provision that we offer, the pastoral support that we offer. (Deputy Head, FE college, Cheston)

The holistic inclusive ethos of Cheston LEA drew heavily on the county's strong commitment to celebrating and valuing cultural diversity. In that respect, having ASR families seemed a positive addition rather than a burden.

Establishing clear indicators of successful social inclusion and integration

The ethos and agenda around social inclusion encourages notions of integration by celebrating, rather than ignoring, diversity and difference, linked to rich notions of culture and a celebration not just of the school but of the cultural communities it serves. Although not entirely dependent on prior experience of diversity within the school, certainly embedded notions of multiculturalism and cultural pluralism helped

LEAs and schools locate the positive cultural (if not political) aspects of ASR students' presence.

Officers, headteachers and school support teachers in all three LEAs spoke with pride about the strong traditions embedded in their schools and communities of coping with and celebrating diversity:

> The Council has, as part of its policy, valued diversity and that principle of valuing diversity permeates through everything. I think people are genuinely signed up to it. [...] So when you get asylum-seekers and refugees, there is a genuine and not a patronising view that they have a contribution to make to this. This is a new benefit to you as a community, rather than it being seen as a challenge and difficult [...] I think this notion of valuing diversity makes a difference, so instead of accommodating the difference I think we promote the differences. (Deputy Director, Cheston).

> Over many decades, the citizens of [Cheston] have welcomed people from all around the world [...] Each new influx of immigrants has brought to [Cheston] the diversity of culture that we enjoy today. All have contributed to the economy of our town in different ways. It is important that we know something about the cultures of our newer communities and the geography of the countries from which they have originated. (From the county's sixth-form college booklet — foreword by a Cheston MP)

By engaging with the resilience of these young people, by developing empathy and arguably compassion for their predicament, and by considering the positive aspects of their cultures, schools could enrich the ways in which they used and demonstrated the principle of social inclusion and belonging *to all students*.

Not surprisingly, given the history of educational policy since the 1970s and the role of schools in attempting to tackle disaffection and social exclusion, teachers and LEA officers reconstructed the image of asylum-seekers and refugees. Rather than seeing them as potential criminals, or as a threat to the social cohesion of British society, the new image was one created by humanitarian discourses that treat ASRs with compassion. The ways in which the three LEAs represented compassion was through an *ethos of care*. Expressions such as: 'welcoming', 'creating a secure environment' and 'caring' were some of the most frequently used phrases by LEA officers and teachers when discussing the education of ASR pupils. Below are some examples:

> Just welcome them to the school really, just know that people care for them. (Governor, primary school, Cheston)

> ... you work here because you care about them and you want something positive to happen [to them]. (Asylum-seeker and Refugee Pupil Support Officer, Greenshire)

For these officers and teachers, caring and welcoming ASR pupils was part of what they defined as good educational practice:

> Good practice is about welcoming in young people to the school. (Headteacher, secondary school, Cheston)

> [Good practice is when] asylum-seeker and refugee pupils or families are actually welcomed into the school and then supported. (Senior Advisory Support Teacher, Greenshire)

Welcoming ASR students and their families was also about creating a safe space for them, making them feel they can belong, that they are part of a community:

> It is all about welcoming them, caring about them and making them feel secure. (Head of Inclusion, Greenshire)

> We try to ensure that they're welcomed into the school and they feel safe and secure. (Headteacher, primary school, Cheston)

> The school just wrapped its arms around him [an asylum-seeking student], welcomed him into the school family, and we all got on with it. He is simply one of us. (Headteacher, secondary school, Greenshire)

The rationale for such an approach relied on a strong commitment to social inclusion:

> The school policy is to include all children regardless of their background and their previous experiences and that all children come

with their own experiences and to value that, to value their culture and their language. (EMAS teacher, secondary school, Horton)

The ethos of inclusion arguably can make the difference between a school that welcomes and caters for these pupils and a school that struggles to do so:

> I think actually the biggest challenge is for schools that ... don't have an inclusive ethos. If you have an inclusive ethos then basically you've got a routine for meeting the needs of any child whether they are asylum-seeker or refugee or not. (Head of Inclusion, Greenshire)

A speech delivered by the headteacher of Fairfield School in Greenshire took the most overtly politically controversial and risky stance when describing the school ethos to a new intake of parents. His view was that being an all-inclusive school, welcoming asylum-seekers and refugees was part of what the school stood for, something parents needed to consider when choosing the school:

> We are a genuine multi-class, multicultural comprehensive school. Every child here has equal value, and one way we make that absolutely clear is by opening our doors to refugees and asylum-seekers. We have more than any other school in the county — in fact we almost have more here than all the other schools in the county put together. Many schools don't want them — we welcome them and have created a special induction programme to help them to settle into the school as quickly as they can. We are a global village school. But if you don't want your child to be sitting beside such students in class, befriending them, accepting them, making them welcome, but above all learning from them, then perhaps it is definitely not a good idea to come to [our school]. (Headteacher's speech, Greenshire)

These three LEAs and schools saw their role as catering for the needs of ASR children in the best way they could – by giving them a better future, regardless of whether this future will be in the UK or elsewhere:

> Schools can play a pivotal role in providing refugees with not only a new beginning, but also a very real sense of the future. Inadequate or inappropriate provision runs the risk of compromising the future

life chances of asylum-seeker pupils who fought so hard to hold on to those chances. (EMAS bulletin, Greenshire, 2004)

We can't assume that they aren't going to be here very long so let's not bother. From my point of view it is to let them access that right, to integrate them to school, to society at large as quickly as possible. If they get permission to stay, you're aiding that transition into becoming UK citizens. If they don't and they are deported ... we have to think about the positive things that we gave to that child and the family while they were here. If they end up speaking English, it's a gift that they can use forever. *You've given them an insight that all of humankind isn't like that, that there is a way to a better life and if they go on to be the citizen that goes on to create that better life in their state or their country then all to the good, you know, but to give them the possibility to move on to better things ...* (Asylum-seeker and Refugee Pupil Support Officer, Cheston, our emphasis)

The challenge to performance models

These LEA approaches to social inclusion directly challenge that of the Home Office and immigration authorities (2004b, 2005a) discussed in Chapter 4. Paradoxically they employed the DfES/DCSF language of *Every Child Matters* and address concerns about social exclusion of marginalised groups to develop this challenge. At the same time, local government appears to have indicated an unwillingness to adopt in any simple fashion the priorities of successful integration (mainly attainment in national examination) put forward by the DfES (DfES, 2002b, 2003a). In contrast, the three case study LEAs articulated different understandings of the indicators for integration, in general and of ASR students in particular. A number of the officers and teachers we talked to were convinced that educational attainment could not be achieved without reference to the wider experiences of the child and their families:

It's not just about doing well in school, they can be successful in other ways, you know, I mean if they are doing well it's a bonus, but if you aren't happy, you're never going to be successful. (Asylum-seeker and Refugee Pupil Support Officer, Cheston)

You know I could pore over their results and ... what they've got in school, but that's not necessarily going to tell me a lot [...] I think, especially in their first two years the social element is the big indicator and the most important to me and is whether they parti-cipating in clubs, are getting involved in choirs, in music and other extra-curricular things. (EMAS teacher, secondary school, Horton)

The difference between the central government approach to inte-gration and these LEAs can be described as the distinction between concepts of *integration* and of *inclusion* (although often teachers drew on both concepts interchangeably). Whereas integration tended to be seen as a process where the individual child needs to adapt to the mainstream educational culture, including the discourse of school achievement, inclusion appeared to be understood as a process where efforts are made to create a school climate that celebrates diversity in such a way that allows it to include a group or individual students and their cultural differences (Corbett, 1999). In other words whereas in the case of integration the burden is laid on the individual stu-dent, when a social inclusion approach is adopted it is the school's responsibility to enable the student to belong:[9]

You know we have to be careful that integration doesn't always mean about the other person changing because that isn't integra-tion. (Head of EMAS, secondary school, Horton)

Criticisms of the goals that were set by the government in terms of what education is for were voiced by some officers:

The Home Office has got indicators for integration, and for edu-cation. I think it is appalling. I told them so myself, because it is basically down to SATs results, GSCEs results, numbers of students going on to higher education, and that is fine, but this is not inte-gration. You can achieve academically, and not necessarily be inte-grated as a person. So it is things like ... the quantitative but the qualitative indicators which are often ignored – things like whether actually parents feel safe to come to the school and question and talk to the teachers, find out more, that they are empowered. (Head of EMAG, Greenshire)

Criteria such as academic attainment were referred to as a *means* of inte-grating children rather than as a tool for measuring their integration:

When they come into school we make the best assessment possible of where they are actually at, what their educational level is and then as quickly as possible integrate them into mainstream classes so that they are learning alongside other children. (Headteacher, secondary school, Cheston)

They also shared an emphasis on a) the social aspects of integration; and b) whether the children felt safe and secure in school. Some officers and teachers working closely with ASR students argued that the main indicator for successful integration was whether ASR students made friends, and whether they joined in activities and felt comfortable enough to open up to others in the school:

They need to be settled well within a group of friends. [...] They need to be involved in as many extra-curricular activities as they want to be. (Head of EMAS, secondary school, Greenshire)

Well I think if they can join in school activities, parents will turn up on parents' evening because that's another important issue isn't it ... it's just taking part in normal everyday life I think, that's what they need to provide the opportunities for. (Deputy Director, Cheston)

Well, if I see a happy child who feels safe, is able to interact with people, his peers and with adults and he's settled in school and able to communicate his feelings and his thoughts and ideas then I think we've done a good job. (Head of EMAS, secondary school, Horton)

The Cheston ASR officer described what she believed was a success story of one ASR female student:

I went into [a school] last week and there's [...] One of the girls ... came waltzing down the corridor with a girl on either arm, and I actually didn't notice her at all, she was just breezing along, laughing and joking with the other girls and as she walked by me, like that, she stopped and turned round and said, 'Hello miss, what are you doing here?' That's integration, when she's just one of the other kids, you know, she's happy, she's got friends, she's joining in the after-school activities. (Asylum-seeker and Refugee Pupil Support Officer, Cheston)

The following extract from an interview with the senior advisory support teacher in Greenshire LEA sums up the high expectations which these LEAs and the schools we visited had in terms of what they hoped to achieve with ASR students:

> I would see a family who was comfortable with connecting with the school first of all and had an understanding of what the school was seeking to achieve. And I would see a pupil who was comfortable with their own identity, had a sense of value about their own experiential background ... was well socially and emotionally well integrated, had a good sense of self-esteem both in the school and outside in the community and was able to access the curriculum and develop their own skills, whether they are academic, social or linguistic, to the highest possible level, who felt safe and secure obviously not just within the school but within the community.

Conclusions: holistic approaches

The case study LEAs and schools which had adopted a holistic approach to the education of ASR students appear to have developed their own criteria for integration. These include notions of social inclusion, safety and the happiness of the child. In order to support these broad-ranging ideals, officers and school staff we interviewed in the three LEAs tended to establish strong parent–school and community relationships, and to develop a multi-agency approach which addresses the needs of the 'whole child'. The schools and officers in the three LEAs appeared to want to offer such pupils the prospect of a 'better future'.

Whether prepared or ill-prepared for such arrivals, the three LEAs we researched all expressed what appeared to be a common language. Each in their different ways actively expressed, through their structures, processes and strategies, notions of what was the morally 'right' way to engage with issues of asylum and immigration. The morality of their response was based on, but not necessarily limited to, the individualised assumptions associated with ECM (Arnot, 2009). As we saw in this chapter and shall see in the next chapter, the moral positioning of these three local educational authorities and the schools in their area had more in common with caring and compassion and concepts of human rights and social justice than with the hostile politics of immigration and belonging.

The multi-agency approaches appeared to be on their way to achieving some of the goals of the Children Act 2004 and ECM (DfES, 2003a) in ensuring all-round support for some of the most vulnerable children.

Children's Trusts[10] also encourage the development of a multi-agency approach, establishing new services (and reviewing existing provision) for ASR communities, families and children.[11] Bringing together the knowledge of the various practitioners who engage with vulnerable ASR children provided an opportunity to address the latter's complex emotional, psychological, medical as well as educational needs.

In the event, we found little reference to the traumatic aspects of pre-migratory experiences of asylum-seeking students, and far more reference to the ways in which the presence of such young people in school, with their resilience in the face of sometimes terrible pasts, was a resource for the school. Here the concept of 'the whole child' rather than specific educational needs lay at the epicentre of the school approach to social inclusion. However LEAs generally moved outside these narrow frames and, for some, the opportunity to apply a child-centred approach was key to the way in which they could address the needs of ASR students. Child-centredness encouraged a focus on individual ASR children's needs and progress. For others, child-centredness could be used explicitly to refocus the politics of immigration on to children's rights and to encourage broader, more collective notions of social inclusion, community and ultimately a common humanity. In the next chapter we use data collected from research in three very different secondary schools to explore the understandings of social inclusion and the associated forms of compassion which are expressed through such child-centred discourses.

7
The Migrant Child as a Learner Citizen

Within schools, there are as many educational frameworks and discourses which define the ASR student as there are in LEAs. Here our exploratory study of the world of schooling moves deeper into the framing of ASR students, focusing now on the perspectives of teachers and later students themselves. By moving deeper into the politics of compassion at school level we are able to uncover the repositioning of the migrant child from being a refugee or asylum-seeker, a legal entity, into a learner – a child who has come to learn at school and who has the rights of any other child within the education system. Using the child-centred approach that we uncovered at local authority level, teachers in schools that prided themselves on their inclusivity offer care and support for the ASR child. They expressed a caring form of compassion by being aware of such students' sensitivities, applying imaginative pedagogic strategies and offering surrogate parenting (Arnot, Pinson and Candappa, 2009). For some, such compassion even becomes the litmus test of the genuine inclusivity of the school and therefore of its self-image. At the same time, by moving the needs of 'the stranger' in their midst, intentionally or unintentionally teachers and support teachers like the LEA officers we interviewed were repositioned *vis-à-vis* the actions of the state. What we found amongst teachers who worked closely with ASR students was their active engagement with the disrupted lives of every ASR student, by employing not just the rhetoric but also the principle which the government had already proposed – that *every child mattered*.

The evidence we have already presented suggests that the education of migrant children cannot be isolated from the general politics of asylum, but also that the world of the ASR student cannot be separated from that of teachers and students in mainstream schooling. The worlds of teachers and that of ASR and other students are interconnected as well as being influenced by external contexts, although often in different ways. The world of the teacher is shaped, as one teacher told us, by the politics of the community which the school serves. Outside the school, among parents and in the community, one can find what she called euphemistically the *'Daily Mail* readers', supporters of the BNP, and the 'middle-class world' of *'Guardian* readers'. The politics of some communities are deeply shaped by the use of casual foreign labour, high levels of unemployment, and local violence against immigrant communities (for example, the Irish attack on Romany families and the attack in 2004 in Thetford, a rural market town in Norfolk in England, when after a football match locals outside a pub turned on members of the Portuguese community).

These economic, political and geo-spatial demographics of the UK shape school politics and frame the possibilities of school actions. Hostility to the presence of ASR students and their families could add to local tensions around immigration or, as teachers argue, if handled sensitively and with compassion, their presence could be the catalyst which reinforces the culture of social inclusion.

In the previous chapter, we heard from the LEA officers and school support staff working within three case study local authorities who wished to promote a holistic inclusive school culture. Here we draw on the views of headteachers and teachers to describe how this ethos was delivered in their schools. We refer to interview data from our first project on LEA policies and practices and the individual semi-structured interviews with key members of teaching and support staff in each of the three schools researched as part of the *Schooling, Security and Belonging* project. These three case study schools – Fairfield School (located in Greenshire LEA), Fordham School and City School – were sampled because we knew that not only were they more likely to know who were the ASR students in the school but also that they had a commitment to developing strong inclusive practices in relation to ASR students. As we saw in Chapter 3, the political and educational contexts in which these teachers worked were very different. Fairfield was an ethnically mixed school in Greenshire which was strongly committed to social inclusion and to making that a public and explicit aspect of its ethos. Fordham School offered ASR students a different environment since it was a large, predominantly White school without a strong history of anti-racist and multicultural work. The small number of ASR students that teachers spoke about were unaccompanied youth. In contrast, ASR students in City School were encouraged to fit into a typical inner city multi-ethnic school. The school had a strong history of anti-racism, anti-bullying and a commitment to social justice.

The average teacher may or may not know who is the ASR child (nor necessarily want to know). Many teachers were purposely not told who was an ASR student in their class by the Head or Deputy Head. The values we tapped were of those teachers who, for different reasons, were drawn into close proximity with ASR students. These teachers were involved in the admission of such students, helping them cope with the demands of a new language and culture, and the demands of learning. They worked with staff in developing appropriate responses. They became, therefore, the public spokespersons for the schools' ethos in relation to the education of new arrivals and vulnerable children.

Our concern in our various projects was to learn from such teachers, albeit in a tentative and cautious way, about their assumptions and the ways in which they conceptualised good practice in relation to ASR students. We asked them how they described compassion and belonging, and whether (and if so how) they tried to engender compassion towards such students in their classes (see Table 7.1 below). It was noticeable that the teachers we interviewed appeared keen to reflect on their role in relation to ASR students.

ASR students by definition have no pedagogic presence. They arrive not packaged as the normal pedagogic subject – they often have no

Table 7.1   Examples of interview questions for teachers

> o What sort of policies, initiatives/strategies have you been involved with that might prepare the school for ASR issues?
> o Is there any particular scheme that is set in place for ASR students?
> o What sort of contact do you have with individual ASR students?
> o How would you describe the approach you are taking in terms of helping such children?
> o What are the educational issues associated with ASR students' learning?
> o How have pupils been affected by the presence of ASR children in the school, if at all?
> o What, in your opinion, is the teacher's role in relation to ASR students?
> o What is compassion in your view? What are the obstacles to compassion?
> o Is compassion with ASR children something that you would seek to encourage, or is there a better emotional response?
> o How safe would you say ASR children feel in the school?
> o What would be the most important thing that you would want ASR children to feel even if they did not stay a long time in Britain?

knowable pedagogic history, no records of achievement, there are no statements or certificates to show for their past – in fact their unknown educational pasts, which still affect their present experiences, pose a professional challenge to teachers. As one EMAS teacher in an all-girls' secondary school in Horton described:

> They come with their different needs, some children have been well-educated in their previous countries, some come with a great thirst for learning and are very eager to progress with their English very very quickly ... but every individual is different. We get individuals where they are learning to write the alphabet for the first time, they are illiterate in their first language too and the whole concept of organising a schoolbag and getting to school on time and being prepared for school is quite difficult.

In some sense, ASR students are the ultimate *tabula rasa* since so little is known about them and the lack of language only adds to the educational silence around them. Their pasts are not only unknown but also not to be spoken of and become largely irrelevant within the educational world they enter. The EMAS teacher in Horton commented on the difficulties this meant:

> I also find it very difficult, they are naturally quite closed about their experience and we try not to pressure them too much, I mean we don't pressure them at all to tell us anything [...] I think that can be a little bit frustrating, wanting to know how much education did you have, what was it like, whereas we are often told, don't mention, you know, a student might come with a brief ... don't mention the war ... so they come as a canvas with no past history and I find that difficult and we want to value that because we value prior learning, but if there is a block ... this child will be upset.

For teachers used to the normal regimes of schooling, its assessment modes, its definitions of different achievement levels, and teacher reports, the ASR student transgresses all the boundaries of their professional knowledge. Teachers' responses, as we shall see, involved rethinking their professional understandings and in that process ASR students are redefined not as migrants, not as children, but more importantly as learners. And by a curious process of transduction, the migrant child acquires the status of what we call the 'learner citizen' (see Arnot, 2009) – perhaps not as a 'soon to be citizen' but a citizen 'in the making' (Rose, 1990) nevertheless. In that context, the school educates the asylum-seeking child as if he or she *were* a citizen.

From the teacher's perspective, ASR students, whatever their legal status, present a challenge and an opportunity. Here again, like LEAs that use a holistic approach to ASR education, the teachers we interviewed in the three secondary schools identified the inclusive culture and ethos of the school as central to their response to the educational needs of such students – in the process redefining ASR students' needs into those which can be seen through the lens of that ethos. In other words, the highly individualised largely educational and pastoral needs of student members of this localised community came to overlay the political and far more controversial issues associated with ethnic conflict, with global inequality and poverty and with controversial government policies. As a result, in our research we learnt more about the school and its values – 'the morality of social justice' within such schools – than we learnt about the experiences of the ASR child. Below we explore the ways in which teachers' compassion for such students expressed itself first in relation to the reconstruction of the ASR child as a learner citizen, secondly in terms of caring pedagogies creating compassion and thirdly in attempts to prevent any bullying or racism against ASR students.

The centring of the asylum-seeking and refugee child as learner

In the context of UK pedagogic approach of the 1990s, children are seen as responsible for their own learning. Contemporary educational discourses are centred on the need to encourage personalised pedagogic approaches which bring out the talents and abilities of each individual child. According to Arnot and Reay (2007), these pedagogic models have created almost mythological discourses around notions of individual student choice and performance, masking the realities of social inequality. This model, while represented as democratic in its goals of promoting a learner's self-determination and independence, avoids recognition of the impact of social stratification, poverty and social exclusion. Teachers therefore, especially in schools committed to social inclusivity and new individualised pedagogical approaches, have needed to consider how best to address this exceptional group.

Teachers in our case study schools identified caring as the most important professional response to ASR children alongside a strong focus on individual student need. For example, as one interviewee said, compassion involved 'caring for somebody, caring and understanding their plight or situation' (Sue Barclay, Pastoral Support Team Leader, Fordham School). Like Nussbaum (2001) who argued that pity can subject the individual to victimhood, thus denying them agency, Maureen Hunter (Assistant Headteacher and Head of Inclusion, City School) recognised that pity was not helpful – compassion should mean giving ASR students the maximum benefit from education: 'I don't think, you see, that a lot of these students want people to sit around feeling sorry for them.' Similarly, as a professional teacher, Sheena McGrath (Inclusion Coordinator, Fordham School) acknowledged the need to relate to students' experiences of trauma while not pitying them. Her reflections on compassion are reminiscent of Hume's argument that sympathy is needed as a prerequisite for compassion – allowing a person to see the other's suffering through their own experience. However, as she honestly pointed out, she tried but failed to 'relate their [ASR students'] experience to any experience of mine'. When asked to define compassion, Sheena responded:

> Blimey! Compassion, in my view, is trying to put yourself in the shoes of the victim, and showing you understand or are trying to understand their position, ensuring that the victim doesn't feel at fault. I suppose showing that, as far as possible, you're on their side. I tend to show compassion by trying to relate their experience to any experience of mine. So whilst I might not be able to say 'I've experienced what you've experienced' [...] And I think sometimes sharing ... offers the victim – can we use the word victim? – offers them, or opens the door for them to share their experience [...] I suppose the word pity always has a connotation of almost being condescending, doesn't it, and even that's why I questioned the word 'victim' because, that has a kind of negative connotation. But what was it, pity and sympathy? I mentioned sympathy, because I was going to say empathy, but then I thought well, can I use empathy, if I've not been in their situation.

Compassion also needed to be linked to action. Like other teachers we interviewed, Sheena grappled with the difficulty of offering an active empathy that could make a difference to that young person's life, and consequently legitimated the view that ASR children's needs were not any different from those of other vulnerable children. Here her approach had more in common with Simone Weil's emphasis on the need to look at someone's needs and rights as equal. Compassion for her was a professional ethic that encourages 'equal treatment for all':

> But I think compassion also has to be demonstrated through action. So it's then 'this is what I can do about it. Or if there's nothing I can do about it, this is what I can do for you'. It's a big question isn't it? Because I talk a lot about compassion ... I'm still coming back to individual need. Because all the children I work with, whether they have a learning difficulty, a behaviour difficulty, they are just children with English as an additional language, or they're asylum-seeking and refugee children, or they're looked-after children, or they're abused children, *they will come to you with a level of need at any time, and my response is to react to the need that is expressed in the best way I can* (our emphasis).

Child-centred pedagogic discourses such as those embedded in ECM and the forms of personalised learning introduced by the Labour government assume that students should be taught to make their own decisions, to be in charge of their own learning and to participate fully in a school community (DCSF, 2008). In such a competence-based pedagogy, as Bernstein (2000) pointed out in the 1970s, communication between teachers and students is essential since more of the child needs to be made public. For the ASR child whose first language is not English, the hurdles involved in such communicative encounters are even greater. Their silence and the silence around them are of great concern to teachers, keen to show compassion by helping them participate as students within the school world. Not only do teachers have to think carefully about drawing out such students' personal narratives (which might be about trauma) but also they would wish to respect that silence. However, the silence of ASR students restricts teachers who are concerned about encouraging student friendships and ensuring that ASR students are safe and happy in their new environment.

Teachers in our project argued that ASR students needed to be able to decide when and if they wanted to share their experiences. These teachers seemed to agree with Weil's assertion that compassion was defined by respecting someone's wishes and needs without reading them off (Weil, 1971 in Teuber, 1982: 227). As Jenny Douglas, Headteacher at Fordham School, observed, '... some children ... want to share that [their experiences] ... other children wish it to be very private. It's respecting their wishes'. The teachers we interviewed, such as Paddy

Thompson (the citizenship education teacher at Fairfield School) were very aware of the fear ASR students might feel in being in a British school for the first time, and not speaking the language:

> It is challenging for them, and I think they're amazing people, actually, to just come and sit there and turn up on time every day. [...] If *they're willing to talk,* then great, I would never push them to. Because that has to be completely when they're ready and when they feel safe enough, or secure enough, to deal with what basically, is a bombshell, actually, it's really, really tricky. But if I think that someone *is ready to talk,* even if it's just to say 'oh, left my country because – ', or whatever, definitely they will be given a platform to do it. And I'd encourage it, but I'm not going to force it.

Teachers worried about how to use refugee experiences to create compassion amongst other students without exposing the ASR students to potential discrimination, bullying or even just embarrassment. John Ford, EAL teacher and Refugee Contact Person for City School, for example, could clearly see great benefit to other students if they were to hear ASR students' life stories. However he recognised that he had to tread carefully:

> ... *it's got to come from the refugee kids really.* I can't say, 'Ooh, look at this person. He's experienced all these awful things and ...' It's finding the right form. So probably citizenship is a good place where we know that it will always be dealt with...

Paddy Thompson tried to address this silence in a most unusual way – taking them to the gym to experience rock climbing. He commented:

> So the kids who couldn't speak English and had had the most awful experiences ... make them climb the wall and let them be scared of that height instead of a life [...] Kids are supposed to be scared ... as opposed to all the nightmares that they must have. And watching them build their towers and not actually using any language apart from body language and basic communication in terms of building blocks and then little bits of English kind of snuck in and they got stronger and stronger – it was fantastic.

Also embedded in the responses to the ASR child is the concept of *deserving* – both of respect, and protection, but also essentially of an education. For teachers working with models of social inclusion, there can be no discursive place for the state's distinction between the deserving or the undeserving even if there is in reality strong social stratification within the school (Gillborn and Youdell, 2000). From the perspective of teachers closest to ASR students, all children were deserving of their commitment, attention and resources, even those, as one teacher pointed out, who were not legally entitled to any special assistance. Although the teachers we interviewed were aware of the lack of specific institutional entitlement to support ASR students, nevertheless they wished to ensure that such students received a 'fair slice of the cake':

> [The] kind of discussions we've had recently in the department have been along the lines of how much time Mrs Brush is giving to some of these children, and the fact that there are, you know, dozens of other children who have equally desperate needs. And nobody has said to me *'oh, those boys don't deserve that degree of support'*. Nobody's said that. But what they're saying is 'what about the others?' ... [statemented children] have a legal entitlement to a certain number of hours' support. [...] *asylum-seeking and refugee children don't have that legal entitlement.* So we're not comparing like with like, in a way. What I always say is that for whatever reason, the children are in *our school, and once they're in our school, they have an equal right to fulfil the school's aims which are presumably about each child fulfilling their potential and so on.* So if it takes a higher level of support for us to do that, we should, where possible, be offering that. But at the end of the day, it has got to be a fair slice of the cake. (Sheena McGrath, Inclusion Coordinator, Fordham School, our emphasis)

By redefining the ASR child as equivalent to other learner-citizens in their class, schools were able to resist popular discourses that saw them as 'the problem'. The professional response was to see such students as nothing more or less than an educational challenge:

> We don't have 'pains in the arse' or 'little buggers' opposed to learning, we've got barriers to learning and we systematically find out what those barriers are and find ways to overcome them. (Philip Watson, Headteacher, Fairfield School)

Teachers and support staff in our two school-based studies revealed an exceptionally positive attitude towards ASR students, surprising perhaps when we consider the pressure on performance and examination targets or even in light of the negative images of asylum-seekers in the press. As Philip Watson, Headteacher of Fairfield School, pointed out in a speech to new parents:

> Ultimately their courage in the face of almost unimaginable hardship and trauma is an inspiration to us all, and without exception, they bring us far more than we ever give to them.

What might have helped create such positive responses was the perception that these students were by and large high achievers and role-models in terms of school values.[1] Expressions such as 'dedicated learners' and 'committed students' were repeated by LEA officers, support staff, headteachers and teachers we interviewed, as these quotes illustrate:

> A lot of my children have been fast learners so, after a while of settling in, they just kind of pick up with the rest of the work you are doing. (Teacher, primary school, Cheston)

> Demonstrably they do very well, we can point out examples of extraordinary achievement from pupils who have come here with very little education and experience. (EMAS teacher, secondary school, Horton)

ASR students' motivation and academic achievement could also contribute to a better learning environment for all. As an ASR pupil-support officer in Horton commented, 'these pupils quite often are more focused in their achievement to try and get on'; while the head of EMAS in a primary school in Horton thought: '[T]hey bring an added dimension to the school population and, in terms of our language profile, it increases that and makes the school a richer environment.' The headteacher of a Catholic primary school in Cheston commented:

> What I would say is that the [ASR] children that we have got in have brought many qualities to school and to a large extent set an example to our own children because many of them are desperate to learn, keen to make something of themselves and keen to please, eager to please and want to work hard and learn.

A booklet published by a secondary school we visited in Cheston entitled *Valuing Cultural Diversity* introduces the ASR students in the school by listing their achievements under the title, 'The success of inclusive partnership'. For example: 'Rim arrived in England Summer 2001, Prefect, June 2002'; 'Alex arrived in England 2001, star basketball player and expert dancer'.

Teachers' morality: social inclusion and pedagogies of caring

The ethics of British immigration policy – the morality of statecraft as it were – have been found to prioritise economic development, national security and the national identity over and above the ethics of asylum. The morality of the schools we researched confirms their counter-stance – that of compassion and social inclusivity. The compassion towards ASR students involves an open approach to school admissions. Although the project of the educational system is about securing national civic identities and identifications within the new generations of 'citizen' children, although citizenship education is about practising those national values and political identities, and although schooling recreates social exclusions, nevertheless schools associate the education of the ASR child with civic inclusion and community integration.

This professional ethic provides the 'non-citizen' child with the opportunity to belong to the school community and to enjoy the same rights as the 'citizen' child – opportunities which are denied them by immigration policy. In contrast with the country's borders and the exclusionary mechanisms imposed on entry through the second gate, an ethos of inclusion appears to have shaped the crossing into the school system, according to the teachers we interviewed. As Jane Brush commented, the open-door stance of Fordham School promotes notions of community and social integration irrespective of the child's origins, legal status or experiences:

> I think it's a wider compassion in the school. *That is what the school community would do for an English person that was having difficulties, so why would they not do it for somebody else?* I think that it's not about this is a refugee, we need to help – it's about this is what we would do for a member of our community, they are a member of our community, this is what we'll do. Which is quite nice, because that's integration, really. (Jane Brush, Assistant Headteacher/Pastoral, Fordham School, our emphasis)

Similarly Maureen Hunter, Assistant Headteacher and Head of Inclusion at City School, recognised that by ignoring the temporary or migrant status of the student, the school explicitly distanced itself from the actions of the state:

> I don't think we've ever refused somebody admission if we've got a place, simply because they haven't had the right documentation. We tend to put them on and worry about it later [...] Because to be honest even if it turned out that they were here illegally, in a way *that's not our concern* [...] We would still not refuse because we honestly don't know the circumstances *and that's not for us, the school, to judge* (our emphasis).

Philip Watson, the Head of Fairfield School, also commented:

> [W]e have never, ever questioned a refugee or asylum-seeker who's come in. We've never thought 'shall we have this kid or not?' They just come, and we integrate them straight away.

Greg Smith, Deputy Head of Fairfield, added:

> I don't think there's an attitude that, this student's case might come up, you know, in immigration or something, they might be sent back. That concept, we don't even talk about that. It's not our business to talk about that.

Teachers' compassionate approach to the admission of ASR students into the school community was based on their professional knowledge about how to create a harmonious culture that focused on the development of the child's potential, recognition of their achievement, and a celebration of difference rather than the promotion of any singular political notion of citizenship and belonging. The years of multicultural activity in British schools in the 1970s and 1980s (Tomlinson, 1987) created a legacy that can still be called upon to frame an appropriate political response to the admission of ASR students into their school communities. Below we first describe some of the ways in which this response to diversity is expressed by teachers in their classrooms and the school as a whole. Our first theme is how they hope to create compassion among 'citizen' students.

Encouraging compassion in 'citizen' students

When asked directly about the strategy they use to develop a sense of compassion amongst 'citizen' students, the teachers we interviewed referred to the challenge of countering negative public discourses created by, for example, the BNP and the media (discussed more fully in Chapter 10). We glimpsed the history of multiculturalism when some of the teachers in our study talked about their goals of trying to encourage among 'citizen' children a tolerant, respectful engagement with different cultures and self-awareness about the vulnerability of their own lives. In that respect they see the school and themselves as responsible for ensuring institutional compassion (Nussbaum, 2001) as a means of moulding compassionate individuals. Some teachers used the fact of being children as a common denominator in encouraging sympathy, while others wanted the 'citizen' child to put him/herself in the 'non-citizen' child's shoes. For example, Maureen Hunter at City School described how she hoped to encourage compassion among students by using the GCSE unit 'Poems from different cultures' as an entry point into discussions of diversity, identity and different experiences of conflict:

> They [students] have to study about eight poems and they're all by different poets from different cultures and the themes that the poets tackle are conflict, language, identity and displacement – and moving from one country to another – which is very helpful because whenever we're teaching it [...] I would always say there's people sitting in this room who will probably understand this poem more than others. And it just helps students who are, say, indigenous British to understand what it must be like to move to another country and think you're going to lose your language or have been beaten up and then suddenly come ...

John Ford (EAL teacher and Refugee Contact Person at City School) argued that he wanted to use a TV programme, *My New Home*, to encourage his students to think about what ASR students face:

> *My New Home* is good because it does make you see the whole situation through those kids' eyes. About what it must be like to come. When everything is totally different. And, of course, they're children too so students here would be able to relate to it, imagine if that was me. I was in their place. Wow!

Some, like Aisha McGregor, the citizenship education teacher at City School, saw the issue of asylum-seeking as a matter of human rights. When asked if these strategies were effective, she argued that students were on the whole 'more careful with their responses, because they know that people could be affected by the experience'. These teachers did not expect 'citizen' students to feel sympathy or empathy for those in pain – they wanted them to understand the experiences of ASR students within the framework of rights and justice and to assume responsibility for it.

Preventing conflict, bullying and racism

However, ensuring the safety of ASR students in their schools was a challenging task. The extent of ethnic and religious diversity in schools such as City and Fairfield could either discourage or encourage student conflict and bullying. Fordham, as a predominantly White comprehensive, faced the challenge of reducing tensions between locals and the new 'strangers in their midst'. Interestingly, the teachers we interviewed almost unanimously spoke positively about the success of their schools in preventing or just containing the different types of conflict associated with the presence (particularly unexpectedly) of 'strangers'. The possibilities of conflict were many – whether between hostile groups of ASR students from the same country of origin, between the students in the school and newly arrived ASR students, or the ASR student encouraging aggression as a result of their own experiences of violence.

Philip Watson, Head of Fairfield School, for example, talked to us about how fitting ASR students into a multicultural school context rather than the concept of a monocultural Britain was helpful, although later he admitted that, even here, there could be conflict from those not prepared or ready yet to adjust to the school ethos:

> We've got loads of different nationalities here. So it's a fantastic place for a refugee and asylum-seeker to come. Because they don't arrive and feel self-conscious. I mean, they do, but they think 'oh my god, another Black kid. Oh, another kid from Nigeria' or 'another kid from Zimbabwe' [...] But, no, so it's an ideal place. I mean, if you had an all-White school and suddenly somebody arrived from Nigeria, and you stuck them in a classroom, everybody would turn round and look at him, and think 'who's the new Black kid?'. But that doesn't happen here. So it's an ideal place for them to come.

In the predominantly White Fordham School, Head Jenny Douglas also talked about the cultural shock involved for ASR students. Some ASR students felt safe, others did not. She reported that conflict occurred in many different ways, not always between ASR and other students. The school needed to ensure that it was prepared for their arrival – it had to prepare all students on how to behave towards ASR students, for example, from war-torn areas. As a result it set up a strong personal development programme, created school assemblies which focused on refugee issues, devised a student mentor scheme to help ASR evacuee students from other countries, and arranged for their classes to visit Uganda, Pakistan and Ecuador in order to experience and learn more about the world. This policy framework (rather than individual intervention by the Head) gave the school confidence that it understood the nature of the culture shock that ASR students experienced coming into their school and the need actively to encourage compassionate feelings amongst the student body.

It was noticeable that, despite the very different ethnic and religious contexts in which teachers worked, many expressed pride in the record of social harmony in all three secondary schools. Maureen Hunter, for example, at the inner London multiracial City School, reported that:

> Our last Ofsted [inspection] which was about two years ago now [...] the inspectors actually remarked on the sensitivity and the compassion of a lot of our students. [...] I think it would be fair to say we have very good whole-school response on students from other countries. There is a welcoming sense. And I don't think students who come here get a feel of being bullied. [...] I think a lot of the students don't understand the level of trauma suffered, but are very willing to learn. And certainly there's a good deal of sympathy …

She re-read conflicts between opposing groups as cultural difference rather than power plays between ASR and other students:

> [Ofsted] talked about a very harmonious relationship between different groups of students. [...] There was one lesson where there was a mix of students who otherwise politically would have been violently opposed to each other, and they noticed how well they got on in the discussions. Our students … are very able to voice their opinions without causing undue tension. But when there has been tension we have tried to address it. And sometimes there has, but again we wouldn't say it's to do with refugees or asylum-seekers, it's the inherent sort of cultural differences …

ASR students have themselves to adjust to the school's inclusive ethos, not just have the school get used to them. There are a number of ways in which conflict can enter into student relationships before such adjustments can be made. Philip Watson at Fairfield observed the tensions which arose when a particular student's physical display of an aggressive masculinity was a cause of conflict:

> But I'm phenomenally proud of our kids and the way they open their arms and wrap them round new people. It's almost part of the culture of the school, that's what you do. [...] We had it a few years ago in a kid who, again, came from Albania, who was hard, tough. And he used to walk round with a body language that said 'don't mess with me, don't mess with me 'cos I'm hard'. Well, you've only got to go round doing that to some of our tough kids, and they do ... you know. 'I'm looking at you', 'Who are you looking at?', 'Do you want some?', 'Come on then'. And we had a bit of trouble, 'til we taught him how to get his body language right, and how not to go and stick himself in the faces of some of the tough groups round the school. Because, I mean, the kids here aren't all angels, but they have ways of getting on with each other ... because we won't have bullying here, they learn how to interact with different power dynamics as well.

Maureen Hunter from City School talked about how the school had to deal with cultural differences that it had not been aware of. Despite being welcomed, ASR students from the same country could find themselves embroiled in major cultural conflicts within their own national group:

> Well it could be that you have students from one area of the world who when they were in their own town might have been a member of a particular group depending where they lived. [...] We can't make everything wonderful when they come in but we can certainly do is keep aware of any tensions and try and do something about it. [...] It would be very, very simplistic to think that just because somebody's coming from one part of the world and you have 10 other students from there that everything's going to be wonderful, it's not. [...] But what's good for us is we have to learn at the school what the problems are, where the tensions might be, and try and do something about it. That's the challenge for us really.

Similarly, John Ford, teaching in the same school, referred to conflict between two Iraqi boys who could not settle in the school and caused trouble. He describes them as having a 'sort of macho gangster-type mentality' that was very anti-school and anti-authority. They appeared to be 'just running riot'. Such conflict between ASR students was reported to be one of the trickiest moments for Paddy Thompson at Fairfield:

> My trickiest moment? That was in Bristol, with the Somalian community, and they were bringing with them a lot of their tribal problems from Somalia and having fights at school, and agreeing [sic] with different friends. And that was really hard to deal with. And in fact it took one student, Hoban, to actually stand there and shout and scream in Somalian, at the top of her voice 'Ah! This is why we left our country, and you're going to bring it over here, and I want to be able to stop here because it's safe, aaagh!' And it worked.

Outside influences such as community territorial disputes or political events such as 9/11 (which created conflict for any Iraqi or Muslim student in the school) were also important:

> We're a very multicultural school and although sometimes there can be friction between groups of students I wouldn't ... I couldn't say it was because of asylum-seekers, no. It may be that there are cultural conflicts, depending on what's going on out in the world. For example, after 9/11 we did have friction.

Interestingly, most teachers in the study reported that there was relatively little bullying and racism among students in their school. For example, Maureen Hunter answered a resounding 'yes' to the question of whether students in the school 'got on' with ASR students, but at the same time she was aware of tensions and what teachers needed to learn more about. Aisha McGregor, from the same school, acknowledged that there were subtle nuances to bullying and that, on occasion, it could be the 'citizen' child who was being bullied by other 'citizen' students:

> ... generally speaking I think it's ... a school ... that's not gonna victimise someone for being an asylum-seeker. I think an asylum-seeker may have, well they definitely will have, specific issues to do with it being alien environment. But apart from that I think they'll probably feel as safe, or as unsafe, as any other kid in the school. You know, a host child will feel unsafe on some days in this school. If there's a fight that's kicked off in the corridor.

Teachers such as those we interviewed admitted that they were not always able to see conflicts between students outside of their class: 'Of course, there's bullying but there's bound to be but I think that it's very low level. [...] I don't think it's a very big issue' (John Ford, EAL teacher and Refugee Contact Person, City School).

Although bullying was not an acute problem at Fordham, Sheena McGrath also realised that teachers were never really sure whether there was racial name calling, pushing, shoving – she suggested it could be the 'normal sort of high jinks between boys':

> I know these things go on ... and to what degree they feel they could come and talk to us. Because they are in such a minority. So when I'm saying you know, how safe do they feel [...] And I've been surprised at how few ... you know I was saying ... about this sort of misguided comments that White English children can make, which aren't overt, meant to be overtly racist, but reflect a racist attitude. And you do hear that, you would hear those, because the children often don't realise they're racist. [...] And you know, I'm not naïve enough to think that those boys and Lena go around school without comments being made or things being said or things being done. And if you happen to have quite an annoying personality, as I suspect [an ASR student] might have with some of his peers, I would imagine he gets involved in quite a lot of... How much of that is overtly racist and how much of that is bullying because he's different? [...] Now how much of that is just Year 8 boys jostling for position, and how much of that is [him] being a good target? ... and it's very difficult to gauge from [him] how happy or not happy he is with that sort of situation.

For many teachers, having a compassionate and inclusive school ethos was seen as a means of countering racist bullying. Philip Watson, Head of Fairfield School, however, put it differently, arguing that racism was not really an issue in his school. He claimed that the school was not about countering racism, it was fundamentally an anti-racist institution, 'we do it as part of our breathing in and breathing out' – diversity was 'part of the main tapestry' of the school. As a result the school did not have an anti-racist programme – 'we are just not a racist institution, and anybody who was would be shown the door, kids and staff'. People who tend to come to the school are 'inspired by our multicultural, multiracial vision'.

At City School, a multi-ethnic London school, Maureen Hunter reported that there was no active vociferous BNP student presence in the school and that, like Fairfield, there appeared to be few feelings of resentment among the students against ASR communities:

> We do come across some students who have, I suppose, a kind of inbred resentment. Although it's not too bad in this school. I mean we don't have, for example, actively vociferous students quoting the British National Party. Some schools do. I think it depends on the area. [...] So if there are one or two students, they almost remain without us knowing. [...] It's my perception anyway, but again students may tell you otherwise. [...] I think it's a very tolerant school. [...] And again I go back to Ofsted. [...] And I think there's more understanding and compassion than resentment and intolerance, to be honest. And I hope you find that when you interview the students but that'll be – that'll be, I suppose, the test of them for you, whether our feeling is what the students feel. [...] Yeah. I'm not saying it doesn't happen. Of course it must. But I don't think the school has a reputation for that.

Aisha McGregor, a citizenship education teacher at the same school, similarly commented on how positive the students were in her school towards ASR students and how they took a stand against racism:

> [T]hey're not tolerant of racism at all. And I was surprised ... [in citizenship education with Year 9s] I got hardly any negative comments from the kids at all about refugees and asylum-seekers [...] I did a series of lessons and discussions about refugees and asylum-seekers and there was very, very little negative stuff coming out of those. Which is really, really impressive. But anecdotally when I talk to asylum-seeker or refugee children, or students in the school, they have told me about teasing in the playground. But on the face of it in lessons, that doesn't come out. [...] I consider them to be very, very open-minded about the issue. Very. Which is surprising, because I don't think that's the case in the wider population at all.

Her colleague John Ford confirmed her impression about the strong anti-racist sentiments amongst their students:

> Like racism. I don't think there's a particular problem, you know. Because most people are very vocal and very anti-racist so you can't be some White NF [National Front, the precursor of the BNP] thug

in this school. Even if you think it you've got to hide those views so, but they're never expressed. I never hear racist statements.

Even if there are some students with 'inbred resentment' against ASR students, this was not 'active, loud, and visible'. City School had tried hard to create more 'understanding and compassion than resentment and intolerance'. Year 8 students were reported to be particularly intolerant of racism, but it was not clear whether this applied to all year groups.

If anything, the diversity in a school such as City can be so great that asylum-seeking students may experience not so much bullying but a lack of interest in their lives and their culture. The silence and invisibility of ASR students can be met by students' indifference – potentially a form of indirect discrimination:

> When you've got people coming from Iraq, Sudan, Somalia, it doesn't matter. It's just another new face. Probably refugees and – I suppose in a way it could feel quite unfriendly. That's the impression I get. Kids are not very interested ... unless you make the move like we do, to try and get the kids involved. (John Ford, City School)

Such a lack of interest could be seen as a sign of indifference or unfriendliness to refugees which, from the perspective of social inclusion, was perhaps more of a problem than bullying and racial hostility.

Ensuring a safe learning environment

Maintaining safety in schools is not just about reducing bullying and racial harassment, although these are clearly critical. As John Ford recognised, the two issues went together – the creation of a 'safe learning environment' would mean there would not be any intolerant, disrespectful language and 'it [would be] completely unacceptable to bully someone'. The challenge for teachers was to ensure the safety of ASR students by helping them integrate into classroom learning and into the culture of the school. The Head of Fairfield School, with his strong global–international ethos, was particularly proud of the spaces which the school made for such students, and of the fact that 'the spaces are comfortable' and that 'the people they encounter in those spaces and the activities in which they engage feel welcoming'.

In order for ASR students to integrate into the culture of the school – 'not a comfortable process' as Mary Jones, EAL Coordinator at Fairfield School, pointed out – ASR students had to change as well: 'You have to let go of something, and you have to make space for something new to come in.' The hardest transitions are those of age, gender and culture. She commented:

> [F]or some of these children – they are adults, they have worked. And then suddenly they've come here, and they're children and they have to be in school. And their definitions of themselves, how they define themselves, how they represent themselves to the world has become different.

She described one student who behaved like a 10-year-old in his class (perhaps because of the presence of female teachers), but acted like a young man outside the school. Other male ASR students had trouble with the way they engaged with female students in the school – the latter's short skirts being an invitation to touch. Others came back into school married and even as fathers without admitting their adult experiences.

The transition to being considered 'one of us' is not just dependent on the response of 'citizen' students to ASR students; the latter also have to want to fit in. 'Belonging,' according to Sheena McGrath, 'is in the heart.' Students have to want to belong, for friendship to develop. Some make a success of it because they have adapted their aspirations, their 'life plan'. Integration in the safety of the school also involves national 'belonging' at some level – becoming to some extent like British students. However, not all ASR students can make that transition, particularly if 'you're black or brown or speak with an accent ... or find English difficult' (Sheena McGrath, Fordham School). 'Becoming British' for boys can mean playing football and mucking about in lessons. Some manage, some try but fail, others do not try. Key to this transition is to find groups to become friends with. This can involve a range of skills – not least eating fish and chips or talking 'gangsta', as Sheena McGrath explains:

> [I]t would be harder for the ASR children to find groups to latch on to and you've got to have the right kind of personality and skills to do that. But from the point of view of the host children, I don't think it's about the colour of your skin or where you're from. It's how English can you behave? Or British ... Because in fact ... a lot of Black culture's very popular, and if you can speak gangsta, then you're cool.

Maureen Hunter, Assistant Head of City School, described the dilemma of wanting to belong and of desiring 'assimilation' at the same time as wanting to hold on to cultural origins as one which affected parents who wished to retain their identity and networks but also be part of the new country.

> Again they are very adaptable aren't they? And I think a lot of them want to belong to the place they're in. But clearly they can have great problems at home because one doesn't always know what their parents want for them. Some of them want them to be really assimilated within society and others want them to retain very much their own cultural identity.

Teachers found that many ASR students and their families are very articulate about what they want from the country and from the education system, often with high aspirations. The diversity of ASR students (some of whom experienced horrific events, others who come with wealth and have had an easy voyage) makes it difficult to generalise. For some ASR students, for example, belonging to a school culture may have the effect of allowing them to think critically about (or even to counteract) their parental culture and values. But from a teacher's perspective, key to the experience of ASR students was, as Maureen Hunter described, that they will have experienced 'a tolerant understanding place where education is seen as essential to their development'.

The teachers we interviewed carry with them models of compassion ingrained in the ethos of teaching as a profession about good practice, fairness and student welfare. Teachers are positioned by the state as being responsible for ASR youth, and in response they mostly seem to position themselves as caregivers. Their compassion is an emotional as well as a political response to state regulation of asylum-seeking children and/or their families. Compassionate reactions in our three case study schools involved pulling out the stops for these youth, often offering unpaid extra work. In Fordham, the support provided for ASR students included a county peripatetic teacher going round to the students' homes to teach for up to three hours in the evening, as part of the package of care for unaccompanied minors. As one teacher commented:

> [W]e're trying to support them in lessons where we can ... I'm teaching the boys maths; I do that in my free periods. I'm not paid ... I just do that because how else are they going to cope otherwise? ... Farah is a trainee teacher ... she's Iranian, and when she was on placement here, gave up every lunchtime when [Ishaq and Hassan] first arrived, to work with them, because they couldn't speak any English, they couldn't communicate with anyone ... So people give

up a lot to help them when they can. But, you know, there's a degree of goodwill, I guess. (Jane Brush, Assistant Head, Fordham School)

The teachers we interviewed went out of their way to provide moral support for these students – support that was underpinned by a deep level of commitment to help them as a mother or father might, and keep watch over them at a very personal level. Jane Brush at Fordham School showed this care in relation to Hassan, an unaccompanied asylum-seeking youth:

I try to nurture all the kids, but be additionally nurturing of them, I think, and it's just really small things like ... it was Hassan's birthday on Sunday, so I bought him a card. Just little things that just show there's someone ... that you don't arrive on your birthday and no one's bought you anything [...] They do need, I think, that the nurturing carries on.

Such a personal response to ASR youth is not restricted to female teachers. John Ford from City School, for example, similarly talked about such quasi-parenting responsibilities towards these youth:

It's a bit of a long-term mothering, fathering type of role we've had there. You've always got an eye on them ... I feel confident that if they're experiencing any big problems, I'll know about it. [...] you try and keep in touch with all of them.

Such caring on the part of teachers did not go unnoticed: some ASR students (particularly those who were unaccompanied) spoke highly of their teachers' help and understanding, their openness, their personal support, and the protection offered by their interventions:

[If] anything happening in the school, tell [ask] the teacher – 'Why this happening?' They can explain to us. (Theodros, Year 11 boy, City School)

If there's like a really strong racial thing that's going on, the school could help. They could call the police or anyone to sort it out. And I have to say that the school has helped a lot with many of our problems. Me and my friends. (Aziza, Year 11 girl, Fairfield School)

> They help me to – like when you've got a problem like in science or
> maths or every subject, you go there [Learning Support], and they
> help you. (Rashid, Year 10 boy, Fordham School)

Teachers helped these students find friends, gave them homework
that helped them learn and achieve more independence. Like all students, not all teachers were helpful or friendly but the image of the
caring teacher comes through our data. Edona from City School, for
example, talked with warmth and enthusiasm about her own experiences of having a 'great teacher':

> [Mr Ford is] great at teaching, great at helping, and speaking, and
> everything. He's like, okay, like speaking to the parents or some-
> thing, he'll like arrange translators to speak and, you know, do
> things. 'Don't be shy' and he's like, 'Okay, just talk'... I mean, he
> doesn't speak any Albanian, but ... how he explains it I can under-
> stand.

Similarly, Lena from Fordham spoke in glowing terms about the
Learning Support staff who had shown her how to progress from being
needy and dependent to developing a sense of her own agency:

> The Learning Support staff's brilliant, they're really helpful ... [they]
> taught me to be more independent than always get help ... They
> kind of, like, when they give you work, they make you try and do it
> without asking for help all the time. Like, so you can depend more
> on yourself than other people to help you all the time.

Rashid, an unaccompanied minor, who had joined school in the UK a
year and half previously in a different authority before coming to
Fordham, summed up the feelings of many of the ASR students we
interviewed when he commented: 'The teachers here care about you.'
  Indeed, such was the level of feeling for teachers that we found that
some ASR students were worried about how teachers in their schools
were treated by others in their class who in their eyes were disrespectful, if not downright rude – a view which distanced the ASR students
from the rest of the class:

> I find different because my country if it's lessons, everybody is quiet
> all this time but here no one ... if you want listen or want study it's
> up to you ...Yeah, here they no listen. Nothing. Basically, teacher

they shout and they [students] want to all go out. They not 'I need to go', they go directly ... (Lauryn, City School)

Well, the first time I came here and I saw the school, like, and I saw to teachers saying bad words, I was kind of surprised and shocked. I mean, how can they say. (Edona, Year 11 girl, City School)

Ishaq, an unaccompanied minor, who was in Year 10 at Fordham School and had been living in the UK for the previous nine months, commented:

I want to stay in this school. This is a good school. I like this school [...] The teachers are very nice, they are helpful [...] If I ask a teacher, she will help me to understand.

Conclusions

The levels of compassion and care expressed by the officers and support services in Greenshire, Cheston and Horton Borough LEAs described in the previous chapter were reflected in the responses to ASR students of the teachers we interviewed in the three case study schools. Teachers in these schools who worked most closely with ASR students had in effect repositioned the ASR child as a learner. The individualised learner citizen replaced the migrant, the Other, by transforming them into children in need and children with needs. These individualising discourses allowed the teachers we interviewed to address the wide range of social, emotional and physical needs of the ASR student. They became not 'the migrant child' or the asylum-seeking child, but 'a child' who has an entitlement to learn, a human right to be treated with respect, to be cared for, and to be protected from violence and harassment. Even more importantly, they needed to be shown a humane world. The humanity of the teachers in our study realigns and applies professional discourses associated with equal opportunity with the ethos of *Every Child Matters*, and with holistic models of caring. Later we discuss what sort of more direct action teachers take when addressing the national politics of compassion and belonging.

We obviously cannot make claims about the majority of the teaching profession since the project findings relate to only a small and highly committed sample of teachers and schools. Such compassion does not necessarily challenge, as Boyden (2009) pointed out, the critical politically deep agendas which lie behind immigration policy. To some extent the caring by teachers belies any more critical engagement with the reality of state exclusion. Nevertheless, despite these limitations, the views we heard suggest that there was considerable moral value in their stance. In other words, the normalities of schooling – those microcosmic moments, processes, understandings and professional values – have to be rethought and engaged with actively by teachers. Given the hostility of UK immigration policy to asylum-seeking families and children, these teachers represent the front line of a compassionate society both in terms of showing compassion and creating the conditions for compassion to flourish within the school, and offering the ASR child the chance, through their actions, of gaining confidence, safety, self-esteem and a sense of agency in taking control, despite their past, of their future world.

Our data also show that teachers' contestation drew on notions of compassion associated with caring and empathy but also on a more political notion of compassion that related to notions of equal rights and entitlements to equal treatment. This ethic, although not always overtly politicised, was strongly expressed in the language of social inclusion, in the focus on child-centred learning and in the personalised commitment of teachers hoping to make a difference to every child's life. In the next chapter, we consider whether or not these caring responses were mirrored in the relationships between 'citizen' and 'non-citizen' ASR students inside and outside class.

8
Finding Security and Safety in Schools

I wasn't looking for sympathy or pity. I was just looking for equality.
(Jamil, Year 10 refugee boy, City School)

One of the main concerns of social and educational research in the field has been the effects of different government policies and services on the integration of ASR children in the UK. Concerns, for example, have been expressed about the negative consequences of immigration policy on ASR children's experiences within education.[1] As a result of dispersal, for example, a pattern of disruption and discontinuity, according to McDonald (1998) often features in their education. In addition they experience the continuous changes in asylum procedures and especially the growing use of welfare restriction as a means of control and deterrence (which we documented in Chapter 4). As a result of tightening controls, ASR children are more likely to experience poverty, mobility[2] and uncertainty in relation to their future, which in turn might affect their ability to access education, and to benefit from it. In effect, having parents who have restricted access to the welfare state and who, in addition, are not allowed to work, positions asylum-seeking children socially and economically as an underclass. Indeed, many ASR children have reported that they experienced an unsatisfactory standard of living, including financial hardship and inadequate accommodation (Candappa, 2002).

The national invisibility of ASR youth in government planning and funding and the lack of records about such students at local level can also jeopardise their full rights to education. As well, the extent to which ASR students are aware of existing services and their ability to make best use of such services can be a major factor shaping their educational careers. Candappa and Egharevba's study (2000) of the social and school lives of ASR children in and around London illustrated the considerable variation in the level of support which students received at school. Sporton and Valentine (2007) found that Somali ASR young people in Sheffield received very limited support with learning English and being integrated into the British education system. Indeed, as we have already demonstrated, not all local authorities or schools employ an inclusive ethos in relation to such students.

Difficulties in integrating can be exacerbated in the case of unaccompanied minors who are looked after by local authorities. Stanley's (2001) study of 125 unaccompanied young people across the country found wide variation between areas in relation to terms of their access to educational opportunities and the type of support available to them. Even though most were determined to succeed, many expressed feelings of being socially excluded. Similarly, Chase et al.'s (2008) research in London with 54 unaccompanied asylum-seeking youth found, among other things, that concerns about accommodation changes or their immigration status had negative effects on the young people's ability to benefit from education.

The government's dispersal policy, which, as we have seen, often places asylum-seeking families in deprived areas that are unused to multi-ethnic populations, has been found to have particularly negative consequences for children's education. Candappa et al.'s (2007) and Macaskill and Petrie's (2000) research in Scotland reported a number of negative consequences – significant amongst these was the presence of racism and bullying within the community. Young asylum-seekers were found by both studies to be plagued by racial harassment and racist attacks. This left families feeling unsafe in the areas in which they lived.[3]

Research on ASR children's experiences of schooling in the UK also reveals the effects of trauma associated with migration, seeking asylum and trying to settle in a new country. These experiences may not be easily recognised by the school. For example, ASR children's experiences of war and loss (Richman, 1998; Rutter and Stanton, 2001) can manifest itself in signs of trauma – something which could be interpreted in a school setting as behavioural problems (Candappa and Egharevba, 2000). Some might also harbour guilt feelings about having to escape, leaving family members behind (Richman, 1998). Upon arrival in the country of asylum, these children have to cope with displacement, and have to develop a familiarity with, and attachment to, a new place (Anderson, 2004). They have to adjust to a new culture and language (Rutter and Stanton, 2001) and to construct a new sense of identity/belonging (Richman, 1998); at the same time they often have to cope with changes in familial relationships, when their parents become more vulnerable and dependent on their children, or more protective and authoritarian (Candappa and Egharevba, 2002; Rutter, 2001b). They may also have to deal with anxiety as a result of the asylum process and the uncertainty of their future (Richman, 1998). They might have special or more frequent health problems (Rutter and Hyder, 1998), and encounter difficulties with the quality of physical and mental health care provided due to a lack of health-care providers' expertise in the needs of ASR students. Not surprisingly, these experiences could present themselves in a wide range of emotional difficulties among ASR youth, including feelings of isolation and loneliness, general anxiety, panic attacks, depression, and sometimes more serious mental-health problems (Chase et al., 2008). One of the ways in which ASR children handle trauma, exclusion and discrimination is to use silence as 'a mechanism for dealing with a traumatic experience' in their present lives (Christopoulou et al., 2004: 5).

These political, social and emotional factors, independent of the school, can affect the ability of ASR children to make the most of their school experience. Many ASR students have experienced an interrupted education and some had very limited, or no, educational experience (Rutter and Stanton, 2001). They need to learn, as we heard the teachers say in the last chapter, how the British school works,[4] the assumptions teachers make about learning, and classroom behaviour. Learning the English language is, of course, vitally important but so too is maintaining their mother tongue.[5] But also, as teachers were aware, the ASR student needs to get on with strong local youth cultures, dialects and youth languages (such as rasta, gangsta); they need to acquire the confidence somehow to make friends and feel part of what could be a working-class urban school community, or even on occasion a White rural setting. Their relations therefore with other students are critical to their integration and personal safety within the UK. As we saw in the previous chapter, relating to classmates is fraught with difficulties because of possible racial stereotyping, harassment or because of ethnic conflict. Gender power relations, described later, also add to this complexity.

To date, there has not been much research on the significance and impact of asylum-seeking status on these students' identities, their relations with other students, and their positioning *vis-à-vis* British culture. Of particular interest, therefore, is Sporton and Valentine's study (2007) of the importance of place and context in shaping young Somali students' identities. A British identity among these youth was imagined as a White identity. Such a construction of citizenship has clear implications for those students who are 'non-citizens' but it also has implications for the social and political dynamics within schools, not just between teachers and students, but between students themselves. Sporton and Valentine found that 'a sense of "belonging" develops where a community has a sense of security and space to define its own identity beyond … narrow perspectives of national identity' (2007: 14). As Lord Goldsmith's report *Citizenship, Our Common Bond* pointed out in relation to 'non-citizens' in the UK, there are:

> … specific issues relating to the integration of threatened migrants. Refugees have often had harrowing experiences. They may have lost their livelihood or home: they may even have come close to losing their lives. Hence, even though they may obtain physical security by coming to the UK, they may not immediately experience psychological security – a sense of being settled and safe. (Ministry of Justice, 2008: 112)

These notions of physical and psychological security have particular resonance for our study of the politics of compassion and belonging since we can assume that the concept of compassion involves encouraging those seeking asylum to achieve a feeling of belonging to a common humanity but also to recognise they have the right to 'feel safe, secure'. While there is not as yet a universally agreed definition of human security,[6] the UNDP *Human Development Report* (UNDP, 1994) has been an important forerunner in the debate. This report posits a universal, preventive, 'people-centred' approach that focuses on 'freedom from fear and freedom from want'. More recently, Alkire (2002: 1) suggested that a working definition of the objectives of human security (in keeping with the ethos of the 1994 UNDP definition) should be 'to safeguard the vital core of all human lives from critical pervasive threats, in a way that is consistent with long-term fulfilment' – here the 'vital core' describes fundamental human rights or absolute needs such as the right '*to survival, to livelihood, and to basic dignity*' (ibid.: 2).

The notion of *human security* therefore, is intimately linked to the 'politics of belonging', as Yuval-Davis et al. argue, 'how subjects feel about their location in the social world which is generated partly through experiences of exclusion rather than about inclusion per se … [and] about both formal and informal *experiences* of belonging' (2005: 526, emphasis in the original). Belonging involves 'an important affective dimension relating to important social bonds and ties' (ibid.: 528). We know, as Yuval-Davis et al., pointed out, that 'being labelled as a member of a racialized group, such as asylum-seekers, often has determinant effects on their position in the world and how they see themselves and in terms of ideas of belonging and otherness' (ibid.: 530). It was therefore an important and pertinent question to ask, especially in the context of research on the politics of compassion, whether the 'non-citizen', the ASR student, feels not only welcomed but sufficiently supported and included by the school for them to be able to feel safe, to be respected and to belong.[7]

The school in principle is well-placed to foster such a sense of security and belonging in ASR youth and indeed is often the only statutory service from which many derive support (Candappa and Egharevba, 2000). However, as we have seen, the contradictions in the policy context, together with the unavailability of dedicated funding to support such students, make this a challenging task for schools. It is not guaranteed that schools with an inclusive ethos of the sort described in Chapters 6 and 7 necessarily succeed at their task of 'wrapping their welcoming arms' around such students. A lot depends, as teachers were aware, on youth cultures, where the ability to make friends really matters.

The aim of our second research project was to explore in depth whether the inclusive ethos of the schools we sampled prevented, from the students' point of view, the building up of feelings of hostility, hatred or indifference towards asylum-seekers among mainstream so-called 'citizen' children. We sought here to explore the other layer of social inclusion, that of youth culture. In doing so, our study needed to develop an appropriate set of qualitative research instruments to investigate the shaping of a compassionate society in schools by interviewing ASR and other students about what they felt would constitute the social conditions for safety, compassion and belonging. Our strategy was first to see whether young asylum-seeking students felt supported, secure and safe with 'citizen' students at school. Did ASR students encounter compassion, empathy and fellowship? But we also hoped to find out whether they experienced feelings of security, belonging and compassion not just within the school but also in British society. Similarly, we wanted to explore how 'citizen' students in the same schools engaged with the issue of asylum and the politics of belonging in the UK. What were their notions of security, belonging and compassion? We explored how these two groups of young people interpret, navigate and respond to the different and sometimes conflicting messages they might receive in relation to asylum and forced migration from key players in their worlds – their teachers and school, and the media and public in the world outside it – and the extent to which they themselves worked on 'being compassionate'.

The students whose accounts we draw on come from the same schools (Fairfield, Fordham and City) as the teachers described in the previous chapter. We know that these three schools presented different demographics and contrasting locations, some where ASR students fitted into a school's diverse ethnic profile, and some where they formed part of a small and visible ethnic minority (see Chapters 3 and 7). The ASR cohort included young people who had arrived as unaccompanied minors as well as those who arrived with a parent or family member, those whose applications were still pending and those who had already received refugee status (and even citizenship) and had already been in the UK for long periods of time, and from home countries in Africa, Asia, Eastern Europe and the Middle East. The 'citizen' students were similarly not a homogenous group: while they were all British nationals by birth, many had roots in as diverse a set of origins as Italy, Morocco, Nigeria, Pakistan, Spain, and in one case, with Roma heritage.

Our data collection strategy was twofold. First we chose to interview samples of ASR students and 'citizen' students individually. This aided conversation on such a sensitive topic. Twelve interviews were conducted with 'citizen' students, four in each case study school. Five interviews with ASR students were conducted in Fairfield School, and four each in Fordham and City schools. In individual interviews with 'citizen' students, we showed participants separate written scenarios depicting experiences of war traumas and tragedy, poverty and hardship, and the violence and brutality endured by two refugee children who were part of the *Extraordinary Childhoods* study (Candappa and Egharevba, 2000). The two stories of Rathika and Sheik (both pseudonyms) shown in Table 8.1 were used to provoke responses to asylum issues, evoking students' feelings of compassion. It was possible then to stimulate a discussion on whether these refugees and their families should be granted asylum in Britain, and whether they might come to feel at home in their school and eventually become British.

With ASR students, in the interview, we did not explore their personal narratives of forced migration, but instead focussed on issues around compassion, security and belonging in Britain, particularly their experiences of schooling, of friendships and whether they felt they might eventually become British. Secondly, we ran focus group interviews with an average of four ASR students (ethical difficulties were discussed in Chapter 3) and discussions with members of their peer group of 'citizen' students (with four students in each school).[8] Beside the group discussions in Fordham which had only a few ASR students, all other group participants were different than those individually interviewed. In total 25 'citizen' students and 20 ASR students participated in our research. The 'citizen' group interviews used Bazi's (another pseudonym) story, also from Candappa and Egharevba (2000), to explore compassion, and notions of 'being' and 'becoming British' (see Table 8.2).

Table 8.1 Refugee stories used in interviews

RATHIKA'S STORY

Rathika is a Tamil girl from Sri Lanka. She lived in Jaffna in the north of the country during the civil war between guerrilla rebels and the Sri Lankan government. When she was seven the guerrillas tried to recruit her brother as a boy soldier into their army, and fearing for his life her mother decided to flee their home with her six children. They had to make a difficult journey overland to reach Colombo, the capital of the country, in the south, and they felt safe there for a while. But then things started to get dangerous for Tamils there, and her mum decided to try to escape to England where her brother lived.

Rathika's mum had to pay lots of money to agents to arrange their escape. But the agents did not just put them on a direct flight to London from Colombo: they had to travel first to Russia, and then to Nigeria, staying in a number of different places and under difficult conditions. It took them four weeks in total to get from Colombo to London.

In England they felt safe, but they were very poor, because as asylum-seekers they had to live on benefits. In their home in Jaffna they had led comfortable lives, but now they had very little money for buying clothes, they never went to the cinema, and could not afford many of the things they wanted.

SHEIK'S STORY

Sheik comes from Somalia, where, with the civil war, there has been a breakdown of law and order. Sheik is Bravanese, which means he belongs to a minority group, with its own language.

When Sheik was ten and playing outside his home one day, some thugs came up to him and told him to go up to his neighbours' door and, speaking his language, to get them to open the door for him, threatening to shoot him if he did not do what they asked. Sheik knocked at his neighbours' door, but said in Bravanese, 'Don't open the door, there are robbers here'.

The door was not opened, and the thugs told him to ask again. But Sheik said to his neighbour, 'Don't open the door because they are still here. They kill people'. The thugs then suspected that Sheik had been warning his neighbours, and they beat him with the butts of their rifles, so he was badly hurt. When the thuggery and robberies became more frequent, Sheik and his family became very frightened and fled to Kenya.

In this chapter we focus on the tension between inclusive schools and exclusive youth culture and their consequences for ASR students' safety and sense of security. In the next chapter we then explore how ASR and 'citizen' students negotiate the meaning of Britishness, belonging and immigration.

Table 8.2   Refugee story used in focus group discussions

BAZI'S STORY

Bazi comes from Somalia in Africa where, with the civil war, there has been a breakdown of law and order, making many people flee the country. Bazi is Bravanese, which means he belongs to a minority group.
 	
    Bazi left his home with his mum, dad, grandma and four brothers. They took a boat along with a number of other people, including some relatives, to try to get to Kenya, but the boat was overloaded and faulty, and ran aground on a nearby island. Some people, including one of Bazi's cousins, lost their lives in the sea that day.
 	
    When they reached the island they were exhausted and just slept on the sand, and the next day they were very hungry but had no food. Then some of the islanders found them and gave them food, and they stayed there for a week, until another boat arrived, which took them to Kenya. In Kenya they stayed in a refugee camp, where they were safe, but there was disease there, and their grandma died of malaria. They then came to Britain.

Acceptance and inclusion

We begin our account of our findings by exploring ASR students' emotional experiences in the school through the lens of inclusion, friendship and security in order to build up a sense of what belonging means. We use the term 'security' here as deriving from friendships and human relations, and 'safety' as in the UNCRC to include freedom from fear and aggression. The ASR students we interviewed wanted to be allowed to get on with their lives without fear or harassment. Most ASR students were very clear that they did not want to tell their stories, that the silence that their teachers allowed them was what they wanted. Farouq, a Year 10 Afghani boy from City School, explained that 'we don't really talk about it':

> *Farouq*: ... I won't talk about – speak about that because they ['citizen' students] don't understand and they laugh at us. And I feel down...
> *Interviewer*: Would you have liked it if they [teachers] asked you?
> *Farouq*: No ... I think I'd be upset. [...] I think I'd be feeling – I'd be alright if I'm not talking about it.

Farouq's comments show his feelings of vulnerability about his peers' lack of understanding and their misplaced humour. He did not feel he could cope with talking about these experiences in public – his silence is a weapon of self-preservation. There were, however, a few students who, in principle, would not have minded sharing their experiences, but chose not to do so. When asked whether she would have liked to stand up and tell the class about her experiences, Edona, a Year 11 Albanian girl at City School, replied:

> Well, kind of I suppose. I don't know. I suppose some people would like it and would like to hear my story, but some of them wouldn't. Like, okay, 'This is boring' – is like saying, 'I don't wanna hear this'.

Her thoughts were similar to Farouq's in that they both perceived an insensitivity in their peers' reactions. Sharing their stories could therefore diminish their social standing in the school, as well as their own self-confidence, jeopardise their inclusion into the school's youth culture, and therefore make them feel less safe, even more different and ultimately visible.

ASR students in our study were clear that they wanted to gain a good education and to succeed at school, and were prepared to work for it. Many came from countries where education was the province of the wealthy, or the social infrastructure had been damaged by conflict, and they were eager to avail themselves of the educational opportunities presented in Britain. They mostly had aspirations to go on to higher education, some wanted careers in areas as varied as medicine and fashion design – one student aspired to high political office in his home country. A safe learning environment was therefore crucial to them.

On the surface, all three case study schools, as we have seen, offered these students a supportive environment. The students saw no difference or discrimination between how 'citizen' and 'non-citizen' students in their school were treated, echoing almost the words of their teachers (see Chapter 7). They became just like British learner citizens, something that they noticed:

> *Daran*: We're all the same, no matter if you're British or not British. We're all like treated as the same.
> *Sabeen*: They [the teachers] welcome you here, right? They don't make you feel like a stranger or anything. (ASR Group, City School)

As we saw in Chapter 7, the ASR students we interviewed were aware and appreciative of the extensive support they received from their schools and teachers. At Fordham School (a predominantly

White school), where these students were a small minority, Lena, a Year 11 Nigerian girl, confirmed this view:

> [T]hey have like a system, which is learning support, which you can go in there and they help you with things such as reading. They do help you ... and you have [a] teacher to talk to if you're like ... And they do look out for problems, so they do definitely help. They don't take anything, like, such as bullying ... (Fordham School, ASR Group)

The primary role these learning support departments played was usually by providing intensive English training, often in a separate class or with special support in mainstream classes. Toma, a Year 9 Croatian boy, explained how it was in the Fairfield School group discussion:

> [I]n my middle school ... when Miss sat on my English lessons and went to learning support ... and they like made the work easier, and helped me to like, adapt to like normal kind of work ... when you're in learning support you get talked to as an individual, so you get like, more attention, and they just like, take time to talk to you, and see what you feel and that.

Kim Robinson, the LEA peripatetic teacher at Fordham School, like others, even provided help with homework in the students' homes, as part of a total package of care for children looked after by the local authority. Hassan (a Year 8 Pakistani boy) reported that she came for about two to three hours each week to his house to teach him English. Similarly Ishaq (a Year 10 Afghani boy) commented, 'she come into my place one day a week ... in my home ... she help me ... After the school. Evening'.

Another scheme provided through Learning Support/Language Development departments supported new arrivals in their first few weeks by establishing 'buddies' or 'class friends' to take them to lessons and familiarise them with the school and help them to integrate into the student body. 'Buddies' are usually volunteers who, if possible, speak the home language of the new student. The scheme helped Farouq at City School build lasting friendships. He commented, 'I just hung around with them, being a part', and added: 'They are still my friends, and I've got new friends.'

Experiencing exclusions within inclusion

However, despite these positive experiences, the ASR students we inter-viewed also portrayed a sense of exclusion within the school. At one level, they felt accepted and included by teachers within these inclu-sive school settings, but on another level they talked about the difficulties they had fitting in with their peers. Security relies upon being treated as a member of a community, rather than as an outsider. Despite their teachers' efforts, the ASR students we interviewed seemed to experience bullying and harassment, albeit mostly at low level. This harassment was primarily directed at their visible or assumed Otherness. The ASR students were newcomers but they were also outsiders; the foreignness of their language, their lack of English skills, and the prevalence of strong local youth cultures were described as important factors in such feelings of exclusion within an inclusive school environment. The bullying they encountered tended to be of a general nature, as teachers indicated (see Chapter 7), not overtly directed to their ethnicity or immigration status. But as Candappa and Egharevba (2000) pointed out, subtle forms of racism can exist[9] – often where there is a general lack of concern for cultural values rather than direct discrimination because of such values. Similarly a study by Rutter (2006) found that, even when racial bullying did not appear to be present, students might nevertheless draw on media discourses and use anti-asylum and racist discourses interchangeably.

On occasion though, ASR students reported that bullying in the school had a more serious nature, especially when harassment was targeted at perceived weaknesses such as their vulnerability as newcomers or physical traits such as small stature. Farouq, for example, who arrived at City with good English-language skills, having spent three years previously in another British school, spoke of his experiences of bullying:

> I see people getting bullied ... just people asking for money, and they're [victims] quite scared. [...] Sometimes they beat them up for no reason ... not racist bullying, just people who are like quiet, then people just beat them up ... I used to be quite a bully of some friend at the end of Year 9. He took my money [picked his pocket], so I went back and got my money back ... Asked for my money back ... and then we fight, and so I fight him, that's why he's scared of me.

When Farouq reported the matter, the school protected him and the bully was excluded by the Head.[10]

Student aggression seemed most often to be targeted at the most obvious signs of Otherness, such as lack of competence in English and/or 'uncool' dress or an obvious lack of knowledge of youth-cultural norms. Anna (a Year 9 White British girl at City School) spoke about students being 'horrid' to other students because they were newcomers, even though what she referred to was potentially commonplace in school, and directed at all new students. However, an ASR student might not perceive this, and could experience such hostile responses as a lack of acceptance and as exclusion rather than a painful rite of passage. For example, for Toma, the Year 9 Croatian boy at Fairfield, arriving at his primary school without knowledge of English left him open to being the butt of light-hearted student pranks:

> When you can't speak English people just look at you ... In lower school ... my friends ... they used to teach me how to say swear words, and said it was good things, and they would say, 'go say it to the teacher', and I ... went and said it to the teacher [...] They used to laugh but, you know, it didn't get me into trouble ...

For Lauryn, a Year 11 Congolese girl at City School and a fluent French speaker new to English and to Britain, found that the unprovoked aggression she experienced was more upsetting:

> *Lauryn*: When I first come here they say some thing, just disturb me, yeah ... They say to me the bad thing – 'f*** off'. [...] Miss Butcher [Head of the Language Development Department] say to me, 'don't follow [listen to] them. Be quiet and they leave you alone'[...] the first day I come, I can't speak English and they say anything about me. I say nothing and looked at them because I no understand ...
> *Interviewer*: ... and the people who were saying 'f*** off' and stuff like that, they were English?
> *Lauryn*: Yeah, they English people [...] Mainly boys.

The teacher Lauryn approached for support seemed unsurprised at her experience and advised her to ignore the bullies, in other words to remain silent, invisible. However, Lauryn went on to retort: 'well, now they're nice because ... if they speak, I speak loud – "don't want that, don't like it".' Standing up to her harassers seems to have won Lauryn respect, and the bullying ended. Those students who arrived fluent in English but with a foreign accent might also find themselves excluded because 'citizen' students found it difficult to engage with different accents. However, as Lena's experience at Fordham School shows, this could be relatively easy to negotiate:

> When I came to England I used to talk so fast, people could not keep up when I talked. But now they can keep up with me, and I've slowed my pace of talking down.

Lena adapted her speech to be accepted by her peers. However, exclusion through language can be painful to students and carry an emotional cost. This is seen very clearly in the account of Theodros, a Year 11 Congolese boy from City School, now a popular student and leader of the basketball team, who described his experiences on joining the school:

> [W]ith boys it was okay, but not with girls. They were sitting there and teachers said, 'you have to sit next to him'. 'Oh, no, he doesn't speak English, I don't want to sit next to him'... Ask a girl, 'Can you help?', 'No, I don't want to help him. He doesn't speak English, I can't help him'. That was hard. Lasted a whole year ... there was some boys coming around me, sitting next to me, but you can't send any girls next to me.

Theodros's story also indicates that this type of exclusion could be gendered – suggesting that girls only help girls while boys help both sexes. In contrast, two girls at the same school, Lauryn and Rebecca, talked about girls being bullied by boys and being helped by girls. Lauryn commented: 'The girls were nice. Very nice people.' This camaraderie between girls was further confirmed in the account of Rebecca (a White British Year 9 student) who reported, 'We [girls] look out for each other, don't we?' If someone like Rathika joined her class, Rebecca thought:

> I suppose she'd definitely soon make friends and – 'cos everyone would understand her situation, especially if other people helped her. The boys can be a bit annoying, but the girls are – most of them are really nice ...
>
> *Interviewer*: When you said the boys are annoying, are they annoying more to the girls or are they annoying anyway?

> *Rebecca*: I suppose it's just that whole thing about teenagers and girls, and half of them probably just fancy them, that's why they're really horrible ...

In contrast, a Year 11 girl from Albania, Edona, who had been at the same school for two years at the time of interview, recounted a different experience:

> When I first came in class ... students were kind of rude actually ... And I mean still, there are like some good students, like they can like help you and talk to you, but still some of them are bad. I mean, they just don't leave you alone. [...] It's just because ... like 'you don't understand us', or something you know, it's just like start saying bad words and whatever, just picking on you ...

Edona was clear that it was both girls and boys who created the problem, commenting: 'Actually ... it's like a kind of game. It's like "you don't know nothing, why did you came here in this school, why did you came here in England", and things like that.' This type of harassment, this 'game', had persisted over time, and while a few peers had helped her, she had not found a way to gain acceptance and entry to peer friendship groups: 'Even I am like two years here in this school, I feel like I've still haven't find the friends I wanted to find actually.' Gender relations were subtly linked to potentially exclusionary behaviour. But 'games' such as these can have more than one explanation and give rise to new sets of issues, many of which have not yet been researched.

The stranger in 'our' midst

In the individual interviews with 'citizen' students we asked them to consider a hypothetical position where Rathika joins their school. We have already seen that many of the ASR students we interviewed did not wish to reveal their story, as if their invisibility made them feel safer. This invisibility was recognised by 'citizen' students such as Martin, a Year 9 English boy at Fairfield who thought that it might serve ASR students well:

> [I]n our school ... if there's like asylum-seekers ... we don't know who they are which I think is a good thing, 'cos then there's some people that might like, try and take the mickey or something like for not having as much as other people ... I think it's mainly their decision, what they think ... you shouldn't have like someone at the

school making it for them ... *they might not want to be pointed out* and like noticed by other people as a refugee or an asylum-seeker, like ... *a name-tag like that* (our emphasis).

Martin echoed teachers' views at the school about respecting such silences, and also showed a keen awareness of the negative public images of people seeking asylum and refugees.

When other students put themselves 'in her shoes' they argued that Rathika might feel 'scared', 'nervous' 'uncomfortable' and 'alone' and 'confused from moving from country to country' before reaching Britain. If they were aware of her story, most students said they and their friends would feel compassion and want to help her feel more comfortable while, at the same time, not wishing to overwhelm her:

> I'd feel the same as like someone who had just moved from like another London school came ... and try and make sure that she's – I don't know, treated nicely by other people in our class, because sometimes they're a bit rowdy and stuff ... (Anna, City School)

The emphasis here is on treating Rathika the same as another student, not singling her out for special treatment or attention, but rather, as teachers suggested (see the previous chapter), to fit in with what goes on in the school. Students felt that in 'Rathika's' place that was what they would also want.

However, relating to Rathika in the same way as any other student means leaving her open to the vagaries of British youth subcultures prevalent in schools. As we have seen, this involves a sort of rite of passage for newcomers. For example, Emma, a White British Year 7 girl from Fordham, commented:

> Some people might feel, 'she's from another country, let's take the mick out of her'. Some people might want to be nice to her, most people might think she's really strange because they've not seen foreigners – might think she's really weird. If she tried to look at them or smile at them, they might laugh. If they knew her story they might laugh a bit more because they knew she's poor ... If they didn't know ... they might laugh because they think she's a foreigner ...

The situation Emma described represents Rathika as a newcomer in a mainly all-White school; however, her Otherness or 'foreign-ness', in all three case study schools, meant that her language, or lack of

English, was likely to result in her exclusion from the peer group, or her becoming the focus of other students 'taking the mick':

> Some people might think 'she can't talk much English' and leave her alone... (Steve, White British Year 7 boy, Fordham)

> [T]here's a couple of people ... who like think asylum-seekers are just a bit – you know, having a little laugh, with bullying them about ... just probably take the mick out the way they speak or something. (Mustaq, British-Pakistani Year 10 boy, Fairfield)

The testimonies of 'citizen' students suggest that such responses to ASR students as newcomers were widespread and unremarkable – an accepted part of school life. Clearly what was critical to the building of genuine friendships was the facility to speak 'good English'. Anna from City School commented that 'genuine' or 'best' friends with girls would require this proficiency:

> I don't think she'd [Rathika] feel like really best friends with them for a while, until maybe she spoke, like, good English or something ... I think she should try and speak English because otherwise ... she won't be able to take advantage of the teaching she gets and the friends she might make.

A number of the male and female students felt that, in time, Rathika would find friends and be comfortable in their school. For example:

> Most of our classes are quite friendly. In the Year Group we are quite supportive of each other, even though we do, like, take the mickey out of each other and stuff, you still know that if ... something's happening to you, they're going to support you... [If Rathika stayed in the school for some time] ... *she'd just blend in with the rest of us. You don't really get outcasts in our Year Group.* Someone's always got a friend, or lots of friends around them ... It's not on how you look, it's how you act ... (Sophie, White British Year 10 girl, Fordham, our emphasis)

> She should be okay here, 'cos this school honestly is a really nice school ... I think at first she'd probably be scared and nervous, but then, as time goes on she should be happier with things [...] I started this school after half the year had gone ... I had felt comfort-

able really quickly. I fitted in. (Nasreen, British-Pakistani Year 11 girl, Fairfield)

She'd soon get friends, yeah … And we're very nice to new people in the school. […] I have loads of friends who just came into the school and they're our friends now, like really close with them. (Rebecca, White British Year 9 girl, City)

The gendered aspect of friendship which we saw earlier also comes through strongly in Emma's and Steve's comments, both from Fordham:

[If Rathika stayed in the school for some time] … she'll probably start mixing more with … the girls than the boys. […] Because girls are probably … more friendly than boys, sometimes […] They sometimes – they can be okay, but then girls are more sensible with people like her [Rathika]. (Emma)

More girls [will be friendly with Rathika] … Because like, they know what she'll like and all that lot … (Steve)

Niall, a White British Year 10 boy also from Fordham felt that 'mainly the girls would care more' – whether the newcomer was a girl or a boy.

In addition, some students referred to stereotypes or religious differences that could get in the way of friendship. If Rathika had a different religion, such as Hinduism, Steve from Fordham thought it would not make any difference to him, but it 'might to some people. […] I think they might sort of, like, take fun out of her sometimes.' Niall, who we heard speaking earlier about gender differences, was also cautious:

If she was treated and looked at the same as everyone else, she should be happy in this school … At the moment I think they aren't treated exactly the same, although I think after a time they might be treated the same. […] There's still people who judge people by the way – their looks … (Niall, Fordham)

Martin from Fairfield commented that ASR students might find friendship with other ASR students who shared the same experience, where they could be safely visible:

[S]he may become friends with people she can relate to, maybe like other asylum-seekers and refugees or – 'cos there's people she can relate to, people she can talk to, about her, like what happened to her ... and not feel people are going to talk about it too much, 'cos they have their experiences ...

In contrast, Ewan saw friendship as more about personality:

> It depends on what kind of person she is, I suppose. Because ... her background or her race wouldn't dictate what kind of people ... she could be friends with. Depending on her personality. Her own making ... it just depends on her personality. (Ewan, White British Year 11 boy, City)

ASR students told us about the pain of this experience. Yet it seems that, in time, some come to comprehend this peer culture, and learn to deal with it in their own way. For example, Rashid, a Year 10 unaccompanied minor boy from Iran, who had been at Fordham County School for over a year at the time of interview, had experienced this sort of harassment as a newcomer, but when we talked to him he was a confident and outgoing student, allegedly with many friends. He described the soul-searching he went through before being accepted into peer networks:

> When I came [students] take the mickey out of me ... [I felt] sad ... didn't tell no-one ... Sometimes talk to them, 'Why don't you like me?' ... Didn't have friends for year because I didn't know the culture – I think they hate me, because of the jokes you know. [...] Now it's okay – I learned how the culture is [...] They hated me, that was difficult man, they take the mick like, 'you don't know to do your tie' and that. I didn't understand why they hate me. [...] School didn't help – I didn't ask them; they didn't know the problem of making friends ...

For Rashid (unlike other students such as Edona, above), eventual acceptance resulted from his comprehension of and working through the peer culture and the school's social hierarchies. Aziza, a Year 11 Somali girl from Fairfield, also concluded:

> *Aziza:* ... now I just feel comfortable getting out the house, going to the park, going to the shops, and just getting on. And not, not like it was before.

> *Interviewer:* And do you think that's because people are more mixed here?
>
> *Aziza:* No, I think that because now, I kind of, I have, I have friends.

Feeling safe?

The tensions between an inclusionary school ethos and an exclusionary youth culture made it at times difficult for ASR students to feel safe. These were key elements of what ASR students indicated they wanted from Britain at the national level, and from their schools at the local level. In their individual interviews, the ASR students were sometimes ambivalent about whether they felt safe or not. Generally they agreed that Britain was safer for them than their home country or other possible destinations. Theodros, a Year 11 Congolese boy at City School, thought Britain was a safe country because,

> I can see ... everything's friendly, they're all nice people ... like the worst thing was people from Belgium and France. They're not really that good to people from foreign countries. [...] My cousins live there, in France.

Yasmin, a Year 11 Afghani student from Fairfield, compared her sense of safety in the UK with the lack of it in her country of origin: 'I feel safe here. Like in my country I wasn't allowed to go out ... from being a girl.'

The school system played a significant role in helping create this sense of security, especially in comparison with schools in some home countries. For example, Farouq found it a 'quite nice school' with 'lots of friends' and 'nice teachers', compared with his experiences at school in Afghanistan:

> I mean this is much better school here than in my country. They used to beat us there and we used to never go to school. I hated school there. And here I love school and I always want to come to school. I get bored at home. And in my country I just – everyone hated school, they didn't want to go to school.

Safety is relative. Aziza from Fairfield was a bit more ambivalent; 'sometimes I don't feel quite safe, sometimes I do', then went on, 'in the UK I feel free actually, 'cos in Somalia, there's like much of, fighting ...'. Similarly, Lauryn, a Congolese girl at City School, felt there were times it was very dangerous in the UK, but on the whole, 'It's nice but it's very complicated'. Farouq's (Year 10, City) comments also hinted at such complications. On the one hand, he felt that he belonged and fitted in, and that British people 'respond very well. I mean they understand the stuff [problem] and that's why they let us in their country'. He felt safe because the British were very good to him and there were no worries in Britain. On the other hand, he added:

> Some English people they just don't like us. If you argue with them they just tell you 'go back to your country, why are you in England'. And they don't understand why you're here, so there's no point in talking about it.

Hassan, a Year 8 Pakistani boy from Fordham, explained that he liked his school, and that the UK was better than his home country because '[here] I'm safe'. Similarly the group of unaccompanied ASR students in the same school talked about Britain as a 'safe country'. Lena, a Nigerian student, used a typical youth expression to say, 'It's well safe'. However in her individual interview she continued cautiously:

> *Lena*: [Britain is] Yeah, a very safe country...Yeah I do, I think it's safe. I think people are jumping to conclusions, and they blame the innocent. So it's not, they're not talking to them, it's just too much with the jumping to conclusion that all Muslims are bombers. And if they see the good side and the innocence and the worries there ... so I think it's a very safe country.
> *Interviewer*: You think this is a good country for people to come to if they're in trouble?
> *Lena*: Yes of course, this is a perfect country.

As Lena suggested, behind the image of Britain as generally a safe place one could find concerns that Britain was not safe for everyone. Dina, a Croatian Year 11 girl from Fairfield for example, voiced her concern that the level of racial violence in the UK meant that her country of origin was actually safer:

> I think it's like, much more dangerous than there [Croatia] now. A little violent ... yeah a lot violence here, and there's quite a lot of racism here ... people are more, you won't go there and see people

you know, spitting and swearing at you, and smashing up cars and anything like that ...

The ASR students we interviewed were aware of community violence, and especially anti-Islamic feelings outside the school, and the potential effect on their security and belonging. Elena, an Afghani-Russian Year 13 girl, also from Fairfield, explained what could be the reason for the hostility she had experienced: 'I think it depends on the area, and the people who live [there] ... because for example when we moved to our house, the people in the area don't really like us, because they are mostly British ...'. At City, a school which had a pervasive loud and boisterous culture and where violent incidents in the playground were commonplace, the discussion between Aasera (Year 10), Sabeen (Year 9), both Iraqi girls, and two Year 10 boys – Daran from Kurdistan and Jamil from Lebanon – brought out all these worries:

Interviewer: I think you said that a refugee child will feel safe in this school?
Daran: Yes.
Interviewer: Do you think this is a dangerous country for foreigners? What do you think?
Sabeen: It can be ...
Aasera: Sometimes it is, sometimes it isn't ...
Jamil: I think any country is a danger – could be a danger to foreigners.
Aasera: It could be, but it's not. You can't say it is.
Interviewer: Do you think that Britain is a good place for people to come to if they were in trouble?
Sabeen: Yes ...
Jamil: They've got an idea now from the media. The media always has some issues. And they make it worse I think now. So people ...
Aasera: People used to get scared to go on a train in case they see a Muslim person in there. Or a woman with a scarf on, or a guy with a beard. Now me, I'll say it honestly. If you ask me – I wear a scarf and ... I'm a Muslim myself. And I am scared to get on a train. Even more than an English person I'm scared to get on a train ... Because I'm scared in case I die at this age ...

Conclusions

These different accounts raise a number of complex issues relating to gender, bullying and dominant cliques, among others, which require further research. Students' accounts of their peers' responses to ASR students suggest that even in these allegedly inclusive school cultures, there are exclusive youth cultures which see the Other (such as someone who is not fluent in English or in 'youth language' such as gangsta) as a fair target for low-level bullying, swearing and harassment (being 'mean' or being 'horrid'), 'for having a laugh' (similar to the 'game' Edona referred to earlier) or for 'taking the mick'.

The data discussed in this chapter suggest that, while teachers strive in these schools to create the conditions of belonging, the politics of such belonging is still very much something to be unravelled and recognised. The micro-moments of interaction between ASR students and other students are fraught with the tensions of disadvantage, youth cultural signifiers, and intolerance of English language learners. The ASR students we interviewed experienced these tensions. Perhaps they did not report on instances of overt racism – however, they encountered moments of exclusion within the inclusive cultures of their school where markers such as language, style and also skin colour became obstacles for belonging and encouraged them to remain silent about their pasts.

Inclusion within the school setting is premised on the ASR students' ability to decode the school's youth culture and its norms, language and hierarchies, but especially the ability to form friendships. This was also a crucial element in gaining a sense of security and safety in a hostile community environment. In the next chapter we describe what it would mean to ASR students to 'become British', and the ways in which 'citizen' students relate to immigration and the conditions for 'being British'. Here there are strong notions that British citizenship is a 'filled space' in which there is not necessarily any room for compassion, even if desired.

9
Britishness and Belonging

In his review of citizenship in the UK for the Labour government, Lord Goldsmith (Ministry of Justice, 2008: 115) asserted that: 'We have been open in this country to allowing people to acquire citizenship, even if they were not born in the UK or have no ancestral connection to the UK.' For this to happen, the report argued, the 'non-citizen' should not only learn English but also learn how to 'become British' – to acquire 'a knowledge of the British way of life'. However, with little prospect of ever reaching the specially provided citizenship test or the much-vaunted citizenship ceremony, there are unlikely to be many opportunities for asylum-seeking students to feel that they could or would belong to British society.

In this chapter we explore ASR and 'citizen' students' conceptualisation of being and becoming British. We asked ASR students whether they would like to become British and what that would mean for them in terms of belonging, and we asked 'citizen' students what they would consider to be an appropriate strategy for the British government in terms of allowing Sheik, Rathika and Bazi and others like them into the country.

Becoming 'British'

It is one thing to feel safe, it is another to feel that a person belongs within a community. Anthony Heath and Jane Robert, in a study conducted for the Goldsmith Report on citizenship (Ministry of Justice, 2008: 86) found that having a positive experience of Britain and British people certainly helped non-British people to acquire a positive British identity. Not only was paid employment very important to this sense of integration but so too was cultural knowledge which enabled 'non-citizens' to make friends. However, most British were reported to have found it hard to define Britishness.

These themes were clearly present in our discussions with ASR students who sought ways of reconciling their national identities, their experiences of Britain and the pursuit of that elusive concept of 'being British'. For all but one of our ASR student interviewees (who felt that being a British national might prevent him from contributing to his home country in later years), the security of having British nationality and a British passport was described as important to their future well-being. For some, it guaranteed their safe travel to the home country and elsewhere, and offered them a legal status that would be respected there. For others, British citizenship and a British passport could add to their feeling of belonging in the UK. For example, Yasmin at Fairfield School commented: 'if I had a British passport and then if I call myself British, then I feel that I belong to this country.'

However, a range of differing views emerged in group interviews about the value of having a British passport and what difference or not it might make to a person's sense of belonging. At City, the group of students comprising refugees and former refugees (some already with British passports) were cautious about the difference the official symbol of British citizenship would make:

> *Aasera*: Before I had a British passport, and when I had it, and when I became like, you know – well it's the same thing. [...] it doesn't make any difference [...] It's like even if I'm born here, I know just like that that country [home country] will be there. It's my country and I will still feel the same.
> *Sabeen*: You don't feel different at all ...
> *Jamil*: Yeah, but you don't feel nothing different. But I think you enjoy yourself better, because you feel –
> *Aasera*: I'm like that's it ... you can do anything you want
> *Jamil*: Yeah, you're belonging now. *You're really belonging.*
> (City, ASR group, our emphasis)

Aasera identified strongly with her home country and having a British passport changed nothing. For her 'my country', the one she belonged to, was her country of origin. Sabeen felt no difference. For them, having a British passport provided a sense of security which they then distinguished from having a sense of belonging. However, Jamil, while seemingly agreeing with Aasera and Sabeen, then changed voice to express the sense of wellbeing and of belonging that having a British passport had given him.

For a few students, their identification with Britain as the country that gave them refuge seemed to be complete, and this was particularly the case for three young people at Fordham who had arrived in the UK as unaccompanied children. For example, Hassan commented: 'I like to become British. I say to everyone, "I come from England!".' Similarly Ishaq answered that he wanted to become British: 'I want to be in this country forever.' Hassan and Ishaq had both been in Britain for less than a year at the time of interview, and as unaccompanied children they seemed to have mentally cut ties with their homeland. Majeed, a Year 10 Afghani boy at Fairfield School who had gained British citizenship, described similar complex shifts in his sense of belonging:

> ... now I forgot from Afghanistan everything, but now I am thinking I am, I like here ... when I'm thinking at home, anywhere, I'm thinking with English, not with *my language,* because I live here, and if I am still here and I forgot Afghanistan, I think here *my country* (our emphasis).

For Majeed, language seemed to hold the key to belonging yet he seemed to cling on to something from his birthplace, as he spoke of 'my language' and tried to negotiate between his belonging to 'my language' and 'my country'.

Some former refugee students who were already permanent residents or British citizens used the same terminology as other 'citizen' students with antecedents from other countries, and spoke of a hyphenated identity, such as Croatian-British. Such identities recognised a depth of feeling and identification with their country of origin that, for these students, could sit unproblematically alongside their identity as British. ASR student identities were often tied up with where they considered 'home' – where they felt they belonged – as Jamil from City School suggested: 'I feel here's home and there's home ... If I'm here I'll say I'm British, if I'm there I'll say I'm Lebanese ...' (ASR group interview). Dina, a Year 11 girl from Fairfield School, talked about the importance of retaining her strong cultural identification with Croatia, her home even if she became more British. She still wanted to

> keep the cultural side ... and like, when I have my children, I still want the names to be ... Croatian names [...] So I still want to keep all that, but I think it'll be like, I'll be like, norm... – like everyone else here, like all the people.

Dina's hyphenated identity meant that she wanted to retain aspects of Croatian culture within a multicultural British context – 'like all the people' in Britain she will have more than one identity. This was inter-preted and voiced in different ways by individual students.

For some, such a hyphenated identity would come with a British passport. Yasmin argued, for example, that she was an Afghan girl until she received a British passport and then she would be Afghan-British. Thus, although the legal status recognised by the British passport gave the holder a British identity, some ASR students still wanted to hold on to the identity deriving from their 'roots'. Lauryn at City School com-mented: 'If they give the card [passport] and they say 'British' – you can be British, but my root is Congolese, African ...'. Similarly, when asked why she would continue to say she was Nigerian, Lena from Fordham answered: 'Just by knowing where I've come from' – if she got a British passport she would be Nigerian, African and British.

Other ASR students expressed greater ambivalence towards 'becom-ing' British. There was the issue of what might be involved at an emo-tional level in becoming 'fully' British. For example, Elena from Fairfield School felt that she wouldn't mind becoming British, but she would still 'feel in *myself* that I wasn't British, but if I did feel British, I don't think I would mind'. She did not actually believe that people could 'become British':

> I don't think so. If you were brought up in like a different country, you kind of, always have memories that would somehow affect the present, so you can't really become completely British.

Those ASR students who sought to belong understood that belonging might come with a price. The difficulties they described about being included by their peers (the conditionalities of belonging, as it were) meant adopting certain aspects of youth cultures which were an obstacle to achieving and performing belonging. Rashid explains that, although he wanted to be British, he could not just copy other students:

> *Rashid*: I want to be like one of those guys when they talk about me. [...] I want to be like one of these English boys, because I want to understand what they're talking about. Because sometimes I just keep my mouth shut, because I don't understand exactly what they're talk-ing about, you know what I mean? And then they ask me, 'why you quiet?', and I just tell them that I'm down today, stuff like that ...
> *Interviewer*: Do you think that you could feel the same things as British kids, or do you react differently?
> *Rashid*: I can't be like them because – I don't know why, but I can't ... I can't be like them, like acting like too stupid.

Interviewer: In, like, the things that you mentioned [earlier]? – about getting drunk and smoking, or what – ? Stupid in what way?

Rashid: Yeah, that's stupid. What you want to get drunk or thingy, smoke, or all those stuff ... And they go to a shop and rob something. I don't want to do that.

Similarly, Farouq at City School distanced himself from what he perceived as British youth values:

The way we think. Things we do. I can't – I'm not a thief, yeah, not like most people ... most of the people at school are thief, so whenever I find something I give it to the office, and most of the people laugh at me. They say, 'Oh why didn't you just keep it!' I give it back ...

Farouq's rejection of British youth values was based on moral grounds. His religious values were important in shaping his life, but he was mocked by his peers for it and, in turn, he felt that he could never be like them. However, the rejection of aspects of local youth cultures might be just symptomatic of much deeper and fundamental issues. Indeed, both Farouq and Rashid went on to discuss why neither of them could ever really be British:

Interviewer: Okay, so do you think that people who are born somewhere else can never really become British – is that what you're trying to say?

Farouq: Yeah, they cannot.

Interviewer: And however long you stay do you think they'll still be seen as 'not British'?

Farouq: Yeah, as long as they're born somewhere else like. But their 'race' and their colour of their skin are different. And their minds are different.

Interviewer: You would like to get British citizenship?

Rashid: Yeah, and I might bring my dad down here to visit me ...

Interviewer: Let's say you do get British citizenship, OK? Do you feel you will be British, will you feel British?

Rashid: No, I don't think – I think so – I'm not sure ... No, I don't think so. Because right now they think I'm British, you know what I mean? But I don't feel like it, because they are different, man. I can't be like them, and they can't be like me [...] When you're Black, you can't be White, can you? Or when you're White you can't be Black. That's same thing to me, inside of me. But I feel comfortable, you know what I mean? I just talk to everyone.

Both Rashid and Farouq perceived a fundamental Otherness between themselves and British youth which Farouq expressed as a different mindset that comes from being born elsewhere. This feeling of Otherness persists despite being comfortable in Britain and among British peers, and even being seen by them as British. The difference was 'inside' and was unchangeable.

Who can belong?

Belonging is a reciprocal relationship; on the one hand, a person must want to belong and, on the other, that person must be allowed to belong. Aasera and Sabeen in the City School ASR group interview described what was involved in achieving a sense of belonging:

> *Aasera*: Belonging. It's like to feel that you belong somewhere, is that to other people – other people treat you nicely. Not treating you like a stranger.
> *Sabeen*: It makes you feel good.
> *Aasera*: Making you feel that you are here and you're one of them.

Crucially, what makes a place 'home', a place where a person feels they belong, is the notion of respect. Jamil (a Lebanese student), when talking to other ASR students at City School, put this well:

> As long as the community is respecting you and you feel part of the community. That's the main bit. When you feel part of the community you're gonna feel safe. You're gonna feel that you are at home.

However, Rashid from Fordham raised a new and complex set of issues about safety and belonging in the group interview. The first might be a precondition for the second, but it does not necessarily guarantee it:

> *Lena*: What will make you feel you belong somewhere? Somewhere when you fit in, people treat you the same, so you belong with a group of friends ...

Rashid: ... I don't actually – I don't feel like that ...

Lena: You have to make an effort to belong, to be honest ... you have to go and talk to people ...

Rashid: I got loads of friends ...

Interviewer: ...To feel you belong somewhere, do you need to feel safe? Is that part of it?

Rashid: No. No.

Lena: I think so ... If you belong somewhere, you feel safe.

Rashid: Yeah, I think I belong in my country yeah, but I didn't feel safe.

Belonging for Rashid is more complex than feeling safe or gaining friends. As we have seen, ASR students in the three schools we researched were encouraged to feel that they belonged – that they were part of the school community. The strategy used by teachers was to turn ASR students into learner citizens by, as ASR students indicated, treating them like everyone else – like British students. However, as we have also seen, youth cultures are more exclusive. Belonging in terms of 'being one of us' is more problematic to achieve not because of exclusionary practices directed at the Other, the 'foreigner', but sometimes also (as in the case of Farouq and Rashid) because ASR students did not want to belong or did not feel they ever did belong, especially to English as opposed to British culture. This view resonated with the answers groups of 'citizen' students' gave us when we asked them to define Britishness and who they believed could be or become British. There was a clear distinction between 'Englishness' and 'Britishness' for some:

> You know, I think that if people call themselves English, it's like because they've got no sort of other kind of mix of blood in them. (Shada, British-Moroccan Year 10 girl, City School, group interview)

For Martin, from Fairfield, Britishness denoted a multicultural inclusive identity while, in order to be English, a person would have to be born in England:

> English, I see like this one where it's kind of, like being born in the country, and that's like the main language and stuff. Whereas I see British as like becoming – you can become British and stuff, whereas

English, I see as more of like uh, roots, kind of like your background.

However, there was a possibility that this might change, over a long period of time:

> I think maybe like, over a period of time maybe if you come from another country, over a period of time or like generations you become English, but not straight away.

Yet for another student, Steve, at Fordham, the terms 'English' and 'British' seemed to be interchangeable – foreigners in his view could become British 'if they were born somewhere else, and then they moved here, like when they were still young, they could speak, like two *languages,* and would be classed as *quite English'*. For Steve, as in official discourse (including the Goldsmith Report mentioned above), knowledge of English language and the British culture were fundamental aspects of the route to citizenship and meaningful membership.

In contrast, Anna at City School thought that a common language and culture were not essential to being considered British – other factors such as residence were very important:

> *Anna*: It means that you live in Britain ... I don't think just because you were born somewhere else you are not British. I think if you live here, like not if you're on holiday here, but I think if you live here, then you're British.
> *Interviewer*: ... are there other things like to do with language and culture and food perhaps? – are those important things?
> *Anna*: No, I don't think they're important. I just think if you live here then you're living in Britain, so you're British. I think ... if you eat other food or anything it doesn't mean you're not British really, 'cos like especially in London, there's so – like so many people from all different places and that, really everyone's British. I don't think it matters if you can't speak English, I still think you can be British.

While Anna saw Britishness as a multicultural, all-inclusive identity, the boundaries of belonging for her were very broad – a person simply needed to be in residence on a permanent basis. In contrast, the 'citizen' group in Fairfield school saw bloodline and country of birth as the main factors shaping Britishness and Englishness. Tim (a White British student), Jena (White British-Italian) and Michael (White British), who were all in Year 9, argued that anyone could *become* British citizens, but not everyone could *be* British:

> *Michael*: But then you'd probably still call yourselves from wherever you are from, because if you were born here – aren't you a British citizen? So if you move here from another country ... say from Africa, you would call yourself African even if you get a British passport. You won't call yourself British just because you've got a passport, you'll say, 'Well, I was born in Africa, my parents are African, so I am African'...
>
> *Tim*: I'd say that, I ... I mean you can become a British citizen or French citizen or whatever, but I'd say it actually does come from your background and your actual blood ...
>
> *Interviewer*: But you are saying that being British is something more than a citizenship or passport or something ... ?
>
> *Tim*: Yes. Yes, I think it is.
>
> *Interviewer*: What is it?
>
> *Tim*: I think it is just blood from your family. Like I said just then, I think like if you have a mum who is just like – if you have a dad who is English and a mum who might be French and Spanish, I would just say you are English, I think.
>
> *Interviewer*: ... But what does it actually mean to be British?
>
> *Jena*: You can tell if someone is like not – like if someone is from Africa or Asia you can tell that they are not British, but that is only by skin colour. That is the most obvious thing that you can tell ...

For this White group of students, the passport seemed to be just a legal document, and did not confer Britishness; this came through a bloodline, defined by Tim as patrilineal. For Jena, Britishness could be defined by what it was not: drawing on a racial discourse of belonging, Britishness also meant Whiteness.

The discussions of the 'citizen' group of Year 10 students from City School, which comprised an ethnically mixed group, not surprisingly had different emphases. Two boys, James (Black British), Aaron (British dual heritage) and three girls – Shada, (British Moroccan), Larita (White British-Spanish) and Catrin (White British) – explored the conditions for Britishness using a bundle of criteria that included 'race', culture, residence and passports:

> *James*: Maybe you could say that being acknowledged as a British citizen... You could be one but people still might not think of you as one ...
>
> *Shada*: Depending on the way you dress and the colour you are, people might not see you as British ... I don't think you have to do anything or to be the way you have to be, to be known as British. [...] Like I don't think ... eating fish and chips shows that you're British. Or, you know, going to the pub shows that you're British.
>
> *Larita*: Or being Cockney and you know... I think being British is having – being a British citizen. Being born in Britain.
>
> *Catrin*: If you live here and you're like permanently here, or you like have a future for staying over in Britain, then I think, yeah, and you actually want to – you like the country, and you want to stay here. And you don't have future plans to go and like live in France or whatever. Then I think that makes you British. Because I know if I went like to a different country, I'll always feel – I classify myself as British. Even if I lived there for like a long time ...
>
> *James*: ... like you could be born here and like been raised here and that, but if they still don't class you as that – people still might look at you and say, think like otherwise ...
>
> *Aaron*: ... I don't think like ... to be patriotic ... matters
>
> *Interviewer*: Can foreigners become British?... If they get a British passport?
>
> *James*: You don't need your passport, you just need your stay. Because ... in order to get your passport you need to stay in England ...

For Larita and Catrin, being born and/or raised in Britain, living permanently in the country and choosing to build a future there would make a person British. By implication, this definition allowed Britishness to be multicultural. However, Shada and James pointed out that, to be British, someone had to be *acknowledged* as British, to be allowed to belong. Public perceptions of Britishness being seen as synonymous with Whiteness and Western dress and norms could thus exclude you, whether or not you were born and raised in Britain or had acquired a British passport through domicile.

'Citizen' students from the three secondary schools clearly did not speak with one voice, not least because of their own very mixed ethnic and cultural origins. Many of these students had hyphenated or hybrid identities and therefore they themselves did not necessarily 'feel British'. Most, whatever their background, were prepared to discuss issues of national identity. It was only Rebecca and Alex, both London students, who seemed to reject the concept of nationality. They saw everyone as part of a common humanity, making any argument for Britishness null and void in their scheme of things; they adopted what might be seen as cosmopolitan identity:

> *Interviewer*: What is it that makes somebody British?
> *Rebecca*: Nothing really... I suppose speaking English and – I don't know really. I haven't thought about it. [...] I'm not really that kind of person who thinks that we're all – I just think, we're not really different are we? We're all the same really, we're all human.

> *Alex*: My feelings are that nationality means nothing any more. We're all the same, whether we're Black, White, Somalian, Pakistani, whether we're a refugee or born in the same country. We're all the same. We're all human beings. [...] We're all the same.

The diversity of meanings attached to British nationality and perceptions of how to achieve belonging among 'citizen' students were important not least because such meanings influenced in turn the ways in which citizen students responded to the politics of asylum and immigration policy. 'Citizen' students not only drew on different public discourses on Britishness (including multicultural Britain) but also on youth languages and cultures to differentiate between those ASR students who fitted and might achieve belonging and those who were likely to be excluded from their friendship group. Consequently, the micro-level of interaction between youth shapes the conditionalities placed on ASR students' sense of belonging and safety.

A matter of compassion?

As expected, the scenarios of Bazi, Rathika and Sheik drew an immediate emotional response from 'citizen' students, who reacted variously with expressions of pity, concern, sympathy, incredulity and outrage at the children's predicaments. When they considered the issues in greater depth, it was possible to see different types of compassion at play: compassion as pity; a notion of compassion as 'fairness' which involved something similar to what Aristotle described as the first cognitive judgement – moral recognition of the suffering of another (see Chapter 3); and the more radical conceptions of compassion in terms of social justice and human rights, associated with Simone Weil's theory.

Compassion as pity was much in evidence when discussing the experiences of Rathika; in individual interviews, nearly half of the students responded initially with pity and sadness:

> It's sad because she had to leave the place where she grew up and everything and where she was like reasonably well off or something and then she came here and ... even though ... she's not in the war any more, she still can't really afford as many things as like other people can afford. (Anna, City School)

> Just like, a little bit sad ... She would have had to like leave all her friends and all that lot behind her, and just move to another country where she didn't really know about. (Steve, Fordham)

> I feel kind of sorry for them. Like they have to leave their countries and their families ... just to come down and be safe. (Diane, White British Year 9 girl, Fairfield)

These students expressed sadness for the suffering of a fellow human being. They seemed to understand the gravity of the consequences of being displaced or forced to move. For Steve and Diane, this was mainly to do with loss of people – family and friends – but for Anna it was more to do with lack of material things and the loss of a lifestyle. Compassion, nevertheless, remained very much at the level of the individual. Some responses to the more shocking scenario of Sheik also remained on this individual level. Anna expressed this view clearly:

> It's really sad 'cos he was only ten. Must be really sad to threaten someone to shoot him and then ... when he's only trying to help ... they beat him ... it's quite scary. (Anna, City School)

For one girl, Sophie from Fordham, who had expressed sadness at Rathika's story, the enormity of Sheik's story shocked her into a sense of moral outrage that made her feel not just sad but 'horrible': 'I just feel all horrible really, because the people are coming over to him, and ... *they're using him like a weapon* ...'. Her reactions went beyond feeling sad or pitying someone's bad fortune. She saw the moral wrong in the circumstances that led to Sheik's situation. A sense of injustice comes across in Fordham student Steve's comments that he felt 'sad and just annoyed that there is people out there that does stuff like that'. Similarly, Niall started out with an expression of pity at Rathika's story, but then 'changed voice' to a moral position on what is 'unfair':

> It made me feel a little bit sorry for her, because they're having to move around and not feeling safe where they live, all the time. Or when they finally get to a place where they do feel safe, they don't have enough money to live a comfortable life. I don't really think that's very... *that's not how someone should really live.* (Niall, Fordham, our emphasis)

He kept this 'voice of fairness' in discussing Sheik's story:

> It made me feel sad that ... he actually got beaten for actually helping his neighbours not to open the door. It was quite brave, like, to actually say ... not to open your door even though his own life was being threatened.

Other 'citizen' students responding to the three ASR scenarios seemed to employ the equivalent of Aristotle's second cognitive judgement underlying compassion – that of being aware that suffering was not the responsibility of the sufferer (see Nussbaum, 2001). Bazi, Sheik and Rathika were represented as deserving of compassion first and foremost because their suffering was seen as not their fault:

> I kind of feel sorry for the people that have to go through that experience, 'cos at the end of the day it's not, *it's not their fault* they have to move from their country, whether they are going to be risking their lives and things, and have to travel, like, ... and when they come to, like, Britain and that, they haven't got much money to get the things they want, making their life that bit harder (Martin, Fairfield).

Ewan at City School explained how he felt about Rathika and her family: 'I suppose sympathy towards them. *They had no choice* but to leave their country and a comfortable life through civil war but ... Yeah, it's a bit ... Sympathy for them.'

When asked what Rathika might feel, he replied: 'She must feel quite shaken up. *Like, having to leave her homeland through no fault of her own.*'

Compassion towards these children's lives tended to be based on the scale of their suffering.[1] For instance, Ewan's outrage at Sheik's story led him to a position that focused on social justice:

> It makes me feel quite disgusted by the violence that goes on in that country. [...] It doesn't seem like there's much law and order in the country. That they can come up to someone, a ten year old, and butt them in the face with a gun. *There's no social conscience ... Well, there's no conscience* (our emphasis).

Martin, another 'citizen' student whom we have already met, responded in a similar way to Sheik's story:

> [Y]ou kind of fear for their safety in that one, not so much feel sorry for them ... you're kind of, really scared, I think, 'cos you've got people coming up to you telling you to do something, and then when you warn other people, *doing the right thing, the right thing,* to get beaten up, I think *it's just quite terrible ...* (our emphasis).

Since Sheik's suffering involved not only displacement as result of threats to his safety and life, but also physical abuse, his suffering was perceived as grave. 'Citizen' students looked at the wider moral circumstances and consequences of such a story. It made them reflect on issues such as the right to safety and the vulnerability of children, perhaps also of themselves – as Martin had simply put it he felt 'really scared'.

A few students, such as Nasreen at Fairfield and Rebecca and Alex at City, expressed their compassion at Rathika and Sheik's stories through a language of human rights and social justice from the outset. The response by Alex (whom we saw earlier demonstrating a more cosmopolitan identity) to Rathika's story offered the most detailed and illuminating example of this position. When talking about Rathika, he argues:

> She needs security. Yeah. I feel that if the government was to see this ... and if the government was to understand, even though this is one person, *a life is a life.* If the government was to see this then they'd ... They'd be appalled at what they've done. What they've missed. They're missing these things and it's really sad that ... if I was to be in these circumstances, I'd want as much as help as I could

get to help me through my life. Whereas the government isn't actually giving this ... giving Rathika the help that she needs. *It's her rights. We deserve the right to live. We deserve the right to have money. We deserve the right to have a job. She's not having her rights. We deserve the right to be secure. To have our own house. She hasn't got the right there. She hasn't got her right to be secure.* The government is missing that. They're letting it slip (our emphasis).

Alex not only empathised with Rathika and was able to put himself in her shoes, but he saw her rights and their fulfilment as part of his own interest. He and Rathika were part of the same 'we' – her interests and rights were part of his scheme of things. When discussing Sheik's story, he revealed how much the language of rights was central to his thinking:

Crikey! That appalling ... That's crazy ... There's no words to describe that. [...] There's no way out for that kid ... That is the worst case scenario that somebody can have ... But also *I feel really appalled that this is allowed to happen. Once again, I come back to the fact of rights. People have rights to live. People have rights to have friendship anyway. This kid didn't ... was denied his rights* (our emphasis).

Alex's responses revealed the emotions he was grappling with as he considered the children's stories – compassion, outrage, admiration, based on a strong notion of human rights and of social justice, which, in his scheme of things, have to be upheld by government, his government.

Blair's dilemma

Whatever the level and type of compassion shown to the stories of Rathika, Sheik or Bazi, the question of whether Tony Blair, the then Prime Minister, should allow asylum-seekers such as these three into the country led to considerable disarray amongst 'citizen' students. The need to contemplate the political case for offering long-term asylum raised new concerns and gave expression to different politics of belonging among the group we interviewed.

The main reason for allowing ASR youth such as Rathika, Sheik or Bazi into the UK would be in order to secure their safety. Here compassion on the grounds of asylum was clearly strong amongst the 'citizen' group in all three schools. The messages of the 'citizen' students we interviewed in the three schools came through very clearly – the UK should offer them refuge, they should be allowed in. Martin, at Fairfield, even personalised his feeling of compassion and guilt that might come of not offering safety to those individuals in need:

> It's a human life that's at risk ... you shouldn't base it on who they are or where they're from and stuff, it's that they need somewhere to go ... I'd feel guilty knowing that our country has turned someone away in their time of need.

Rebecca, Ewan and Alex at City School in London were also strong in their compassion and their convictions that the children in such scenarios were deserving of UK protection. Rebecca's reply to the question of whether they should be let in was: 'Yes, of course, why wouldn't you?' Ewan commented: 'I'd let them in ... they're being mistreated. [...] haven't got a secure life ... There's always going to be a limit ... but you should help countries in conflict or people in danger ...'

However, Alex also showed himself to be aware of national concerns about population numbers and costs to the country even if in the event compassion would outweigh such concerns:

> I'd let him [Sheik] into this country ... We shouldn't deny anybody but if they're poor then, yeah, the government should be able to help them. But ... the government doesn't have enough money to help every single poor person in the area, but they have got [a] facility to help them develop their own business. Help them to develop their own ways of making their own money. With Sheik's and Rathika's story, yes, they're in a war and if I was the Prime Minister I'd happily let them into my country. I'd happily give them a home to live in. I'd happily help them out with the right school because, as I said, *a life is a life, and a life is worth living*. And I'd be ... I'd be inclined to help them out as much as I can (our emphasis).

Concern about the size of the British population and the number of potential asylum-seekers was something which the rest of the City 'citizen' student group was concerned about:

> *Larita*: ... there's loads of other people, and if you're gonna make an exception for one, you have to like look at ... what's happened to everyone else's lives ...
> *Shada*: You can't just think about one. Because there's probably so many other families, and then if you let them all in there's gonna be no more space ...

Catrin: But not many of them have probably gone through what he [Sheik] did. And, yeah, but they've all had different experiences, and some of them probably worse. Some of them a lot less –
James: ... courage he [Sheik] showed, basically to sacrifice himself like that. I think we should let him in. (City School, 'Citizen' group)

These London students in a sense replicated the government discourse of the 'deserving' and the 'undeserving'. They were clear that the country could not just randomly protect some and not others; but also that the government could not accept everyone because then there would be 'too many of them'. In their search for a 'fair' way to determine those who are deserving of protection the group suggested that Britain should rely on assessing the scale of the suffering of those seeking refugee.

The group of White 'citizen' students at Fairfield struggled even more with the idea of how to respond. Although based in a multi-ethnic school where many of the students come from different ethnic backgrounds, in the discussion these students battled between the human dimension of asylum, the need of safety and protection from war, and the need to protect the country from becoming 'full up':

Michael: They could go to other countries ... because Britain has got a lot of asylum seekers [...] But we could help them but I don't know how you can say 'No' to them really...
Interviewer: So you wouldn't say 'No' to them because ...
Michael: You wouldn't really say 'No' because if they were in danger [...]Well the first thing you'd say [...] Well you would try and make them safe and [...] Most people would think that if they come to this country then they are safe and the government will keep them safe ...
Tim: The detention centres they are for refugees who come over aren't they? [...] they could make more of those I suppose for the people who arrive but maybe people would hear about it and think, 'Oh that is a place we can go'. And then they get all full up and more and more keep on coming in. I mean I don't have a problem because it doesn't seem to affect ... well in the short term ... I don't think any of us would notice any difference in the way we live because of it. But maybe in the long term there might be ...
Ines:[2] ... at the same time ... you usually don't let a lot of people in, and then they are going to start families off anyway ... And then if they have their own families here and they start having

more children, and more people come in [...] Eventually there is not
going to be any room for like anymore people to come in ...
Michael: ... our towns will just be like houses with estates and stuff
... (Fairfield School 'citizen' group)

Finally, in Fordham, a predominantly White school, the students' discussion below on how to advise Tony Blair on the admission of asylum-seekers exposes the various criteria which they would use to choose who could stay which showed remarkable similarity to the criteria put forward by the government and the media:

> *Connor*:[3] If they haven't got, like, if they just, like, was in poverty,
> then yeah. Probably would.
> *Rakim*:[4] ... it may sound cruel, but I'd only really let them in if I was
> Tony Blair, I'd only let them in if they came in legally; ... if they just
> came to the country and just expected everything then I wouldn't
> let them, but if they were legal, yeah [...] If they came in asylum
> thing, yeah. If they just, like, got false identities and everything,
> then, if they just were completely illegal immigrants, then ...
> *Lisa*:[5] I don't know if I'd let them in, because on one hand they're
> like, they need somewhere to stay and they need to be safe. On the
> other hand they could cause like more problems, and like racism
> and things, and people saying that they're illegal and things, if
> they're not. So I think it would be quite a hard decision.
> *Interviewer*: So you said you're not sure, is that right? Because you
> said on the one hand about being safe, you said something like
> that?
> *Lisa*: Yeah, they would be ... they could be safe, and they would be
> happy here, and they wouldn't get diseases. But on the other hand,
> they could, like, people could bully them for racism.

The influence of official, public and media discourses on asylum in this conversation is evident. They used the legal, criminalised discourse to suggest that there are genuine and unlawful asylum-seekers, they feared Britain becoming swamped with asylum-seekers and they raised concerns about the influence of a large intake of asylum-seekers on race relations, an expression of racism, while allegedly worried about the safety of asylum-seekers.

Indeed, for this group of 'citizen' students, of equal importance to asylum policy is where ASR youth and their families 'would be safest'. This could mean that these students wanted to protect ASR youth from racial harassment or violence in the UK. Alternatively their views could represent examples of racial stereotyping, discrimination and exclusion – that good race relations are only achieved by blocking the immigration of Black migrants:[6]

Interviewer: So ... is this for their sake you're saying you don't know if it's a good thing, about the bullying for racism? Is that what you're saying?
Lisa: I think it would be for their sakes.
Interviewer: Right. And do you think it might be, it might be better for them to stay in the refugee camp?
Lisa: Yeah.
Connor: Yeah. Rather than going out and other people, like, pickin' [on] 'em ...
Interviewer: Right.
Rakim: But then they was, there was lots of diseases there, so ... they could just move somewhere –
Connor: – else in the world.
Rakim: Yeah, 'cos, like Britain has got a ridiculously high population, because it's such a tiny island, so –
Lisa: Or a special place where they could all go together, so they're all, like, the refugees are all together, and then there would be no one there to, like, bully them, and they could be free from disease and be safe.
Rakim: I think it would be safer for them and us if they stayed in a certain area, so if they did bring disease in, then it wouldn't spread ...
Lisa: They could, like, still come to the UK, and, like, they could build an island, somewhere like the Isle of Wight, and then they could put them all on there ...
Rakim: What about Ireland?
Interviewer: You want to send them to Ireland?
Rakim: No, no, it's not, not really, it's more of a joke, really. But, yeah.
Connor: If they could go to, like, America or some other big country, then it would be easier for us, and for them, because they would have more space, and it wouldn't crowd England up too much.

Here compassion for asylum-seekers is mediated through the lens of where to put asylum-seekers and refugees – for example sending them to different countries (such as Ireland or even Russia according to the

Fairfield group) or settling them all on an island. Compassion was also affected by the fear of the Other (they might bring diseases) and their association with an increase in racial conflict given existing racist sentiments.[7] It seems that, despite the compassion that the same students were able to express towards individuals, when the larger political issue of asylum-seekers coming to Britain was considered, they became the 'human waste' which 'we' should dispose of in as practical a way as possible. The morality of this latter position, of sending ASR students to 'some place' noticeably worried those 'citizen' students at Fordham, who were keen to retain some notion of fairness:

> *Lisa*: Or they could, like, every so many years, about a year or two years, then like all the leaders of the smaller countries could come together, and then they could divide up the refugees like evenly between all the countries.
> *Connor*: But you'd have to keep families together though.
> *Rakim*: Yeah.
>
> (Fordham School 'citizen' group)

These three group discussions suggest, at minimum, that when forced to consider asylum issues on national and not an individual level, such students are confused and ambivalent, finding themselves caught between the politics of compassion and the politics of belonging.

Conclusion

Paradoxically, we could see that it was in fact the visibility of individual asylum-seeking stories (which we presented to them in the form of three scenarios) that encouraged compassion among 'citizen' students. However, when confronted with Britain's best interest and with immigration policy questions, the politics of belonging prevailed, suggesting that those 'citizen' students who suggested that ASR students should remain silent might have been right. This begs the question, as Stead et al. (2002) argued, of how we encourage safe visibility for ASR students – a form of visibility that not only will encourage compassion for the individual but also will transcend to offer a different politics of belonging. In the following chapter we explore the moments in schools when their visibility becomes a catalyst for political action.

10
The Politicisation of Compassion: Campaigning for Justice

> Becoming political is that moment when the naturalness of the dominant virtues is called into question. (Isin, 2002: 275)

In previous chapters we explored the many-faceted concept of compassion which the notion of asylum generates at governmental, LEA and school level, and amongst 'citizen' students. Different forms of compassion emerged from our empirical data. For example, we have seen government attempts to restrict compassion only to the 'deserving' rather than to those seeking asylum. While the schools we researched expressed compassion as sympathy and caring for the whole child irrespective of their political history and civic status, another form of compassion based on humanitarian principles and human rights came through our data. Our research in secondary schools and LEAs suggests that compassion for ASR students, when linked with professional ethics and an inclusive ethos, can move teachers to empathetic personal and pedagogic responses. Schools can value the presence of ASR students as one way of engendering compassion in the community as a whole. They become a resource rather than the problem characterised by the media and by government. However, the policing of immigration control described in Chapter 4 challenges these moral stances and can create the circumstances where compassion becomes overtly political, galvanising schools, teachers and students into political action in the name of social justice.

In his insightful work *Being Political: Genealogies of Citizenship*, Isin (2002: x) posits an ontological difference between politics and the political. 'Being political,' he states, 'among all other ways of being, means to constitute oneself simultaneously with and against others as an agent capable of judgement about what is just and unjust.' 'Being political' is when the 'naturalness of the dominant virtues' is being called into question. We suggest here that, when the unjust ceases to be a condition in the abstract, when the unjust can no longer be ignored because of its proximity, then a political moment is created which calls the dominant discourses around asylum into question, transforming compassion for those seeking asylum and refuge into praxis. For some schools, teachers and students, such a political moment is created when faced with the actions of the UK government through its immigration and asylum policy, which seem that much more unacceptable given asylum-seeking and refugee children's past experiences of violence and when unexpected violent moments of forced removal and threats of deportation of asylum-seeking children and their families are brought into the everyday life of a British school that prides itself on tolerance and inclusion.

At these moments and in these circumstances, a local politics of belonging is activated that leads either to a more politicised teaching around the notion of human rights or to the involvement of teachers, students and even parents in a political campaign in support of asylum-seeking children against a hostile state. In both these scenarios, compassion becomes something more akin to what Nussbaum (2001) described as the type of compassion embodied within 'just institutions'. This type of compassion can be achieved when Others are respected by the community as people who have not lost their own agency but who are temporary victims of circumstance, and when there is recognition that the relieving of their suffering is part of 'our' (or the institution's) goals – 'our' own scheme of goals.

Narratives of endurance

Our starting point is the silence of youth already discussed at various points throughout the book. The form of caring compassion within schools we found amongst teachers and 'citizen' students was largely based on the silence of ASR youth. Teachers and students reported that on the whole they were not given access to the life stories of ASR students, partly as we saw because of their invisibility in the melange of multi-ethnic schools and the lack of data on the numbers and individuals involved. This lack of information is compounded by the chosen silence of ASR students who are constrained by language difficulties and, even more importantly, by the fear of being ostracised, stigmatised or bullied. They prefer not to have their privacy invaded and, in return, wish to be accepted like any other young person. However, as a stranger, such 'normality' is hard to achieve – the conditions for belonging are not just that they should acquire the cultural identity, attributes and habits of British youth described in the previous chapter. They need to have had 'ordinary' childhoods. The testimonies of ASR youth about their childhoods would immediately place them outside the parameters of what constituted the ordinary lives of British youth. As Candappa and Egharevba (2000) argued, ASR students have had 'extraordinary childhoods'.[1]

The points at which their narratives become public or are publicised, therefore, are pivotal moments not only for ASR students but also for their schools. The hostility of the state towards such vulnerable and traumatised children appears then to challenge the notion that compassion is 'caring' and that good teaching is sufficient. At these points, compassion takes a different form.

Wars and political conflicts, with the attendant persecutions and atrocities these inevitably bring, create the social conditions that force people to leave their homelands to seek political asylum. The route to freedom is often hard and dangerous and carries considerable human cost. Many ASR youth lose family members both in the violence of their own country but also *en route* to the new country. The stories of their flight, of their travels often across a number of holding countries, and of their arrival and settlement in the UK are filled with fears for safety, loss and trauma, but also with their personal endurance and courage. Refugee children's narratives tell of considerable suffering. For example, Ragi, the pseudonym for a Somali boy who was also part of the *Extraordinary Childhoods* study arrived in Britain unaccompanied when he was ten years old; aged 14 he was attending an east London school at the time of interview:

> Now I live with my uncle. [...] My mother she is in Nairobi. My dad died in Somalia the first day they fight. He fell on the floor and just the people capture him. I heard he was killed, my mum she was telling me. When he was dead, we come. My mum wanted to go. I come to Nairobi in '91, about four, five years there. [...] But sometimes they are going to come, the police, and they're going to check – all the people, if you got passports. [...] We left. I don't know how my mum is, and my brothers and sisters ...

The memories of war in Somalia of 11-year-old Bazi from the Brava community (see Table 8.2) involve experiences of fear, death and disease:

> One day we leave by boat ... but the boat broken in the middle of Somalia and Kenya and some of our family fell in the water and

drowned – our cousin. And we just prayed to God and God pushed us through the sea to the land ... The boat was slowly going down to the sand ... In the sand there was nobody and one day we slept on the sand. [...] Some people came by small boats and they came to collect us and took us to their island. We was very hungry that day. They gave us food. And then we stayed for week. [...] After two weeks, some people say that our family sent small ship from Mombasa to that small island and then they took us and we got to Kenya. [...] We stayed in place for refugees [...] There was bad disease there ... My Grandma, she died from malaria. My Dad ... he said that this is no good country. There is much disease.

Such memories are carried with these youth into their daily lives at school in the UK. Affected by images of war on the television, Sheik, whom we also met in Chapter 8 (Table 8.1), is continually reminded of the emotions associated with his past life in Somalia:

I think about Somalia and the fighting ... It's hard thinking about some of my neighbours. They get – some get killed. Sometimes when I dream, I'm thinking about them. I remember what I used to do with them. [...] I used to be friends with them ... I don't know if they're okay, I don't have any idea ... When I see on TV people getting killed, I get sad. I just keep dreaming about them. Don't feel good to see them – things that happen in Somalia and some different countries like Bosnia ...

Further tests of their endurance had to be faced once in the UK. These youth have to struggle with the harsh realities of being poor – a political underclass within British society. The UK's progressive tightening of the law and its curtailing of asylum-seeking welfare entitlements to serve as a deterrent to so-called 'bogus asylum-seekers' stretches still further the resilience and courage of families seeking asylum. Serap (a pseudonym), a 14-year-old Kurdish girl from Turkey, remembers the grinding poverty they lived in when their family first arrived in the UK:

When we came to the house, there was nothing in there. We had to buy everything ... You know we get Income Support? – they help us, but afterwards they cut it from the Income Support. [...] We got carpet just for our rooms. Last year ... we got carpet for the stairs and middle and corridor ... It was very dirty ... our wallpaper was ripped, some of it was coming off. That is why we had to clean it, it was dirty. You know, pigeon poo was everywhere. Bathroom was like this – all the pigeon poo. (Testimony collected by the *Extraordinary Childhoods* study.)

To add to their distress, as we have seen, compulsory dispersal places such families and their children in areas where there are real poss-ibilities of being harassed. Candappa et al.'s (2007) study of ASR fam-ilies' experiences in a dispersal area in Scotland (created in 2000) found that large numbers of asylum-seeking families were clustered together in inner-city housing in an area where aspects of difference such as skin colour and dress made the presence of asylum-seekers very visible and where the children of families seeking asylum were vulnerable to racism and abuse. In one highly deprived area, Somali parents reported stones being thrown at them outside the school; in another area a Turkish parent told of refugees being spat on by Scottish children in a park, saying (while accompanied by their parents): 'f*** off you Black bastards, go back to your country.' Unaccompanied minors similarly experienced racist abuse on a regular basis in the city centre and while on public transport, so much so that one young man commented: 'they call me names like "Black bastard", I do not respond. Sometimes I feel no freedom because people abusing us.'

Asylum-seeking children's experiences were even further aggravated by the inhumane treatment meted out to such families by immigration officials, especially at the point of a failed asylum claim. The violence of their arrest, removal and detention push such families even further towards the limits of their endurance. A number of children in the 11 Million report (2009) related how they had been treated with violence by officers in such removal raids, including being dragged and thrown to the ground. An 11-year-old child is quoted as saying: 'They pushed me on the floor and got my hands behind me ... then they took me to the van. I was on my own in the van. I didn't know what was happen-ing to my family ...' (11 Million, 2009: 20). Children and parents told of feeling 'like criminals' during their transportation to Yarl's Wood immigration removal centre in caged vans that were dirty and smelled of urine or vomit.

As the 11 Million report states: 'their treatment during transportation impinged upon their dignity and was not consistent with humanitarian principles' (ibid.: 24). In a large majority of cases children reported that officers' behaviour after entry to the house had been aggressive and, on a few occasions, violent. Children reported officers 'shouting', having a 'bad tone of voice' and 'being rude' while others said that officers took pleasure in the family's distress, telling them that they were 'going back to their own country' and laughing and making fun of them when they showed signs of distress or anxiety (ibid.: 19). In testimonies offered to teachers in a children's forum at Yarl's Wood, one eight-year-old girl reported:

> When they come to get you to take you to the detention centre, they knock on your door like they are going to break it. They should wake us up gently, not just shouting. They should call through the letterbox and if the person doesn't wake up then shout but not break the door down. Also just having the key and going inside the house shows no respect. They should have a bit more manners ... (Girl, 8 years old; 11 Million, 2009: 19)

Sir Al Aynsley-Green highlighted the fact that the majority of children and young people encountered on a visit to Yarl's Wood had either 'lived in the UK for many years, or were born here', mainly as a result of 'historic inefficiencies of the asylum system' (11 Million, 2009: 5), making the experience of exclusion and removal probably even more traumatic.

These narratives of endurance are even more distressing when we consider that asylum-seeking children suffer not only from the violent removal process but also from the inadequacy and harsh conditions at detention centres, even in Yarl's Wood which presumably was designed to cater for families with children (see Chapter 4). The distress of asylum-seeking children is clearly documented. They are quoted as saying:

> It's a prison, you can't call it anything else, and it's a prison' (Girl, aged 11, 11 Million, 2009: 29)

> I hate, repeat HATE Yarl's Wood. I never wanted to come here. I just wanted to stay in this country, in Manchester, near my friends. (Boy, aged 14, 11 Million, 2009: 26)

Listening to the narratives of ASR children is harrowing in the extreme. How much harder it is to learn that these children's deprivation and trauma are extended and aggravated by the inhumanity of their treatment by the government in the UK. There can be little doubt, as both the school and prison inspectorates (HMIP, 2008; Ofsted, 2008; see also Chapter 4) acknowledge that the conditions relating to the arrest and detention of children for immigration purposes are unjust and in breach of their human rights and that their treatment in the process is a further violation of their rights as children. Government action in 'the nation's best interests' thus adds to the considerable distress of such children. At such moments, schools, teachers, parents and students are caught up in a new politics of belonging manipulated by the state. Compassion here involves taking action in the name of the values of fairness and of social justice (see Weil, 1970; see also Chapter 3). Below we identify some of the moments when this form of political awakening and action of students and teachers were created.

Political moments: awakening schools

As we have seen, ASR children are mainly invisible in a school population. However, at times, this invisibility is broken and children's refugee past and their current vulnerability, insecurity and oppression are starkly exposed to peers and school. One such moment happened in a north London secondary school participating in the *Extraordinary Childhoods* (Candappa and Egharevba, 2000) study. This was a multicultural school which prided itself on its equal opportunities policies and always celebrated its international intake, but at the time of these events was not really prepared for the different needs of children who had experienced trauma and loss through wars and famine. Athy Demetriades, the Head of Year at the time, recalled:[3]

> Susan arrived aged thirteen years from Mogadishu, Somalia. She spoke no English ... someone was asked to look after her. [...] A week later her class were playing a game ... it was a great game ... verbal communication was not necessary. It was a game of nudge ... [But] Susan suddenly had a panic attack which led to a heart attack ... Two years later Susan did manage to convey to us that the last time she had been nudged was with the butt of a gun before her mother was raped, her father taken to prison and her brother shot and killed.

This incident shocked the school into looking at itself. Athy continued:

> We had 29 such [ASR] children ... whom we knew nothing about. [...] We felt outraged that the usual safety nets for children who had suffered loss or abuse were not in place for our refugee pupils. We felt outraged that we as teachers had no support or guidelines.

With the support of the Head and Governors, links were made with the Tavistock Centre to provide counselling to a group of ASR students and to raise awareness among staff. This started a chain of events which led a group of staff and sixth-form students to provide an ASR support network at the school which evolved into the Children of the Storm project, aimed at helping ASR students rebuild their lives; and to new guidelines and strategies for the whole school. Athy commented: 'the skills we ... acquired by working with war traumatised children have influenced the way in which we deal with all children. Our programme of equality works both ways.'

The *Extraordinary Childhoods* project discovered a different event in another multicultural London secondary school that had been taking refugee students for some time. Mark Stephenson, a humanities teacher, recalled how a Year 7 class he had been teaching had become politicised over the experiences of a refugee student:

> [One afternoon] a whole group of boys in the class were late to the lesson from lunchtime, and then ... they came in very angrily. And the reason they were angry was something that had happened to one of the boys in the class ... he was a Somali refugee. [...] What had happened was that in the playground somebody had called him a 'stupid refugee', and he had pulled a knife. He brought out the knife as a response to this boy ... and because of that he had been hauled in by the Year Head, the school had told him he was being temporarily, short-term, excluded. [...] The reason they [his friends] were angry was, they said, the boy had told what his situation was in Somalia and they knew that what he was used to ... was if anybody threatened you, you had to fight back, because that was the way of survival. They held that the boy [Abdi] was responding in the only way he knew how to respond ... and their words were, 'the school should have understood that'.

Subsequently the school agreed that the class should do a project on refugees, which they called '*Why?*' A local theatre group was engaged to help the project produce a play and a video. In the run-up, a presentation from an outside speaker on displacement and refuge had moved Abdi to tell his story in public to the class, speaking through his friend. Abdi had previously been adamant he would not share his experiences. The storytelling was reported to be a 'cathartic moment', after which the students owned and drove the project forward, with the teacher as support.

The politicisation of this group of students had effects far beyond the classroom. The students' zeal and passion for justice led them to, among other things, visit a detention centre; join a protest against deportations on Parliament Green, and interview a government minister on the subject, all of which went into their video, which subsequently went on to win a Granada TV award. Their play was performed at the school; they were also invited to stage it at various other schools, universities and colleges, and at the request of the Medical Foundation they performed it on Parliament Green before TV cameras. These students' political involvement kept the play going until they completed Year 11. The strong leadership by teachers, with support of the Head, and a school ethos of caring and justice lent support to this process of politicisation.

The experience of admitting large numbers of ASR, minority ethnic and bilingual students for the first time could similarly act as an impetus for political awakening in schools. As Mary Campbell, Curriculum Team Leader at St Xavier's Primary School in a Scottish dispersal city[4] commented, '… this wasn't a multicultural, cosmopolitan area at all. So it was very new for staff and children, and just a lot of learning has happened'. Not only did the school have to deal with a steady flow of dispersed children, it also had to deal with removals by immigration authorities of families of children who had been well settled and progressing within the school. Mary talked about the trauma the school underwent when a child is removed:

> Those periods when families are sent back are very difficult for us in trying to support the children. The children are very apprehensive about what lies ahead, and it manifests itself in school, their progress becomes slightly retarded on occasions …You can find behaviour difficulties, emotional difficulties.

The Head was similarly torn between the injustice of the situation, her helplessness towards families when they are deported, and the wider needs of the school when this happens:

> Finally the public are becoming aware of the way these families are being – absolutely awful! … At first we couldn't believe this could be happening in this day and age and in our city like this. So pleased that the public is actually getting a lot more publicity. It obviously frightens the other families and the other children about getting a knock on the door at dawn. […] It does impact on the type of support that we are able to give the children. It impacts on my management time, it impacts on Mary's time, and it obviously impacts

on the daily interaction of the child's peers in the classroom and with the classteacher. (Fiona Musgrave, Headteacher, St Xavier's Primary)

Politicisation results from being a firsthand witness to the nature and personal consequences of UK asylum policy. The headteacher of another primary school in that city described how one of the first asylum-seeking pupils in the school had had a devastating story of loss even before witnessing his father being marched off in a dawn raid:

> I mean, amongst our first group we had a little boy ... in Primary year one [whose mother had been killed in his home country]. [...] He had a further trauma [in Primary Four], seeing his father marched off in handcuffs in a dawn raid ... (Siobhan Cameron, Headteacher, Robert Burns Primary).

The events led to her and her school becoming aware of what she called 'a whole additional layer':

> I thought when the children were coming that we already were a school who had a heightened awareness of issues to do with 'race'. You know, anti-racism, and bilingualism. And you know, the difficulties faced by some of the families coming in. We have now learned about a whole additional layer, some of it really to do with the bureaucracy and we've all become much more aware of the immigration system, and how that affects our families, and in some cases some of that has been a revelation to us ...

She found the injustices within the immigration system disturbing to her values, particularly her sense of fairness and compassion:

> I was hearing on this morning's radio that there was a peaceful protest outside ... the Home Office, and that really doesn't surprise me from what I've heard ... just about the way they [asylum-seeking families] are sometimes treated, and particularly the dawn raids and the fact that that's happening with very young children in the midst of it, I find hard to believe that it's happening around me, in the country where I have always lived.

Witnessing the politics of immigration at first-hand redefines the relationship of teachers to the state. Teachers are involved in protecting asylum-seeking youth. The strategies they use to encourage their abilities and help them settle into the school, however, are seriously disrupted by the actions of a government attempting to reduce asylum-seeker numbers rather than help them integrate into society. The schools we visited were clear about their professional ethic – they adopted an ethos of inclusion and integration which was very different from that of central government. However, this approach is hard to sustain if one of the asylum-seeking students suddenly has to leave as a result of the government dispersal programme or is inexplicably forcibly removed from the school. The effects reverberate around the classroom, the school, the community – coping with the emotions associated with a child's (a friend's) forced removal are not dissimilar to the strategy for coping with children's grieving at the unexpected death of a pupil. Jenny Douglas (Head of Fordham School), for example, described what the disappearance of a student means for her and her class from an emotional, educational and a school manage-ment perspective. Her professional sense of being a teacher was greatly disturbed by the disappearance of one of her students whose academic progress was then disrupted and the other children in the class were left feeling guilty:

> It affects in terms of having to reschedule resources, because obvi-ously resources have been set aside for that child, and suddenly the child disappears. [...] other children not necessarily understanding why someone's gone ... [b]ecause sometimes the children can take it as a slight on [themselves] ... well they were happy here, why have they been moved? You know there's obviously something wrong with us. Is that why they've moved them?

Some schools actively use the negative aspects of immigration and war to encourage students to consider in an active and highly relevant way concepts of human rights, democratic practice and the rights of the state. The issue of asylum, if part of the curriculum, can awaken students to critical debate around the notion of social justice. For example, some teachers described to us how they used hostile media representations of ASR communities and deportation cases as a means of teaching young people about democracy and democratic processes of protest. For example, teachers in Fairfield School used the media to illustrate the 'dehumanisation' of asylum-seekers in the UK:

> [O]ne of the examples I give is how, when you see pictures of all these poor people abroad looking so forlorn and upset and on the

run ... everyone feels a lot of pity for them ... [b]ut then, as soon as they arrive on British soil, they're suddenly dehumanised people. (Greg Smith, Deputy Head, Fairfield School)

Paddy Thompson, the citizenship education teacher at Fairfield, spoke the same language. His aim in his classes was to 'humanise the whole issue' by 'putting ... more meat on the bones' of the students' knowledge about asylum-seekers and challenging the 'facts' presented by the media: for example, 'the fact that asylum-seekers aren't allowed to work, as opposed to coming over here to steal our jobs ...'. Being more compassionate, he argued, was linked to being more politically aware of the issues, although he was aware that this goal does not mean promoting one position: 'I think it's really important to expose them to all these different political aspects of the world but not to brainwash them.' He therefore challenged students to think about what they would do in a situation such as the Rwandan civil war where in 100 days some 800,000 people were massacred. When he gave a lecture based on his knowledge of the war, the 'kids were clinging to every word'.

Similarly Mark Kranz, Chair of the Manchester Committee to Defend Asylum-Seekers, also describes how his pupils confront the nature of democracy when they explore the ways in which media and politicians create a culture of rejection and hostility. Using a constructed narrative about an asylum-seeking child, he exposes the 'clear contradiction between young people's feelings of common humanity born out of their experience and the world they get explained to them in terms of difference and rejection'.[5]

The space in the GCSE citizenship curriculum module called 'Participating in Society' also provides teachers with the chance to offer students an opportunity to understand other people's realities and to become involved in international and national charities (such as Oxfam, UNICEF, Islamic Relief). Other opportunities were Red Nose Day, Refugee Week and modules such as 'Is Britain a Fair Society?'. Greg Smith, the Deputy Head, observed that the effects of running 'a citizenship in the news' class means that students can engage more critically and more actively with the issue. As a result,

> students are very conscious of their rights. But they also therefore apply that idea to other people. [...] So they pick up that they have rights, but they also apply that to issues like those seeking refugee status or asylum-seekers and so on, and they get in a conversation, they would argue that people have rights here, international rights.

Challenging the system: teachers' and students' civic protest

Teachers' and students' involvement in the politics of immigration is also revealed in anti-deportation campaigns – campaigns aimed at keeping asylum-seeking students in the community and hopefully in the country. The threat of deportation that places the asylum-seeking child and their family back in danger is one which teachers and their students across the country have campaigned against. The numbers involved are not available[6] since these campaigns tend not to be orchestrated through teacher unions or professional associations. Information about such campaigns tends to be found mainly in local newspaper reports or on the campaign websites.[7] Occasionally, news of a particularly controversial campaign involving children, ill or dying parents or deportations to violent countries, such as Zimbabwe, reaches the national media.

At a professional level, teachers might argue that their involvement in anti-deportation campaigns is not in breach of the spirit of codes of conduct that hold that it is illegitimate to bring politics and particularly partisan controversial issues into the classroom. Today, however, teachers are encouraged quite clearly to become actively involved in a 'duty of care' to all students. For example, the Statement of Values issued jointly by the General Teaching Council (GTC), the General Social Care Council and the Nursing and Midwifery Council in 2007 professed that child practitioners (of which teachers are one group) should ensure a child's safety and wellbeing. In this statement, *all* children are considered to have the right to be safe:

> Child practitioners should place the interests of children and young people at the heart of their work. They share responsibility for a range of outcomes. They are committed to ensuring all children and young people have a chance to: be healthy, stay safe, enjoy and achieve, make a positive contribution, and experience economic well being. (GTC/GSCC/NMC, 2008: 1)[8]

The statement adds that child practitioners are meant to concern themselves with 'the whole child'; be 'committed to equality of opportunity for all children and young people, and actively combat discrimination and its effects through their work'; and 'to pursue positive outcomes for children and young people whose circumstances place them at risk of exclusion or under-achievement' (ibid.). The GTC's own statement of professional values for teachers develops this further, affirming that within the legal statutory framework and school policies, teachers should challenge stereotypes, 'opposing prejudice, and respecting individuals regardless of age, gender, disability, colour, race, ethnicity, class, religion, marital status or sexual orientation' (GTC, 2006: 3). These values speak directly to the needs of ASR students – however, the boundaries separating legitimate and illegitimate levels of concern about such students are matters of interpretation.

Similarly under Section 11 of the Children Act 2004, teachers have a 'duty to safeguard' all children.[9] The key principles here are those enshrined in the Children Act 1989, that the welfare of the child is of 'paramount consideration', and that any decision made in relation to a child should 'take into account the ascertainable wishes and feelings of the child concerned'. Of especial note is the principle that children should be safe and protected by 'effective intervention if they are in danger'. However, as we discussed in Chapter 4, the omission of immigration agencies from Section 11 of the Act (at least up until October 2009 under the new Borders, Citizenship and Immigration Act 2009) made asylum-seeking children extremely vulnerable and reinforced the precedence immigration policy takes over asylum-seeking children's rights and safety. Notwithstanding this exclusion, teachers were encouraged to apply the concept of safeguarding to *all* children in their care. The principles of *Every Child Matters,* the safeguarding agenda and the Children Acts 1989 and 2004, as well as the setting up of Children's Trusts, all pointed to a newly defined professional role for teachers in the UK in relation to children. As far as teachers are concerned, they do not have any special duty in relation to ASR students nor in terms of the politics of immigration control which overrides their duty of care to their students.[10] On the contrary, from an educational point of view, what teachers have been given is a professional mission – a duty to safeguard and protect a child's so called 'best interests'. These interests would best be served by their attending mainstream schooling, rebuilding their lives, finding employment, integrating into society and, even more importantly, learning how to trust and become part of a humane society.

With such a professional ethic in mind, teachers in very different communities have become involved in fighting detention and the forced removal/deportation of their asylum-seeking students. The evidence for this comes mainly from the websites where teachers write testimonies about their actions.[11] Here we can find reports of the *causes célèbres* (such as Glasgow, Canterbury and Portsmouth) and information about successful anti-deportation campaigns.[12] Even more importantly, we can trace the debates about the role of schools in anti-deportation campaigns.

Many strategies and political understandings of principles that are at stake are revealed. Below we use these testimonies to offer insights into what underlies such political campaigning by schools in the UK.

Fighting deportation

Given government concerns that teachers should avoid controversial issues and always maintain political balance, a significant political action for teachers would be to sign the *Declaration on the Deportation of Children and Young People from Schools and Colleges under Immigration Act Powers* produced by the Schools against Deportation campaign. The Declaration begins:

> We, teachers, headteachers, lecturers, teaching assistants, students, young people, trade unionists, mentors and others working in the education system are concerned about the damaging impact which the threat of deportation or actual deportation can have on children and young people studying in schools and colleges. Deportation affects a child's educational progress, health and well-being. We are also deeply concerned about the detrimental effect on the wider school or college community when personal relationships are disrupted and friends are separated. (Schools against Deportations, 2005: 1)

Teachers signing the Declaration commit themselves to offering 'whatever support and care they can' to the young person who is threatened under Immigration Act powers.

A number of the websites are devoted to what are called 'images of resistance' – in effect schools, teachers and students working in alliance with other civic and professional groups. Going public with anti-deportation campaigns is a political step in itself – teachers' testimonies describe their success in delaying or even preventing the deportation of young people and their parents. The image is of students taking action and building public campaigns with the help of their teachers rather than teachers politicising students. The grounds for such action is largely compassion, the political discourse is mostly, as indicated above, about what is considered to be 'in the best interests' of the asylum-seeking student and their school community.

As part of these campaigns, some teachers even attend asylum appeal hearings. Schools have no duty to provide or divulge information about particular asylum-seeking students to immigration officials. In fact, schools, as we saw in Chapter 7, do not necessarily know much about the background story of the particular asylum-seeking child.

Hackney Community Law Centre advises that teachers should not engage in political arguments about 'the likelihood of persecution in countries of origin' when attending such hearings – this should be left to the lawyers:

> Where a school can make a significant contribution is in making representations of the area it is expert in – the welfare of the child. The kinds of things which might make a difference are; evidence about the emotional, physical or psychological state of the child on admission to the school; the fears which were expressed or which came out in the child's school work or playground activity; how the child has settled in the school, made friends, etc. If being at school and being a part of the school community has assisted in the rehabilitation of the children's well being, then this should be stated. Likewise, if being uprooted would have a disastrous effect on the well-being of the child.[13]

Those schools, teachers and even students who become actively involved in anti-deportation campaigns find themselves not just interfacing with the government, especially the Home Office, its officials and immigration authorities, but also with the police, lawyers, churches, neighbours, MPs, the Refugee Council and many other asylum advocates. For example, the Head of EMAS in a secondary school in Horton LEA described how the school routinely supported asylum-seeking families in their dealings with the Home Office and especially with deportation:

> For example we've got a Pakistani boy at the moment whose family are in the process of being deported and the school has intervened and helped the family write letters, help them canvass MPs and so on. That's something we would *normally* do with asylum-seekers (our emphasis).

Similarly, engagement with an anti-deportation campaign can involve teachers in the writing of petitions, setting up awareness-raising activities in schools or offering strong personal support to a vulnerable child or family. Campaigns can include lobbying the local MP, attending court hearings, making speeches, dealing with the media or holding vigils. In one city, for example, communities were very involved in patrolling the streets, sheltering families and developing campaigns to save particular families. It can also lead to a major public campaign run by students themselves, with or even without the help of teachers.

Involvement in such anti-deportation campaigns moves teacher and student compassion closer to more general political concerns about democracy, social justice and a more critical position in relation to state action. For example, Forest Gate School teachers and students fought against the deportation of Natasha Matembele, a Year 7 student who came into Forest Gate School in East London as usual on Wednesday morning and told staff she was going to be deported to Angola the next day. Her classmates drew up petitions, collected signatures from the whole school, made banners and posters, and within 24 hours the school marched to the park, having faxed letters of support to the local MP; this resulted in a temporary staying order on Natasha's case. Rosie Mason, Natasha's PSE and English teacher, recognised the importance of the case – it was the first public acknowledgement not only that the school had a lot of refugees and asylum-seekers but that they faced a very different reality:

> I suddenly started to look around me and think about the kids I was teaching from Somalia, Ethiopia, wherever, and I wondered how many of them have been given *leave to remain*. I'm sure it was the minority. They were looking at Natasha and thinking, this is me and, if she can get this kind of support then maybe we can too. We don't need to be afraid of telling people about the situation [...] It's impossible for us to understand the experiences and the pressures and insecurities for lots of those young people. Experiences of fleeing and persecution mean that you do not trust people. Then they would have arrived in England and thought we're safe now, and then suddenly they realise they're not. At any minute that security is going to be taken away and the government will send them back. [...] If they are living under the threat of deportation often for many years in poverty, appalling housing conditions, with parents who cannot work, then those factors will limit their progress and affect their behaviour. These are issues teachers have to deal with. [...] In the media now there's a kind of battlefield where racism, and issues around immigration, refugees and war zones, are played out. So for teachers it's an extension of the human rights agenda and seeing education as an area where you can exert a change of attitudes. Teachers have to be part of changing attitudes towards asylum-seekers. It really is a kind of agenda you can't ignore. [...] We went from a situation where people might not even know the word refugee or asylum-seeker to a point where they understood the subtlety of the difference between the two.[14]

The students (even 12-year-olds) at Forest Gate School were helped by their teacher to organise the school response. Students researched the situation in Angola where Natasha came from, preparing assemblies and writing a play about being a refugee. The public campaign, which won a reprieve for Natasha, and whose family was eventually allowed to stay, had considerable benefits for the school. According to Rosie Mason:

> The campaign gave those pupils involved the opportunity to experience the democratic process directly, and its success, real confidence from realising how they could control it. [...] The result has been the after-school club which provides a space for pupils from Forest Gate school and beyond – to both enjoy activities ... and to have a safe place of their own to informally discuss issues that there is not time for at school. (ibid.)

Another effect of the campaign was to challenge racism and improve understanding of refugee-related issues, not only with the school but outside of it. The students experienced in effect *basic human rights education*. As Rosie Mason explained:

> It was so powerful for the young people because really it made them aware of what it is to have rights ... and to exert and be able to exert your freedom of speech ... The kids were driving the media coverage ... They would go along to demonstrations and marches and speak in front of thousands of people. Twelve-year-old children perceived as being quite demure Muslim girls were primarily the driving force behind the campaign, and it was so powerful for them, and a brilliant kind of role model for how people can become involved in the democratic process and not see themselves as powerless but able to manipulate and control things. (ibid.)

A similar political impact was experienced at a secondary school in Portsmouth where some students came from families with BNP sympathies. Lorin, a Kurdish student, had been subject to racist remarks from some students. Following her family's arrest in a dawn raid in October 2004 and being held at Tinsley House immigration removal centre near Gatwick airport, Lorin got in touch with her school begging them to do something to get the removal halted. A lot changed in the school as a result; teachers began raising awareness in lessons. In the *Independent on Sunday* (14 September 2008), Diane Taylor reported that: 'The school responded swiftly by mounting a huge campaign. In art lessons they made "Free Lorin" posters and received local media coverage' (Taylor, 2008). In addition to instigating a high-profile local media campaign, school actions included 50-page petition letters to two local MPs.[15] The family was later released from detention pending a review of their case – this eventually took place following a march and rally in January at the local town hall; the family was given two years' discretionary leave to remain. Lorin was quoted as saying:

> Some of the pupils were shocked that asylum-seekers could be innocent people. Even though some were sympathetic to the BNP, they just wanted to help me. One girl said she'd even write to the Prime Minister to make sure I wasn't deported. That really touched me. (Taylor, 2008)

Headteacher Derek Trimmer confirmed that:

> Some of our older students whose views on 'race' were a bit hostile needed counselling because they had very strong feelings about what was happening to Lorin and had difficulty bringing their two views together. (ibid.)

These actions by teachers and students are significant morally and politically since they unite concerns about compassionate approaches linked to *Every Child Matters* with egalitarian concerns about equity and fairness. However, as we saw in Chapters 6 and 7, not all believe that public campaigns of this sort are necessarily in the 'best interests' of the child. John Mayes, a headteacher in Manchester, admits on the web that the anti-deportation case in which he became involved tested whether 'the government feels bound to honour its pledge to promote social inclusivity and citizenship studies in schools'. If schools have responsibility to secure the personal and educational development of all its members, then there were compassionate grounds to allow ASR students to have the right to stay in the UK. He was concerned, however, that newsworthy anti-deportation campaigns could become a 'soap opera' – with asylum-seeking students finding it hard being the focus of media attention. In the end, the effect of such campaigns might hurt them since the media could be insensitive to how children feel and view things. What was more important, he argued, was the power of education – the ethos of education – that the government was supposed to support:

> What I can do [as a Head] is to concentrate on the child's developing in the school and their place in the school community. That to

me is fundamental. When a child has been in this country for four years and integrated into society, you don't uproot children at that time, those are the most formative years of their education and emotional development. That to me is the point.[16]

Reflections

Public pressure, particularly from public service professionals and human rights agencies and latterly the arts world, on the UK government to address the welfare of ASR youth has grown substantially in recent years, challenging inhumane and immoral immigration policies which do not support families. The focus of this opposition is to offer children fundamental rights, and to encourage a culture of social morality.[16.] New political alliances have been formed and new information sources provided to stimulate action (such as the Children's Rights Alliance for England and the Refugee Education (RefEd) electronic list).

Those advocating an immigration policy based on the UNCRC argue that migrant children should be defined as 'children first, migrant second' (Crawley, 2006). Bill Bolloten, a leading refugee education consultant, and one of the writers on the NRIF website, argues that these campaigns across communities, and across the social services and the teaching profession, represent a new politics. Schools as institutions located in the welfare state represent the concept of universal entitlements and, as such, they symbolise and represent the child's best interests. In contrast, asylum and immigration policy runs counter to such universal welfare principles as far as asylum-seeking children are concerned. The UK government's immigration policy largely denies asylum-seeking families access to most public services by using a regulatory culture that goes against the principle of the educational service and the work which schools do to integrate and educate all children according to the best pedagogic principles. Dispersal, detention, deportation and the denial of the right of the family to work or to access social benefits when living in acute poverty are policies that make the task of the school in developing the welfare and learning of the asylum-seeking child difficult if not unworkable.

Teachers and 'citizen' students do not stand alone but represent in some ways the voice of educational institutions that are deeply concerned about ASR children's best interests:

[ASR students], by going to local schools, having face-to-face contacts with their non-refugee peers who themselves came from diverse multi-ethnic communities ... that dynamic in schools has enabled a sector of the public sector workforce and large sections of our communities where refugees have settled to understand that the official discourse and the tabloids' media discourse on refugees is not one that they recognise and not one that they subscribe to. (Bill Bolloten, interview, 2 March 2008)

Bolloten suggests that these public campaigns provide evidence that:

The absence [through detention] of children who were loved and appreciated, valued for the contribution they made to the school community, on a personal and family level ... and the rank injustice in what happened has resonated with people who basically dissent and have a sense of fair play and justice. (ibid.)

What is significant, Bolloten argues, about the schools' anti-deportation campaigns is that they have not been generated, as far as he could see, out of the traditional Left. School-based, particularly student-led, campaigns in support of ASR students and families have a particular shape and culture that does not use the conventional language of politics:

School-based campaigns would operate on the level on which they can engage people. They are not going to express it in a kind of ... political language. That is not going to happen. It is ... about defending 'our friends' – 'she [the ASR child] would die if she would be sent back to Angola'. (ibid.)

The presence of ASR students in schools, coupled with aggressive state immigration control and what is seen as the injustice of state asylum policy define the experience of students who are being taught alongside them. The social bonds, and the friendships created between ASR and 'citizen' children, can lead to a new form of politics that is based on compassion of a different sort.

11
Conclusions

They may not be British citizens, but they are human beings, and they are a British responsibility. (Zadie, sixth-form student in the Children of the Storm project)

The status of permanent alienage[1] of 'non-citizens' – which is most notable in the case of refugees and asylum-seekers – is politically, socially and also personally dangerous (Benhabib, 2004). Asylum-seekers especially can find themselves permanently stateless – as Bauman (2004: 76) points out:

> [E]ven if they are stationary for a time, they are on a journey that is never completed since its destination (arrival or return) remains forever unclear ... They are never to be free from the gnawing sense of the transience, indefiniteness and provisional nature of any settlement.

This book has focused on the education of ASR children and the assumption that schooling is a major institution in which such alienage can be reduced. Despite the political vacuum in which ASR children find themselves, schools as social institutions have a moral purpose which is to create the human conditions for social unity and harmony. As Durkheim (1893[1997]) recognised, this moral purpose was to ensure social cohesion over and above the divisions embedded in economic organisation by transmitting a moral code – a *'conscience collective'* ('collective consciousness') – to the next generation of youth. In the case of forced migration such a moral code was established by the 1951 UN Convention relating to the Status of Refugees and in the case of children by the 1989 UN Convention on the Rights of the Child. Both these transnational conventions represent internationally recognised instruments which were designed to ensure that political and human rights are offered to all within national institutions. Each declaration commits signatory governments to support those most in danger of being marginalised and oppressed. The consequences of not addressing the instability and statelessness of asylum-seeking and refugee children are quite major nationally and globally. There is a danger of creating a disaffected and alienated transitory population of (often stateless) young people who have already suffered the trauma of flight, removal, dispersal, detention and neglect and who, without an education, cannot find new ways of supporting themselves. Schools have the potential, as teachers in our study believed, to make a difference to ASR children's lives, if only to show them, as the Asylum and Refugee Officer in Cheston said, that there are people who care, who are able to offer support, who in other words are humane. Schools can, in effect, 'humanise' the issue of asylum-seeking, taking a stand against the dehumanisation of forced migrants by governments, the media and, on occasion, local communities.

The question we addressed at the beginning of this book was the extent to which the school system in the UK was able to transmit such a moral code, encouraging compassion amongst all its students towards strangers in distress. Our focus has been not just on the impact of forced migration on educational policy but on the ways in which compassion has been shaped politically through immigration and educational policy and by the practices of local educational authorities and schools. We explored how the 'politics of compassion' works at different levels – in central government with its different agendas around immigration, asylum, educational integration and educational achievement, and through the actions and policies of local authorities who were given responsibility to address the needs of a heterogeneous group of 'new arrivals' in their region. At the school level, we investigated how headteachers, teachers and students responded to the presence of ASR children and their feelings about what constituted an appropriate response to immigration into the UK. Our investigations offer insights into the different types of compassion and the ways these moral values and emotional responses are expressed and institutionalised within educational policy and practice.

At the same time, we are aware that compassion is shaped by a different politics – that of belonging. While compassion addresses the suffering (in different ways) of ASR children, the 'politics of belonging' defines the national territorial, demographic and cultural boundaries in which such compassion can express itself. Such boundaries demarcate who is allowed to be included in the national constituency – who is physically allowed in, who is allowed rights (whether of access to education and economic opportunities or rights to welfare) and who has the right to keep their dignity and to be treated with respect and fairness. This national boundary-making activity discursively constructs the moral parameters of compassion. It does not determine what compassion looks like but it has considerable impact on those to whom, as a society, we feel able to offer compassion. In the age of globalisation, when developed states find themselves overwhelmed by a fear of globalisation's 'discontents' (to use Bauman's language), the politics of belonging is joined by other discursive practices (such as the criminalisation of asylum) to justify the lack of compassion for the many, and a muted compassionate reaction to a selected few who are considered 'deserving'. Over time, this 'deserving' category itself becomes refined and redefined the greater the political pressure on governments to act in the name of serving the country's 'best interests'.

With this theoretical framework in mind, we have explored how educational policies and practices have been shaped in the past two decades in the context of the particular conditions for belonging in the UK, framed, as it were, by immigration and asylum policy. In turn, such conditions of belonging relate to the transformation of the UK economy in the context of a highly competitive global world. As a result, UK educational policy has been affected by the UK government's attempts, in a series of steps, to reduce the historical legacies which positioned the country as a Commonwealth state and as a state of refuge (Gibney, 2004) while still attempting to sustain the country's alleged reputation of having a liberal, democratic, multicultural and 'open and tolerant' society.

Our analysis of the education of ASR children, therefore, offers a different account from that normally provided by educationalists, not least because it uses a sociological perspective to understand the shifting construction of asylum and immigration within which such children find themselves. We embed rather than distance ASR education within the social context of state responses to economic and political globalisation and the threat that forced migration represents to governmental concepts of an economic order and social progress. Globalisation, especially the movement of large numbers of people, challenges, as we have seen, the logic underlying the ways in which economic, political, social and welfare rights are offered to citizens and the ways in which such rights should be distributed. It is important at this point to be reminded of this political shift both in asylum and citizenship before bringing together the findings from our LEA and school-based research.

The economics of belonging and compassion in the UK

Within the context of globalisation, the framing of a new logic of rights that is seen as more suitable to a fluid competitive economy represents one of the great dilemmas that lie at the heart of liberal democracies and liberal democratic education today. Chapter 2 explored political theorists' understanding of this dilemma, which contemporary governments face when considering the relationship between state sovereignty and citizenship. This debate, while seemingly far removed from the day-to-day work of classrooms, nevertheless is deeply significant for the education of ASR children. While nation-states have the right to protect their interests and boundaries, many have also declared a commitment to protect universal human rights (Benhabib, 2004; Weiner, 1995). From a moral point of view, the global migration of people raises the question of whether, and if so how, such universal human rights can be delivered – and to what extent can those who are not citizens of a particular society expect to be offered their rights under international human rights conventions.

In effect, despite such commitment to universal human rights, nation-states still use their power to define their political and economic borders by closing them. Although governments may no longer be able to offer security to their citizens, nevertheless they may, through such exercise of power, for the time being

> unload at least part of the accumulated anxiety ... by demonstrating their energy and determination in the war against foreign job-seeking and other alien gate-crashers, the intruders into once clean and quite orderly and familiar native backyards. (Bauman, 1998: 10–11)

The argument put forward in favour of the closure of borders and restrictions on 'aliens' is one which juxtaposes national interests with economic benefits. Geddes (2005: 165) suggests that the 'neo-national reassertion of the conditions of membership' in contemporary society is based on the idea of the alleged contribution of a person to the economy. The economic recession of the 1970s, for example, raised concerns about the potential costs of migration which were used to justify a zero-immigration policy (Gibney, 2004; Sivanandan, 2001). However, until the late 1980s the small numbers of refugees arriving in Britain, and their origin (mostly Europeans), meant that the cost of welcoming them was not challenged (Sivanandan, 2001) and the logic of protection for those fleeing persecution was allowed to prevail. However, since the mid-1990s, the story about forced migration has changed because politicians now proffer the view that the very success of the British economy and, in particular, its generous welfare state is a 'pull factor' for the high numbers of asylum-seekers (Wolton, 2006). As a result, government policy turned to announce the dramatic removal of social welfare from asylum-seekers, leading to an increased likelihood of destitution, alienage and misery (see Chapter 4). The new politics of belonging, which draws on economic nationalist discourses, suggests that the UK put 'its economic interests before those of the politically persecuted' (Sivanandan, 2001: 89).

In contrast to an asylum policy that is characterised by an increasing number of restrictions and a dominant official discourse about 'reducing the numbers', government policy on economic migration (at least some types of economic migrants) is more flexible and liberal. Like other European states, the UK government publicly admits that, in order for the country to maintain its competitive economic edge, it needs to be more open to different types of migration (Flynn, 2005). As we saw in Chapter 4, the White Paper *Secure Borders, Safe Haven* (Home Office, 2002) and the Nationality, Asylum and Immigration Act 2002 led to the introduction of the scheme for highly skilled migrants while the processes used to issue work permits were relaxed, allowing more to be issued. Migrant workers are now understood to increase economic growth by setting up businesses, creating new jobs and paying taxes (Home Office, 2002: 27). The Home Office (Home Office, 2005a: 13–15) has even gone so far as to argue that: 'Without migration, the rate of economic growth would be much lower ... Migrants have brought dynamism to the economy.' In the same document, the arrival of foreign workers was represented as 'essential' to British prosperity by the then Prime Minister, Tony Blair (ibid.: 5–6).

As we have seen, this economic argument about the nation's 'best interests' has manifested itself in a discursive distinction between the 'deserving'/wanted and the 'undeserving'/unwanted new arrival (Sales, 2002). The UK government has promoted the idea that only some new arrivals are able to contribute to the economy and could in the future adjust to neo-liberal conditions, that is, by becoming consumer citizens (Bauman, 2004). The 'unwanted' are those whom the government now represents as an economic and social burden as well as potentially even a threat to the economic order (bogus asylum-seekers, terrorists and criminals). The transmogrification of the concept of asylum into economic policy in effect closed the space within which the genuine asylum-seeker who flees persecution can fit.

This arbitrary and highly political reconstruction of those seeking asylum suggests that, in contrast to foreign workers, asylum-seekers are now associated with a negative economic impact (Gibney, 2004). Yet many asylum-seekers and refugees are highly skilled, highly motivated economically and have much in common with the desire of migrant workers to be employed at their skill level, as the following testimony indicates:

> Our group comprises refugees from diverse professional and academic backgrounds, including: former teachers, managers, engineers, economists, lawyers, mathematicians, artists, ICT specialists and scientists, who fled our countries of origin due to political persecutions and settled in the UK. Despite the fact that we arrived in the UK with academic qualifications and substantial experiences, which could have contributed to our host country and enriched our own lives, it has been very difficult for us to re-enter professional lives. Since barriers were beyond our control, we remained unemployed or ended up taking employments which were far below our qualifications, experiences and abilities. We were marginalised in a society which has offered us safe haven. (Mesay Eshete's address at Refugee Week Celebrations at the Institute of Education, London, June 2009)

In order to justify its draconian immigration rules, in effect, the UK government has played havoc with its moral commitment to those in need. The notion that the majority of asylum-seekers are undeserving of access to the British economy and its welfare systems puts out a message, in effect, that compassion is for the minority and not for the majority of seemingly valueless and possibly unlawful asylum-seekers. In effect, the Home Office split asylum-seekers and refugees into two mutually exclusive groups – refugees who have the right to be integrated into British society and those (asylum-seekers in other words) for whom integration was not relevant (see Chapter 4). Here again there is no middle ground in which to locate the 'good asylum-seeker' who does not yet have refugee status.

The crux of the matter is the failure to support the 20th-century image of the UK as a 'country of refuge'. Yuval-Davis (2005: 520) warned that a politics of belonging based on economic rather than humanitarian principles would invite 'cherry picking' of refugees based on their alleged work skills and potential for integration rather than their real need for protection.[2] By 2008 she went further, suggesting that in a globalised world, universal rights 'tend to be restricted to those who have skills to offer to countries of immigration' (Yuval-Davis, 2008: 106). Human rights, it seems, are for those who already have the rights of citizenship within their home country or the state in which they reside. Increasingly there is a denial of the rights of economic and social wellbeing, health and protection to 'non-citizens' (asylum-seekers and refugees). In the school setting, therefore (and even more so in detention centres), the fact that the asylum-seeking child is at the mercy of government immigration policy has serious implications in terms of their rights. Their dependency on their parents means that the asylum-seeking child is classified as an outsider. They are Others and strangers who should not and cannot be integrated, in anticipation, as it were, of their removal. Only those migrant children whose parents offer economic value or who pose no threat to 'our values' are meant to be integrated into the English language, British culture and into the values of 'our society'.

The categories of 'deserving' and 'undeserving', in effect, establish a hierarchy of migrant child rights, not just those of adults. Children of 'undeserving' immigrant parents find their educational opportunities are framed within a politics of belonging that has little to do with their own best interests 'as children'. The processes of dispersal, detention and deportation described in Chapters 4 and 10 have repeatedly been criticised for neglecting such children's short-term and long-term personal and physical wellbeing and their educational development. In terms of alienage, this approach to asylum-seeking children fundamentally denies them their human rights.

The conundrum for teachers is whether to notice these regulative categories, whether to act upon them, or whether to ignore the effects of such policy on their students even though these distinctions greatly affect their students' material wellbeing. Not surprisingly, as our research shows, these political distinctions between different categories of migrant children have had little meaning for educational practitioners – especially since they are anti-educational in their discriminatory ethos and practice. The act of classifying children as migrants rather than as children has little discursive resonance in the world of educational practitioners where all children are assumed to be equally entitled to respect and to receive help in reaching their full potential.

Yet, despite the irrelevance of the above distinction, immigration discourse has a great impact on the work of schools. As we have shown, immigration and asylum increasingly have played a significant role in the political reframing of education policy because it transforms the conditions under which education systems work, and directly or indirectly shapes the ethos and social relations of schools and teachers' classroom practice. Chapters 5 and 6 demonstrated that the hierarchy of rights is reflected in the arbitrary levels of organised and funded support that asylum-seekers and their children receive in different localities where they compete with other disadvantaged and identified 'vulnerable' groups of 'citizen' students – minority ethnic groups, traveller children or 'looked-after' children (see Chapter 5).

Is personhood an alternative?

In 2008, the UK government officially declared that it had withdrawn its reservation to the UNCRC and accepted therefore that the UNCRC applies to ASR children, over and above immigration policy. The removal of the reservation, which asserted that immigration policy could not be compromised by any of the terms of the Convention, means that it is now possible to talk about the human rights of the ASR child. The door is open now to considerations about whether the deterritorialised logic of *personhood* (see Chapter 2) can be developed with respect to asylum-seeking children. There is a new space in which the more universal model of human rights could override the exclusive authority of the nation-state and the asylum-seeking child's social rights can be restored.

However, the extent to which this change of heart over the UNCRC by the UK government will affect the boundaries of national citizenship (Bhabha, 2005) is not clear. The tension between the economic logic and other political, civil and ethical logics such as human rights is likely to remain. This makes it unlikely that the interests of the ASR child can be understood as part of 'our' scheme of goals, or in Weil's (1970) terms, that we will be able to see their interests and needs behind the rights. Currently, the ways in which asylum-seekers are represented in the public domain (especially in the mass media and party political agendas – see Chapter 2) are left unchallenged. This means that it is highly unlikely that the needs of ASR children can be fully recognised and supported. As we saw in Chapter 4, the tabloid press, with its mobilisation of populist discourse around 'race' and xenophobia, gives obsessive, negative attention to asylum-seekers' presence in the country, implying that most, if not all, asylum-seekers are bogus claimants, and that they are a threat to British citizens' rights of welfare, housing and employment and an obstacle to creating harmonious communities. The media currently distances itself from the morality of compassion that those fleeing persecution have a right to expect. As we have demonstrated throughout the book, understanding of these global and national discourses around forced migration and the ways in which the UK has shaped its political and moral response to the arrival of different types of 'aliens' was important for exploring the challenges faced by LEAs, schools and teachers when educating ASR students.

Compassion and belonging in the educational system

The UK government has preferred not to discover or reveal the number and location of ASR children in the country. On the one hand, from the point of view of central government, the decision to avoid data collection on politically sensitive categories could be connected to genuine concerns about possible stigmatisation, hostility and discrimination against asylum-seekers; presumably it is a policy of 'doing good, by doing little' (Kirp, 1980). On the other hand, whatever the reason, the decision not to provide national and local statistical data on ASR students in schools means that there is inadequate funding to help local authorities and schools cope with ASR students' physical, social, emotional and educational needs.

The invisibility of ASR students has been a major theme throughout this book. Silence and invisibility is often sought by ASR students themselves and that desire appears to be respected by teachers. However, such invisibility and silence have implications for the types and level of compassion that is shown to them. For example, those trying to support such students are unable to guess at the depth of their trauma and their educational needs. Also, opportunities are lost to learn from the testimonies of these ASR students about the political, social and human costs of forced migration and war. The increasing importance of children's voices in research has in the past two decades brought ASR children's testimonies into the public domain and has shown that such voices and stories have the power to challenge the lack of morality of government practices (whether related to domestic or foreign policy), to elicit strong compassionate responses among 'citizen' students and to mobilise teachers and students to take action in the name of human rights. Watts (2004: 327–8) found, for example, in East Anglian multicultural schools that the telling of life histories of a refugee enabled a greater understanding among initially hostile students:

> To open up that space, it was necessary for ... [a Chilean refugee] to tell and for the students to hear his life history – the contextualised personal story. Moreover, to keep that space open, the students

needed guidance to see beyond the barriers that had previously filtered out what they did not want to, or could not, comprehend in the wider communities beyond their own.

In these settings, young people appeared to be aware of human rights abuses in distant countries but had not yet connected these to the 'cosy backgrounds' of their world. Ahmed (2000), however, suggests that there is another way of looking at such encounters with 'strangers' and their life stories. In reality such encounters are never 'new' – they are more likely 're-encounters'

> ... with what has been assumed or imagined. Allocated identities facilitate the process of 'stranger fetishism' whereby strangers 'become incorporated into the "we" of the nation at the same time as that "we" emerges as the one who has to live with it (cultural diversity) and by implication with "them"'. (Quoted in Watts, 2004: 325)

The invisibility of many such children in the education system can also lead to a denial of agency, which sustains the view that the ASR child is a victim suffering trauma rather than a human being who has the right to be consulted about his/her future and a right to a full education.[3] There is a fine line between, on the one hand, supporting their choice not to share their life stories with others or respecting their right to share their life stories in their own time and in their own way or, on the other hand, rendering them voiceless. In the context of contemporary pedagogical discourses on pupils' consultation and student voice, the silence of ASR pupils might, in fact, strengthen the distinction between 'citizen' and 'non-citizen' child which the teachers in our research tried to resist. The transition from the 'non-citizen' child to the learner citizen is not complete unless a safe visibility and voice is offered to such children. We agree with Stead, Closs and Arshad (2002: 55) who suggest that 'we need to provide refugee pupils with the choice and opportunity to be safely visible: only then will their visibility be acceptable'. Similarly Waghid (2005: 331) suggests that what is needed is a kind of 'compassionate action that goes beyond the discursive and radical notions of democratic citizenship'. A school system should make 'it possible for [all] students not only to engage in deliberative conversation but, more important, to articulate their personal stories' (ibid.) – to let their inner voice be heard.

The politics of schooling

Our research has demonstrated the various ways in which the political void left by central government in relation to the education of ASR children has been filled by LEAs and schools. Chapter 5 identified a number of discursive framings used to make sense of such children once they enter into the educational system. These frameworks emphasise the individual needs of ASR children rather than focus attention on the requirement to assess the moral-political terrain of asylum. Further research is needed to know how the different LEA services and how the various policy discourses used by local authorities impact on school and teacher practice. We do not know yet what the long-term educational and social consequences of the approaches taken by schools and LEAs will be on the educational experiences and achievements on ASR youth.

Our interviews with teachers and officers in those authorities and schools which had developed a *holistic approach* to the education of ASR students revealed an emergent multi-agency approach that redefined the goals of integration. The three LEAs we researched described their role in relation to ASR students and their families as extending beyond providing access to education and routes to educational attainment. They saw their role as caring and catering for the whole child, and their families. The 'giving of hope' and the creation of a safe and welcoming environment for ASR children were indicative of the level of compassion which can be offered to all children. The deeper we investigated teachers' practice, the more we saw their compassion and commitment to make a difference to these students' lives.

Our research shows how within these schools, the presence of such children throws into relief the social values which schools and teachers, as professionals, encourage within their schools. From the perspective of teachers who work closely with ASR students, all children were deserving of their commitment, attention and resources. The emphasis here is on ASR children as learners – that their education matters as much as that of other children in their class. These teachers call upon the models of compassion that are central to the ethos of teaching as a profession about good practice, fairness and student welfare. They position themselves as caregivers and surrogate parents. As a result, consciously or not, these teachers challenge the hierarchical structure of rights ingrained in state politics of immigration and belonging. The notions of inclusion and belonging frame their professional practice over and above the ASR child's legal status. From the perspective of most of the teachers and LEA officers we interviewed, the main priority was to address the educational and social needs of each ASR child.

For some schools, there is no doubt that the presence of ASR students will just add to the burden of coping with many children's special needs. In these schools, it is likely that ASR students will remain invisible, placing them within very disadvantageous positions in competition for limited resources with other disadvantaged students. More research is needed on the educational experiences of ASR students in schools where, on the one hand, there is little experience with ASR students or ethnic minorities (and hence a lack of EMAG funding) and, on the other, where ASR students might be visible and be subjected to institutional racism (Macpherson, 1999). Our research offers a largely positive picture of the coping strategies of teachers and ASR teams in our three case study schools and LEA holistic strategies in relation to support services.

Asylum-seeking and refugee students paid great tribute to their teachers, recognising their compassion and support. They were critical of some students' disrespect towards teachers, but also of the petty criminality, if not violence, of certain individuals. They were aware of the subtleties and nuances of behaviour required in order to be included within British and English youth cultures. Friendship with 'citizen' students was influenced by the need to speak English, gender dynamics and the display of gendered behaviour, but also depended on the success of ASR students in positioning themselves within a variety of communities, whether White rural or multi-ethnic, often working-class, communities. The challenge was to negotiate these often hidden rules of joining youth subcultures. The complex and subtle juxtapositions of ASR students and youth culture that were captured in Chapters 8 and 9 raise questions which require further research. For example, we are left asking whether ASR students' experience of schooling as strangers is similar to that of any other groups of new arrivals and whether these experiences have any impact on their educational achievement and sense of belonging. We also do not yet know the extent to which the ASR students' positive experience of friendship with other students can counter the negative experience of exclusionary youth cultures and a hostile political environment. Much more research is needed before we can understand the significance of social class, gender and community relations for the integration of ASR students and their security within British society.

Racial bullying and harassment were reported by teachers and by students as not being high, but the exclusionary cultural processes within such inclusive schools that ASR students reported could sustain the dominance of Whiteness as a form of ethnic power. As Harris (1993: 1737) points out, Whiteness may not be a unifying characteristic but rather can be deployed as a means by which to exclude others seen as 'non-White'. Whiteness is a language of power which, in the case of the White 'citizen' student may well have been expressed through indifference, discrimination or avoidance (justified by reference to the personality, religion, language and behaviour of ASR students). More research is clearly needed on these implied racial and religious undertones of the interactions between the 'citizen' and 'non-citizen' student.

We also do not yet know how the diverse group of 'citizen' students in our study, whether White or from minority ethnic groups, construct the Other in relation to their own political identities and within their civic discourses. This requires much deeper research on youth identifications and identities. As we have seen, there are no simple dichotomies or distinctions between British and others (especially given the diversity of hybrid and hyphenated British identities), between White and minority ethnic identities, nor between European identities and different identifications with national and local sites within Britain. What emerged in three different ethnic environments was that the heterogeneous 'citizen' students shared considerable concerns and compassion for individual young refugees and asylum-seekers on account of the terrible tragedies the latter had faced. As a result, they were in somewhat of a dilemma about whether such strangers could ever become one of them. 'Becoming English' was not an option since it is was perceived as based on birth and blood.

The possibility of asylum-seeking students 'becoming British' was raised so long as this identity was based on residence, on having a hyphenated identity or on the ability to fit into British culture (even if this was not clearly defined). Many of the dilemmas of 'citizen' students were revealed in discussions about whether ASR youth and their families should be allowed to come and stay in Britain. In some cases, 'citizen' students adopted the position of the 'host', discussing the boundaries of Britain's hospitality and in so doing reasserted 'the identity and belonging-ness of the host against the movement, shifting, unstable, un-belonging-ness of the guest' (Germann Molz and Gibson, 2007: 5). In other cases, the solutions proposed by 'citizen' students verged on racial discrimination, associating images of disease, overcrowding and danger with asylum-seekers. The compassion expressed here was framed within the pragmatics of demographic and social-order concerns and the wish, as far as we could see, to have the moral issue of asylum transferred to others.

Where ASR and 'citizen' students shared a concern, it appeared to be in relation to the notion of security. Achieving a sense of security and safety was crucial for ASR students who worried about their ability to fit into existing youth cultures rather than the school – in the case of schooling, their aspirations were positive and very high. In contrast, 'citizen' students were concerned about security when talking about the presence of asylum-seekers in the UK. The sense of national (rather than personal or human) security of 'citizen' students was influenced by current views about the potential risks of allowing asylum-seekers to settle in the UK. There was no equivalent sense of threat in the context of youth cultures or classroom learning. The concept of security, therefore, is more complex than safety or wellbeing since it gets to the heart of debates about British values, the limits of inclusion and the nature of belonging and collectivity. Teachers and schools face the challenge of creating a school environment and a curriculum that will encourage an ethic of hospitality and a mutual sense of security.

Citizenship, personhood and asylum

At a more general level, our findings suggest that schools, teachers and students are caught in the conflict between *citizenship* and *personhood* (as described by Brysk and Shafir, 2004). On the one hand, schooling is about educating British citizens into a national unity and, on the other, the presence of non-citizen ASR students whose rights derive from liberal discourses of human rights and the logic of personhood offers a different moral project. These two agendas, which we discussed in Chapter 2, might once have been commensurate. Now, according to Giner (2007), they are discrepant – they represent the conflict between *the notion of a child's best interests* as applied to ASR children and the *interest of the state*. For the teachers in this study, all young people's 'best interests' lie in mainstream education – receiving their full entitlement to quality education, being protected and safeguarded and being given the opportunity to develop all the elements of 'wellbeing' listed in *Every Child Matters*: 'Be healthy, stay safe, enjoy and achieve, make a positive contribution, achieve economic well being.'

Paradoxically the introduction of *Every Child Matters* with the Children Act 2004[4] gave schools the opportunity and the discourse with which to position ASR students within the mainstream and to realise that the presence of children from different parts of the world with such extraordinary childhood experiences could greatly enhance that project. Such pedagogic caring represents just another example of good practice under the teachers' professional code of conduct.

Our research suggests that there are schools which support an ethics of care and compassion – what it cannot confirm is how extensive this approach is nationally or how committed the teaching profession is to this approach. It is increasingly likely that, with the requirements of the Children Act 2004, more LEAs and schools will be encouraged to take such a stance. Bill Bolloten (in interview) suggested that when *Every Child Matters* gave official backing to multi-agency holistic approaches to vulnerable children, it encouraged a move away from bureaucratic hierarchies in local authorities. In effect it should give more voice to frontline people, like the LEA officers and teachers we interviewed who work closely with ASR communities. Far more research is needed before any comprehensive statement can be made about whether this approach has been extended nationally.

The inclusive LEAs and schools we researched provide evidence that a wide variety of mechanisms to support ASR students can be put in place. However, the individualising of ASR children's needs is problematic. Rutter argues that these approaches can render such children weak and vulnerable, as 'traumatised' rather than seen as having been violated by political and personal oppression. Reflecting on the dominance of the trauma discourse in LEA and teachers' responses, she speculated that it might 'make a person appear caring towards the victim' and therefore would not address the 'hard political questions about EAL funding or the refugee policy of local government' (2006: 130). A more extensive argument is put forward by Boyden and Berry (2004) who, in their edited collection *Children and Youth on the Front Line,* argue that individualising psychological discourses depoliticise the ASR children's experiences of government, forced migration and settlement, and the realities of surviving loss, death and destitution. From their perspective, ASR youth should not be defined by the trauma they have experienced but by their resilience, agency and sheer courage in the face of extreme circumstances.

The individualising approach associated with neo-liberal discourses in education and the emphasis of the UK government on 'vulnerability' does not encourage an active engagement with issues of human rights and social justice. Nor, it seems, does a strongly caring approach necessarily lend itself to this agenda. The goal of educating young British students to learn how to cope with and befriend strangers and to reduce xenophobia and racial prejudice while encouraging compassion for those who have suffered persecution is not one that has had any obvious promotion by the UK government. It was quite noticeable that the language of human rights was not obviously present in LEA responses to our survey, nor was there any strong engagement with the concept of creating an explicitly critical curriculum in schools.

Despite the introduction of citizenship education into the primary and secondary curriculum, LEA officers appeared to refer only in passing to the power of this subject when talking about preparing young people more generally about global conflict and refugee issues. The opportunity provided by Education for Citizenship as a curriculum subject allowed some of the more politically aware teachers we met in Chapters 7 and 10 to find ways of engaging with their students in critical analysis of the dehumanisation and criminalisation of the asylum-seeker and refugee, and encouraging them to reflect on the richness and security of their lives. The assumption teachers appear to be making here is that proximity is not sufficient to encourage compassion, and that teachers need to develop appropriate materials, topics, activities and campaigns to link refugee issues to the promotion of democracy, social justice and human rights. This stance shifts attention away from the asylum-seeker and refugee to, for example, peace education, anti-violence or anti-xenophobia education. The discourse of human rights, although itself individualised, could potentially form the basis of such a more strongly critical transformative pedagogy on behalf of the group rights of all ASR children.

Perhaps because of the individualisation of ASR students' needs, the prevalence of racial denigration and harassment of ASR children (on the basis of skin colour, religion or just strangeness) has not been challenged. Nor has concern been expressed at the image within some LEAs that ASR students are 'models' of high ambition, motivation and resilience. While some might read this image as a positive rejoinder to those wishing the school to do more to counteract racial discrimination, Gillborn (2008) takes the view that such representations of minority ethnic students can signify a form of racial discrimination. In these instances, ASR students find themselves differentiated from the mainstream White student body.

Even though we have focused on our two key concepts in our research design and data analysis – compassion and belonging – we were aware of other social dynamics at work. Our data point to the subtle prejudices which Pettigrew (1998: 83) suggests are fed by 'the perceived threat of the minority to traditional values, the exaggeration of cultural differences with the minority and the absence of positive feelings towards them'. Such prejudice among youth carries overtones of institutional racism which can represent and embody discriminatory practices in wider society (Lea, 2000; Macpherson, 1999; Sivanandan,

2001). Some teachers are well aware of the effect of, for example, tabloid hostility and make it their business to use the media reporting on asylum in class to address issues of compassion and citizenship (Chapters 7 and 10). However, for the most part, our research did not reveal whether, or if so how, schools are tackling unsympathetic public opinion, or how more critical messages delivered through the citizenship curriculum are being received by students. As a result, the cause of local conflict between social groups does not appear to have been seriously tackled by central and local government. Racial harassment is not just about subtle forms of indifference and instances of 'taking the mick'. As a number of refugee researchers have revealed, such harassment of ASR youth can also be violent.

The radical potential of race equality policies which were developed in the 1970s and 1980s did not seem to have been called into play to tackle the presence of racially shaped behaviour in schools against ASR students. As a consequence their problems appear to be defined more as issues of language and 'new arrivals' rather than of racial justice. With recent legislation, specific duties have been placed on schools relating to education and to integration. The Race Relations Amendment Act 2000, among other things, places a duty on schools to eliminate racial discrimination and to promote equality of opportunity and good relations between people of different groups. According to section 78 of the Education Act 2002, the curriculum for all maintained schools should promote the spiritual, moral, cultural, mental and physical development of pupils at school and in society. The Education and Inspections Act 2006 also places a new duty on schools to promote community cohesion. In other words, the integrative role schools are expected to play should be extended to all pupils, 'citizen' as well as 'non-citizen', and beyond the school walls into the wider community. Specifically, all schools, whatever their mix of students, are responsible for helping all of them to live and thrive alongside people from a variety of backgrounds. This new equality duty, together with existing responsibilities, suggests the need for a more radical approach by schools towards the issue of racial harassment.

A new politics?

Public pressure on the UK government to address the welfare of refugee and asylum-seeking youth has grown substantially in recent years, challenging the morality of its immigration policies. These campaigns draw upon *a culture of social morality* over and above the state.

Clotilde Giner (2007: 254) argues that the 2004 Asylum and Immigration Act uses 'already vulnerable children as pawns to convince their parents' to leave the UK and carries with it the expectation that social services departments and individual social workers should be involved in controlling immigration, an expectation completely at variance with their professional ethos. Far from complying, Crawley (2006: 9) notes that 'SSDs [social services departments] have tried to ameliorate the worst effect on children by providing support within increasingly hostile practical and political contexts'. Like social workers who are caught up in the government immigration and asylum policy by default (Wade et al., 2008), teachers engage at many different levels in mediating the consequences of asylum-seeking children's poverty and distress. In some cases this has led teachers and students, as we have seen, to joining new political campaigns and alliances which have been formed to fight the deportation of asylum-seeking students and their families.

Asylum experts such as Bill Bolloten suggest that these alliances and campaigns represent a new form of politics which does not fit easily into existing party political frameworks, nor has it been led by professional organisations. What is interesting about actions such as the schools anti-deportation campaigns described in Chapter 10 is that they do not appear to use the conventional language of politics nor to have been generated or supported out of the traditional Left:

> ... these campaigns represent something new. A new development of engagement of a section of young people [...] we saw that happening in a slightly different form, but in a similar parallel form before the invasion of Iraq, where spontaneously children were going on strike and going out of schools and joining demonstrations, often with the opposition of schools that tried to keep them in ... and that really worried the establishment, because they were new forces, they are not controlled by the Left, [...] by the traditional labour movement ... (Interview with Bill Bolloten, 2 March 2008)

A greater awareness of children's rights under the UNCRC, when confronted with the sorts of political moments we described in Chapter 10, could have triggered students to invoke their own rights to fight for social justice.

The phenomenon of campaigns against the deportation and detention of children is not unique to the UK. In recent years such campaigns could be found in many European countries.[5] Fekete (2009: 178–9) argues that these campaigns focus on the

> child as a child no matter what part of the world he or she comes from, challenges the racism (inherent in public discourse) that denies asylum seekers and *sans papiers* individuals their human dignity.

These campaigns, Fekete suggests, reconnect Europeans to their history of combatting poverty, authoritarianism and displacement in the Second World War era, 'reinvigorating Europe's humanitarian tradition and breathing fresh life into degraded concepts such as solidarity' (ibid.: 187). Even if the concept of asylum no longer evokes compassion, the image of the refugee child can still engender a compassionate reaction.

However, even these humanitarian responses have their limitations. Western modernist notions of childhood which have shaped the British humanitarian response to refugee children in the past[6] construct these children as 'passive and vulnerable' and their life circumstances as simply 'a regrettable modern tragedy' (Myers, 2009: 30). This discursive formation, which can still be found in use, leaves no room for considering

> circumstances that had brought the children into exile or any explanation of why they had come without their families ... no recognition of the cultural capital which children bring with them ... no recognition of the complexities of children's identities ... this discourse helps produce a form of cultural chauvinism in which the power to help reproduces the kind of otherness and difference that was central to imperialism. (ibid.: 42)

Such modernist images of childhood, if reused in the post-modern context, can 'maintain prevailing colonial and paternalistic relations' (Burman, 1994: 238). Indeed the danger in the morality of compassion that derives from modernist concepts of childhood lies in the fact that it might be patronising to ASR children. It renders their resilient childhoods as significant not because it was painful for 'them' but because it disturbs 'our' notion of childhood. Consequently, society attempts to 'normalise' their special circumstances, with the result that their special circumstances are ignored (Burman, 1994).

There are, therefore, political risks inherent in the form of compassion as caring that was expressed by some of the teachers we interviewed (Boyden, 2009). A caring ethos distances ASR children from the circumstances that forced them to flee and, in turn, exempts 'us' from the responsibility of considering issues such as community conflicts and displacements. By focusing on individuals, Boyden warns us that 'attention is diverted away from the wider structural conditions that produce and reproduce forced migration …' (Boyden, 2009). She adds:

> Many refugees and asylum seekers reject this kind of thinking because it emphasises their difference and renders them objects of pity, or victims … it risks the implication that only those who are deserving merit sympathy and support. […] the notion of care risks characterising forced migrants as powerless in the face of adversity. (ibid.)

In other words, basing compassionate reactions on pity for the suffering of others places them within a symbiotic care-dependency relationship. This positioning might also offer space to the type of moral reasoning we saw emerging from the government discourse on the deserving and the undeserving. It offers a morality based on outdated modernist conceptions of childhood that is far removed from compassion as a form of social justice. If we go back to Nussbaum (2001), it is important for us to also consider the implications of the suffering of such children to our scheme of goals, particularly those relating to social justice.

Those teachers who believed in developing students' moral agency through the curriculum and through campaigning on behalf of asylum-seeking families took a different stance. They wanted to alert children to the injustices of war, genocide and forced migration. Their sensitivity gets closer to what Weil (1970) and Nussbaum (2001) describe as the desired role of education in developing a more critical compassion. Moral education, Nussbaum argued, should encourage children not just to understand the reality of someone other than themselves but to imagine what it might be to be someone else – not in terms of hypothetical cases but as understanding the concrete reality of someone else. If schools are to create compassionate individuals, they would need to install a sense of shared humanity, possibly through critical notions of cosmopolitanism, or by the developing of global citizenship as a path to compassion (see Arnot, 2009). A compassionate citizenship education should therefore involve more than moral reasoning and argumentation. It should require

> students to make certain practical judgments about how to deal with these different variables in their public and personal lives. The

judgements they make will inevitably be based on their perception of others' distress, underserved misfortune, suffering, injustice, plight, disability and disease. It is in this regard that compassion becomes a necessary condition for acting upon and deliberating about such matters, because compassion ... 'pushes the boundaries of the self' outwards. (Waghid, 2005: 334)

This approach gets closer to concerns about social justice suggested by Simone Weil (see Chapter 3). Teaching about social equality should include the teaching of compassion for others. A compassionate citizenship education should not be passive but should involve ASR students actively in the construction of the subject. As some authors have pointed out (such as Prout, 2005: 31), young people's participation, whether led by teachers or at their own instigation, would be critical since it is 'capable of transcending differences in the social, cultural and economic conditions of children's lives around the world'.

Today there is a real need to engage with the politics of compassion in our schools. This book has identified the ways in which the politics of compassion works against, alongside and with various moralities at work already within society and the school system: the politics of belonging, liberal-democratic values in education, the morality of modernist notions of childhood, as well as the professional morality of teachers.[7] Increasing attention is now being paid by social scientists to the need to create a stronger morality based on a new 'ethic of hospitality' within a globalised world. This revitalised notion of hospitality in our contemporary global world could reconstruct the relationship between citizens, immigrants, refugees, asylum-seekers and the nation-state (Germann Molz and Gibson, 2007: 10).[8] Such an ethic would need, for example, to deconstruct the dichotomies of 'host' and 'guest', and of citizen and Other, which derive from national metaphors of hospitality (ibid.). According to these authors, in order to create a new ethic of hospitality fit for a globalising world, we would need to return to 'ancient questions' about how we should define 'our individual, communal and national self' (ibid.: 1).

However, it is also important to recognise that, according to Bauman (2004), the spaces which were constructed as 'no man's land' in which new forms of hospitality could be created are fast disappearing. The world is filled with nation-states with their closely defined and watched boundaries. Globalising economies amplify the amount of 'human waste' – the 'flotsam' of humanity who are pushed or wafted across such boundaries as refugees or asylum-seekers. The major moral problem lies 'in that gap between the suffering we see and our ability to help the sufferers' (Bauman, 2001: 2). Today, Bauman argues, where once there used to be a match between our moral responsibility and our capacity to act, now 'the challenges of our moral conscience exceed many times over that conscience's ability to cope and stand up to challenge' (ibid.). Arguably our mutual dependence is greater than ever, and our moral responsibility for each other is ever more real. However: 'Our moral impulses are increasingly blunted by our incapacity to act – we feel voyeuristic' (ibid.). In this context, the notion of asylum today is said 'to be dying the death of thousand cuts' (Bohmer and Shuman, 2008: 267) since asylum-seekers are now seen as a threat to liberal democracies.

In this global context, it is important to recognise that for many the role of the educational system is *the* focal point for those who wish to retain the ancient ethos of asylum. After all, as Athy Demetriades, the teacher leading the Children of the Storm project commented:

> *'Education is the only weapon asylum-seekers might take back home one day.'*

Notes

Chapter 1

1. The Convention has been ratified by all UN Member States except for the US and Somalia.
2. Unless unaccompanied, the asylum application of a child is determined on the merits of the parents' case.
3. See for example: Candappa and Egharevba (2002); Closs, Stead and Arshad (2001); Richman (1998); Rutter (1998a); Rutter and Stanton (2001); Rutter and Hyder (1998); Rutter and Jones (1998); or the work of NGOs such as Save the Children, the Refugee Council and NCB.

Chapter 2

1. See Van Selm (2005); Whitaker (1998).
2. In some cases this led to an increase in numbers of other groups of forced migrants such as the internally displaced, returnees and stateless persons.
3. Immigration control as a moral and ethical issue is discussed further by Gibney (2004) and Weiner (1995).
4. For discussions about the conceptualisation of forced migration see also: Boyle, Halfacre and Robinson (1998); Castles (2003); Castles, Miller and Ammendola (2003); Crawley (2005); Kunz (1981); Richmond (1993); Turton (2003).
5. Many Western nation-states still use the 1951 Convention as their main frame of reference in determining their asylum and immigration policies (Boyle et al., 1998; Gibney, 2004).

Chapter 3

1. Until 2005 refugees were automatically given permanent residency.
2. We avoid using the term 'host' since it presupposes a moral obligation to offer hospitality to aliens.
3. Fix and Laglagaron (2002) created a further distinction for the US context between 'permanent non-citizens' such as refugees and 'tolerated non-citizens' such as asylum-seekers, who are granted entry for a limited time.
4. Buddhist traditions have also contributed greatly to the conceptualisation of this notion. In these traditions compassion represents a very significant element of religious belief and practice. It involves a 'desire to relieve suffering' but is also thought to be 'one of the ways in which people could free themselves from destructive emotion' – it 'involves being open to the suffering of self and others, in a non-defensive and non-judgmental way' (Gilbert, 2005: 1). However, it is beyond the scope of this book to explore further Buddhist notions of compassion. Despite the interest of Western

and Eastern religious and philosophical traditions, Gilbert (2005) claims that, surprisingly, the notion of compassion has received little attention in Western psychology and social science in general.

5. The Stoic and non-Stoic traditions differed in their answers to such questions. Whereas the Stoic dismissed the role of emotions in morality, those who emerged from the Aristotelian tradition defended their relevance (Nussbaum, 1998). For the non-Stoic philosopher, compassion is an emotion with special relevance to morality since it inherently involves judgement.

6. This discussion is based on Nussbaum (1998).

7. See Nussbaum (1998).

8. For a more detailed discussion, see Janaway (1994) and Nussbaum (1998).

9. The institution of citizenship, for example, like the formation of other collective identities, is a major site in which belonging is shaped since it is here that societies and states create and maintain their national boundaries (Croucher, 2004; Yuval-Davis et al., 2006).

10. The project was funded by the GTC and the Faculty of Education, University of Cambridge.

11. The project, conducted by Arnot and Candappa in 2006–2007, was funded by the Faculty of Education, University of Cambridge, Research Development Fund.

12. A study funded by the ESRC (award numbers L129251009 and R000222952). In a two-stage project the *Extraordinary Childhoods* study explored the social lives of refugee children. In the first stage, interviews were conducted with 35 ASR students aged 11–14 living in and around London, and an ethnically mixed group of 32 indigenous students in the same age range. ASR students were interviewed in-depth about their lives, and invited to reflect on their experiences of home, school and social life in the UK. Indigenous students, illustrating 'ordinary childhoods' were similarly interviewed about their home, school and social lives, for comparative purposes. The second stage provided indicative, comparative survey data on the contemporary lives of 312 ASR and indigenous students in Years 8, 9, and 10 in the same two London schools from which many of the interviewees were drawn.

13. Funded by the Scottish Government, 2005–7 (Candappa et al., 2007), it explored issues relating to the education of ASR students in Scotland. The study included case study research in two Scottish cities (one of which was a new dispersal area for asylum-seekers); and also in two English LEAs for policy development purposes. As part of the research, two primary and two secondary school case studies were conducted in the new dispersal city selected from a number of schools recommended by the Education Authority as having inclusive approaches towards ASR students. In each school the Head was interviewed, sometimes supported by a senior teacher who worked closely with ASR students, and documentary evidence was gathered in relation to the school's policy and practice.

14. As we discuss in Chapters 5 and 6, to a great extent they are still statistically invisible.

15. For the questionnaire see Arnot and Pinson (2005).

16. In order to draw a sample that reflected the diversity of LEA experience we used two sources of data, neither of which were statistically reliable given

the lack of monitoring by central government of ASR children in the school system. We used the Home Office official data on dispersal areas, and data collected by the survey conducted by the Refugee Council in 2002 on the numbers of asylum-seekers and refugee children located in different LEAs and the extent to which LEA data on the numbers of these children were collected. We cross-referenced these two main sources by dividing LEAs according to three locations: London, dispersal and non-dispersal, and according to the Refugee Council's categories; LEAs with high numbers of ASR students; LEAs with low numbers of ASR students and LEAs that indicated that they did not have data; and LEAs that did not respond. We created a grid of 12 boxes that represented potentially different experiences of LEAs with asylum-seeking children, into which we classified all English LEAs. We then selected a number of LEAs from each box. We initially contacted 62 LEAs of which 58 cooperated with the research.

17. In retrospect this became part of the information we gathered about the support structures of LEAs and we concluded that asking LEA officials to name the responsible officer proved not only to be methodologically useful but also a valuable source of additional data.

18. The taped interviews (with LEA officers and school staff) were all semi-structured and focused on the following themes: the background and history of the LEA and schools with ASR children; the responses of the LEA, the school and the local community to their integration; the ways in which interviewees describe LEA/school approaches; the ways in which they defined their responsibility; what they considered as good practice and information about their policies and support practices.

Chapter 4

1. Cohen (2006) suggests that the open-door policy towards asylum-seekers was a mere myth and never really existed.

2. Enoch Powell, a Conservative MP between 1950 and 1974, was known for his controversial 'Rivers of Blood' speech against Commonwealth immigration which he gave to a Conservative Party gathering in Birmingham in the run-up to the 1968 election.

3. The association between illegal immigrants and asylum-seekers is created alongside the view that the failed asylum-seeker is an 'immigration offender'.

4. Recently, the Home Office attempted to move away from such criminalisation discourse. In its 2008 Departmental Report (Home Office, 2008) asylum-seekers were dealt with under different sections and strategic plans than illegal migrants, border tax fraud, trafficking or immigration crime.

5. This policy trend is similar in other European countries. In 2006, 33,200 people were granted refugee status in Europe; 34 per cent fewer than the previous year (UNHRC, 2007).

6. Those who arrive in the UK seeking refuge are considered asylum-seekers, while awaiting a Home Office decision on their claim. If their application is not denied, they could be granted temporary leave to remain (up to three years) – under the principle of humanitarian protection. Alternatively they could be granted refugee status.

7. Britain's colonial past had a great influence on its immigration and asylum policies and acted both as a force for openness and for closure. As a result of this heritage, it has had difficulty in negotiating the legal meaning of citizenship. Consequently it used immigration policy to define membership. For further discussion see Dell'Olio (2002) Gibney (2004), Joppke (1999), and Solomos and Schuster (2001).

8. After 2003, asylum applications and numbers dropped. Although numbers of asylum applications were high – 28,300 applicants (including dependents in 2007 – in reality, only a minority receive refugee status or exceptional leave to remain. For example, only 16 per cent of initial decisions made in 2007 received refugee status and an additional 10 per cent were granted humanitarian protection or discretionary leave to remain, while the rest were recorded as failed asylum-seekers.

9. The Immigration and Asylum Act 1996; the Immigration and Asylum Act 1999; the Nationality, Immigration and Asylum Act 2002; the Asylum and Immigration (Treatment of Claimants, etc.) Act 2004; the Immigration, Asylum and Nationality Act 2006; and the Borders, Citizenship and Immigration Act 2009.

10. Evidence against this thesis can be found in studies funded by the Home Office which found that the majority of asylum-seekers had little choice about where to flee and were more concerned with leaving their own country than their destination. If there was a choice, the main factor in their decision to seek refuge in Britain was having family and networks in the UK, historical (colonial) links to the UK and knowledge of English. Considerations such as their entitlements and the welfare support they might receive as asylum-seekers were found to be only minor factors in their decision and in most cases there was little evidence to suggest that asylum-seekers had any knowledge of their entitlements prior for their arrival to the UK (Koser and Pinkerton, 2002; Robinson and Segrott, 2002).

11. Since 2002 the Labour government has made great efforts to strengthen distinctions between migrants seen as valuable to the UK and asylum-seekers (see, for example, Home Office, 2002, 2005a).

12. Home Office integration policy is articulated in the following documents: Home Office (2004d, 2005b, 2005c, 2006).

13. The other two reservations related to an unwillingness to provide special protection to 16-year-olds in the labour market, and to discontinue placing young people in custody together with adults.

14. Section 55 of the Borders, Citizenship and Immigration Act 2009, which introduced a new duty on the UK Borders Agency to safeguard children, is expected to come into force in October 2009.

15. Victoria Climbié sustained horrendous abuse and died at the hands of her private foster carers. The government response to the report of the enquiry into her death was to publish *Keeping Children Safe* (DfES, DoH and Home Office, 2003) and the Green Paper *Every Child Matters* (DfES, 2003a).

16. In the White Paper *Secure Borders, Safe Haven* (2002), immigration staff were given permission to interview children about their claims.

17. Personal communication.

18. Many studies of immigration stress the importance of social capital to enable immigrants gain access to societal resources (Coleman, 1988; Kao, 2004;

Pallon et al., 2001). Social capital can help immigrants achieve and benefit from schooling without the risk of losing their unique identity and cultural heritage (Zhou, 1997).

19. See also: Bacon (2005); Bloch and Schuster (2005); Pirouet (2001); Wolton (2006).
20. Today many detention centres are run by private companies (Bacon, 2005).
21. See for example the Independent Asylum Commission's report (2006).
22. The Home Office publishes snapshots of detention facilities on a specific day and every so often cumulative quarterly statistics.
23. For more details on the negative impact of detention on asylum-seeking children see further the studies by Cole (2003) and Crawley and Lester (2005).

Chapter 5

1. In 2005 two web portals were set up to provide information about good practice for LEAs, schools and teachers in relation to the education of ASR children. One is the New Arrivals portal, with cooperation between QCA and DCSF. Another is the NRIF, a Home Office initiative on which DCSF advised: http://nrif.homeoffice.gov.uk/Education/index.asp
2. With the exception of those who reside in removal centres, in which case education would be provided by the centre.
3. Within the new structure of the DCSF there is an officer under EMA, responsible for disseminating good practice and advice for the education of both ASR and traveller children. Responsibility for the wellbeing and safeguarding of these children rests with the Parliamentary Under-Secretary of State for Children, Young People and Families.
4. This particular interviewee did not give permission to tape the interview, hence throughout this chapter we use extracts from the interview as documented and paraphrased by the interviewer. Also, in order to maintain interviewees' anonymity, we did not name them or identify their roles.
5. This was called for by the Swann Report, *Education for All*, in 1985.
6. Interestingly, this role is now being introduced into higher education in the UK in the name of protecting the country in its alleged war against terrorism.
7. In the academic year 2004–2005, more restrictions and cuts were introduced by the DfES to EMAG and consequently LEAs had less money to support EAL students in general.
8. See also Arnot and Pinson (2005), Mott (2000) and Reakes and Powell (2004).
9. Other groups encompassed under the VCG are: looked-after children; children unable to attend school due to medical condition; gypsy/traveller children; young carers; school refusals; teenage parents and young offenders.
10. Although in practice some ASR students (once identified) have been found by teachers to be model, even high-performing students and of great benefit to the achievement cultures of schools as a result of their high motivation and resilience (see Chapter 7).
11. The Audit Commission report *Another Country* (Audit Commission, 2000) noted that some schools resisted accepting children of asylum-seekers because they could not offer necessary support, and/or were concerned that the new arrivals would adversely affect school league tables. The report

cited Refugee Council research which suggested that in 1999 there were around 2,000 ASR children without a school place.

12. Issues around the education of asylum-seeking and refugee students have also been integrated into the Ofsted inspection of LEA support for ethnic minority groups and approaches to inclusion (Ofsted, 2003a).
13. See Mott (2000); Ofsted (2003a); Reakes and Powell (2004); Remsbery (2003); Rutter (2006).
14. Similar concerns were also raised in a study of Welsh LEAs (Reakes and Powell, 2004).
15. From September 2000 to March 2003, schools in the dispersal authorities were eligible for a one-off grant of £500 for each asylum-seeker pupil they admitted. The grant applied only to those families who were supported by NASS (Ofsted, 2003a: 5).
16. This debate is not dissimilar to the educational dilemmas associated with separate provision for children with disabilities and particular learning needs.
17. For more details see Arnot and Pinson (2005).
18. The recent emphasis of the DCSF on pupil mobility may mean that this framework has gained more prominence since the survey was conducted (personal communication from Bill Bolloten).

Chapter 6

1. Under section 17 of the Children Act 1989 local authorities have a duty to safeguard and promote the welfare of children in need in their area; under section 20, every local authority shall provide accommodation for any child in need who has no person with parental responsibility. ASR children are not mentioned specifically, but the category of children in need, loosely defined, allowed local authorities to provide accommodation for asylum-seeking families who were at risk of destitution.
2. A holistic approach, whether employed in education, medicine or social care, is concerned with the whole phenomenon and not merely with its parts (Lewis, 1998). Holistic education, therefore, is likely to have a broader focus, addressing the whole – the spirit, mind and body of the child (Martin, 1997).
3. In Cheston, interviews were conducted with the following officers: Cheston's Deputy Director; the Head of EMAS and the Deputy Head of EMAS acting as asylum-seekers and refugees officer. In Greenshire interviews were conducted with: the Head of Inclusion; the Head of EMAS; the Deputy Head of EMAS; the ASR officer; the LEA's advisory support teachers for primary and secondary education; and one of the LEA's cultural mediators. In Horton interviews were conducted with the following: the Head of Inclusion, the ASR team (including two officers, one for primary and one for secondary education), and the education and welfare officer for ASR children. In Cheston three schools were visited, a secondary school where we interviewed the headteacher and the Head of EMAS; a primary school where interviews were carried out with the headteacher and one mainstream teacher and a primary Catholic school where we interviewed the headteacher and one of the school's governors. An

interview was also carried out with a deputy headteacher of a sixth form college which integrates ASR students. In Greenshire, because of time constraints, only one school was visited – a secondary school where interviews were held with the headteacher, the deputy headteacher, the Head of EMAS and the Deputy Head of EMAS. Finally, in Horton, three schools were visited. In an all-girls secondary school we interviewed the deputy headteacher and the EMAS support teacher; in a comprehensive secondary school we interviewed the Head of EMAS and lastly, we interviewed the headteacher and the Head of EMAS in a local primary school.

4. Welfare/pastoral support involved assisting ASR parents in obtaining free school meals and free uniforms, using a special grant to provide bus passes for ASR students, and providing each new arrival with a starter kit that included a school bag, notebooks and other essentials.

5. Greenshire schools ran induction programmes, assessment, maintained progress profiles, and provided EAL support and in-class support. Pastoral support might include a special tutoring system, lunchtime and after-school clubs in the EMAS centre which acted as a safe space for the children, and courses in community languages.

6. Research conducted in the mid-1990s identified the need in the authority for such a team. Initially it should have included four primary and four secondary officers, but budget restrictions meant that Horton could only afford a team of two officers.

7. The Refugee Council (2008) conducted a study of good practice in breaking down the barriers between ASR families and schools.

8. Council members as well as the LEA senior management made it customary to visit minority ethnic communities and refugee community organisations to allow them to voice their concerns and give their input into life in the county.

9. The 'inclusive education' literature also brings to our attention the relationship between school inclusion and other educational agendas such as school improvement and the marketisation of education (Armstrong, 1999).

10. Children's Trusts were announced in 2002, as a joint initiative of the Department of Health and the Department for Education and Skills. Children's Trusts combined health, social care and education for integrated service provision for children, using existing powers from the Health Act 1999 to delegate functions and pool money.

11. Similarly the Children's Fund was set up in 2000 as part of a catalyst to move forward inter-agency cooperation and children and family-led preventative services in local authorities. The initiative had a total funding of £960m. It was part of a long-term strategy aimed at strengthening communities and families, and targeting young people aged 5–13 years seen to be at risk of social exclusion. It was located in 149 local partnerships across local authorities in England.

Chapter 7

1. These findings also resonate with the images used by schools and LEAs to describe ASR students in Wales (Reakes and Powell, 2004).

Chapter 8

1. See: Hardwick and Rutter (1998); Remsbery (2003); Richman (1998); Rutter (2006); Rutter and Hyder (1998); Rutter and Jones (1998); Rutter and Stanton (2001); Save the Children (2002, 2004); Stanley (2002).
2. Rutter and Jones (1998) suggest that the high mobility of asylum-seekers often meant that they were attending the less popular schools and had disrupted education.
3. On the other hand, Candappa et al. (2007), found that inclusive schools with the support of the education authority were making great efforts to welcome asylum-seeking students and support their learning and wellbeing. One secondary school in particular stood out – in the words of one of the students interviewed, 'four out of the five [school] captains are asylum-seekers or refugees' (2007: 19).
4. About the need to adjust to the culture of a new education system and a new school culture, see Candappa and Egharevba (2000); Hamilton and Moore (2004); Marland (1998); Rutter and Hyder (1998); Rutter and Jones (1998); Rutter and Stanton (2001).
5. See Candappa and Egharevba (2000); Rutter and Hyder (1998); Rutter and Stanton (2001).
6. Various authors present differing emphases; see, for example, King and Murray (2000); Leaning and Arie (2000); Rothschild (1995); Sen (2000); Thomas (2000).
7. The three concepts of *safety, belonging* and *compassion* are interconnected; however, the relationship between them requires further research.
8. With the exception of the ASR focus group in Fairfield which included only three students and one 'citizen' focus group in City School that included five.
9. Racism and bullying experienced by ASR students has been commented on by a number of authors, for example Chase et al. (2008a); Rutter (2006); Stanley (2001).
10. Farouq is slightly built and has a mild manner. However, when he retaliated to end the bullying, a behaviour described as 'life affirming violence' (Ringrose, forthcoming), he then described himself as a bully for resorting to the same behaviour.

Chapter 9

1. See Nussbaum's (2001) description of the first Aristotelian judgement.
2. A White British/European Year 9 girl.
3. A White British Year 8 boy.
4. A Dual Heritage British Year 8 boy.
5. A White British Year 8 girl.
6. This view is not dissimilar to that expressed by Enoch Powell in the 1960s (see Chapter 4).
7. As noted above, Rutter (2006) also found that 'citizen' students often use anti-asylum discourse interchangeably with racist discourse which is rationalised with the state's-best-interest discourse.

Chapter 10

1. There are number of publications which reveal ASR children's stories and their extraordinary and resilient childhoods. For example: Bolloten and Spafford (1998); Chase et al. (2008); Melzak (1997); Melzak and Warner (1992); Stanley (2002).
2. The testimonies of ASR youth reported here were collected by Mano Candappa, some of which were reported in Rutter and Candappa (1998), Candappa (2000) and Candappa and Egharevba (2000, 2002).
3. Taken from a speech by Athy Demetriades, for the charity Children of the Storm, 1994.
4. This and the interviews with the Heads of St Xavier's and Robert Burns primary schools were conducted for Candappa et al. (2007).
5. Available at: www.irr.org.uk/2005/january/ak000009.html, accessed 15 August 2009.
6. This area is currently the subject of Clotilde Giner's doctoral research at the University of Warwick.
7. For example, Justice and Peace Scotland (www.justiceandpeacescotland.org.uk); National Coalition of Anti-Deportation Campaigns (www.ncdac.org.uk); Schools Against Deportations (www.schoolsagainstdeportations.org); Support Hicham Yezza (www.freehicham.co.uk).
8. This is the 'Final Version Released for Circulation (Public Document)', released 3 March 2008.
9. This statutory duty was an extension of responsibilities in the Education Act 2002 where schools were given the duty of care of all their students.
10. See Chapter 4 for a fuller discussion.
11. Notably the National Coalition of Anti-Deportation Campaigns (NCADC: www.ncadc.org.uk), and Schools Against Deportations (SAD: www.schoolsagainstdeportations.org).
12. Anti-deportation campaigns have been mounted across Glasgow, often with considerable success, including the case of Max Waku and family, who were released in February 2008 after huge protests by Glaswegians (http://justiceandpeacescotland.orf.uk/campaigns.shtml); in Canterbury a coalition of students and anti-deportation campaigners rallied together to help student Abrahim Rahim win his right to judicial review, with the campaign collecting 12,000 signatures in support of its cause (www.irr.org.uk/2005/august/fq000020. html); the Portsmouth case is discussed later in this chapter.
13. Hackney Community Law Centre. Available at www.irr.org.uk/sad/guidelines.html, accessed 4 September 2007.
14. See www.irr.org.uk/sad/forestgate/ros_text_f.htm, accessed 27 November 2009.
15. See www.ncadc.org.uk/archives/filed%20newszines/oldnewszines/Old%2051-100/newszine54/amina.html, accessed 27 November 2009.
16. Accessed at www.irr.org.uk/sad/astley/mayes text t.htm, page 2, on 4 August 2007.
17. The President of the Irish National Teachers' Organisation commented in 2005 that deportations were 'terrorising pupils' and that schools were acquiring the 'status of embassies'. See www.ncadc.org.uk/archives/filed%20newszines/oldnewszines/Old%2051100/newszine63/letter%20for%20schools%20and%20unions.pdf, accessed 27 November 2009.

Chapter 11

1. The official status and condition of an alien – see www.thefreedictionary.com/ alienage
2. However, it is important to note that despite this discursive formation of the valuable and lawful asylum-seeker, many female-headed households are given refugee status even though they have few economic skills. Their husbands might have been killed, tortured, arrested and disappeared. Most of the mothers have never worked away from the home and have no requisite skills for a job.
3. Malkki (1996) argues that refugees are invisible both as *a persona* (as a social position) and as individuals.
4. The UNICEF Innocenti Research Centre (2007) ranked the UK in the bottom third in five out of six dimensions of children's wellbeing. It also argued that the UK needs to devote much more attention to the 'excluded, those from ethnic minorities, those from immigration families and those being cared for in institutions' (42).
5. Fekete (2009: 178–9) notes in the context of detention of children all across Europe (in countries such as Spain, France, Greece, Ireland, the Netherlands, Sweden and of course the UK) the emergence of a number of new types of campaigns. These new coalitions include, for example: the European Coalition against the Detention and Forced Removal of Minors, the National Coalition of Anti-deportation Campaigns, Reseau Education Sans Frontières (in France and Belgium); the Swedish Network of Asylum and Refugee Groups, and the Euro-wide No Borders network.
6. For example, offering asylum to Basque children and Jewish children fleeing from Nazi Germany, or taking in Vietnamese refugee children in the 1970s and refugees from Bosnia and Serbia in the 1990s.
7. Boyden (2009) also lists the morality of UNCRC, the morality of democratic citizenship; the morality of the political imagination, and the professional morality of those in the education system.
8. An alternative view is that in the UK context the 'metaphor of hospitality ... functions as an alibi in order to protect Britain's own interests and self-image' (Gibson, 2007: 159).

References

11 Million (2009) *The Arrest and Detention of Children Subject to Immigration Control: A Report Following the Children's Commissioner for England's Visit to Yarl's Wood Immigration Removal Centre* (London: 11 Million).

Agamben, G. (1998) *Homo Sacer: Sovereign Power and Bare Life*, trans. Daniel Heller-Roazen (Stanford: Stanford University Press).

Ahmed, S. (2000) *Strange Encounters: Embodied Others in Post-Coloniality* (London: Routledge).

Alderson, P. and V. Morrow (2004) *Ethics, Social Research and Consulting with Children and Young People* (Barkingside: Barnado's).

Alkire, S. (2002) *Conceptual Framework for Human Security (Working Definition and Executive Summary)*. Paper presented at the Harvard Center for Global Equity.

Anderson, A. (2004) 'Issues of Migration', in R. Hamilton and D. Moore (eds), *Educational Intervention for Refugee Children: Theoretical Perspectives and Implementing Best Practice* (New York: RoutledgeFalmer), 64–82.

Arendt, H (1958) *The Human Condition* (Chicago: University of Chicago Press).

Armstrong, F. (1999) 'Inclusion, Curriculum and the Struggle for Space in School', *International Journal of Inclusive Education*, 3 (1), 75–87.

Arnot, M. (2009) *Educating the Gendered Citizen: Sociological Engagements with National and Global Agendas* (London: Routledge).

Arnot, M. and H. Pinson (2005) *The Education of Asylum-Seeker and Refugee Children. A Study of LEA and School Values, Policies and Practices* (Cambridge: Faculty of Education, University of Cambridge). Available at: www.educ. cam.ac.uk/people/staff/arnot/AsylumReportFinal.pdf

Arnot, M. H. Pinson and M. Candappa (2009) 'Compassion, Caring and Justice: Teachers' Strategies to Maintain Moral Integrity in the Face of National Hostility to the "Non-Citizen"', *Educational Review*, 61 (3), 249–64.

Arnot, M. and Reay, D. (2007) 'A Sociology of Pedagogic Voice: Power, Social Inequality and Transformation', *Discourse*, 28 (3), 311–26.

Audit Commission (2000) *Another Country: Implementing Dispersal under the Immigration and Asylum Act* (London: Audit Commission).

Aynsley-Green, A. (2006) 'Memorandum from the Office of the Children's Commissioner to the Joint Committee on Human Rights on the Treatment of Asylum-seekers.' Retrieved 16 September 2009, from www.childrenscommissioner.org/adult/news/news.cfm?id=1964&newsid=51

Bacon, C. (2005) 'The Evaluation of Immigration Detention in the UK: The Involvement of Private Prison Companies', Working Paper No. 27, Working Paper Series (Oxford: University of Oxford, Refugee Studies Centre).

Barlo, Z. and J. Morrison (2005) 'Refugees and Racism', in E. Guild and J. van Selm (eds), *International Migration and Security: Opportunities and Challenges* (London and New York: Routledge), 113–28.

Bauman, Z. (1997) *Postmodernity and Its Discontents* (Cambridge: Polity Press).

Bauman, Z. (1998) 'Europe of Strangers', Working Paper Series, Working Paper No. 37 (London: ESRC: Transnational Communities Programme).

Bauman, Z. (2001). *Community: Seeking Safety in an Insecure World* (Cambridge: Polity Press).

Bauman, Z. (2004) *Wasted Lives: Modernity and Its Outcasts* (Cambridge: Polity Press).

Bell, V. (1999) 'Performativity and Belonging: An Introduction', *Theory Culture & Society*, 16 (2), 1–10.

Benhabib, S. (2004) *The Rights of Others: Aliens, Residents, and Citizens* (Cambridge: Cambridge University Press).

Bernstein, B. (2000) *Pedagogy, Symbolic Control and Identity: Theory, Research and Critique* (Lanham: Rowman and Littlefield).

Bhabha, J. (1999) 'Belonging in Europe: Citizenship and Post-National Rights', *International Social Science Journal*, 51 (1), 11–23.

Bhabha, J. (2005) 'Rights Spillovers: The Impact of Migration on the Legal System of Western States', in E. Guild and J. Van Selm (eds), *International Migration and Security: Opportunities and Challenges* (London and New York: Routledge Research in Transnationalism), 28–50.

Bloch, A. (1999) 'As If Being a Refugee Isn't Hard Enough: The Policy of Exclusion', in P. Cohen (ed.), *New Ethnicities, Old Racism* (London: Zed Books), 111–22.

Bloch, A. and L. Schuster (2005) 'At The Extremes of Exclusion: Deportation, Detention and Dispersal', *Ethnic and Racial Studies*, 28 (3), 491–512.

Bohmer, C. and A. Shuman (2008) *Rejecting Refugees: Political Asylum in the 21st Century* (Abingdon: Routledge).

Bolloten, B. and T. Spafford (1998) 'Supporting Refugee Children in East London Primary Schools', in J. Rutter and C. Jones (eds), *Refugee Education: Mapping the Field* (Stoke-on-Trent: Trentham Books), 107–24.

Boyden, J. (2009) 'What Place the Politics of Compassion in Education Surrounding Non-Citizen Children?', *Educational Review*, 61 (3), 265–76.

Boyden, J. and J. Berry (2004) *Children and Youth on the Front Line: Ethnography, Armed Conflict and Displacement* (Oxford: Berghahn Books).

Boyden, J. and J. Hart (2007) 'The Statelessness of the World's Children', *Children & Society*, 21 (4), 237–48.

Boyle, P. J., K. Halfacre and V. Robinson (1998) *Exploring Contemporary Migration* (Harlow: Longman).

Brah, A., M. J. Hickman and M. Mac an Ghaill (1999) 'Introduction: Whither "the Global"?', in A. Brah, M. J. Hickman and M. Mac an Ghaill (eds), *Global Futures: Migration, Environment and Globalization* (Basingstoke: Macmillan Press), 3–26.

Brysk, A. (2004) 'Children Across Borders: Patrimony, Property, or Persons?', in A. Brysk and G. Shafir (eds), *People out of Place: Globalization, Human Rights, and the Citizenship Gap* (New York and London: Routledge), 153–76.

Brysk, A. and G. Shafir (2004) 'Introduction: Globalization and the Citizenship Gap', in A. Brysk and G. Shafir (eds), *People out of Place: Globalization, Human Rights, and the Citizenship Gap* (New York and London: Routledge), 3–10.

Buchanan, S., B. Grillo and T. Threadgold (2003) 'What's The Story? Results from Research into Media Coverage of Refugees and Asylum Seekers in the UK.' Article 19 (London: Research Asylum in London). Available from www.researchasylum.org.uk/?lid=451

Burchardt, T. (2005) 'Selective Inclusion: Asylum Seekers and Other Marginalised Groups', in J. Hills and K. Steward (eds), *A More Equal Society? New Labour, Poverty and Exclusion* (Bristol: The Polity Press), 209–30.

Burman, E. (1994) 'Innocents Abroad: Western Fantasies of Childhood and the Iconography of Emergencies', *Disasters*, 18 (3), 238–53.

Candappa, M. (2000) 'Building a New Life: The Role of the School in Supporting Refugee Children', *Multicultural Teaching*, 19 (1), 28–32.

Candappa, M. (2002) 'Human Rights and Refugee Children in the UK', in B. Franklin (ed.), *The New Handbook of Children's Rights: Comparative Policy and Practice* (London: Routledge), 223–36.

Candappa, M., M. Ahmad, B. Balata, R. Dekhinet and D. Gocmen (2007) *Education and Schooling for Asylum-Seeking and Refugee Students in Scotland: An Exploratory Study*. Scottish Government Social Research 2007 (Edinburgh: Scottish Government).

Candappa, M., and Egharevba, I. (2000) 'Extraordinary Childhoods: The Social Lives of Refugee Children', *Children 5–16 Research Briefing*, Number 5 (Swindon: ESRC)

Candappa, M. and I. Egharevba (2002) 'Negotiating Boundaries: Tensions within Home and School Life for Refugee Children', in R. Edwards (ed.), *Children, Home and School* (London: RoutledgeFalmer), 155–71.

Carter, A. (2001) *The Political Theory of Global Citizenship* (London and New York: Routledge).

Castles, S. (1998) 'Globalization and Migration: Some Pressing Contradictions', *International Social Science Journal*, 50 (156), 179–86.

Castles, S. (2003) 'Towards a Sociology of Forced Migration and Social Transformation' *Sociology*, 37 (1), 13.

Castles, S. and A. Davidson (2000) *Citizenship and Migration: Globalization and the Politics of Belonging* (London: Macmillan Press).

Castles, S., and S. Loughna (2002) 'Trends in Asylum Migration to Industrialized Countries: 1990–2001.' Working Papers/UNU–WIDER Research Paper (Helsinki: World Institute for Development Economic Research [UNU-WIDER]).

Castles, S., M. J. Miller and G. Ammendola (2003) *The Age of Migration: International Population Movements in the Modern World* (New York: The Guilford Press).

Chase, E., A. Knight and J. Statham (2008) *The Emotional Well-Being of Unaccompanied Young People Seeking Asylum in the UK* (London: BAAF).

Children's Legal Centre, The (2003) *Mapping the Provision of Education and Social Services for Refugee and Asylum-seeker Children: Lessons from the Eastern Region* (Essex: The Children's Legal Centre).

Chimni, B. (1998) 'The Geopolitics of Refugee Studies: A View from the South', *Journal of Refugee Studies*, 11 (4), 350–74.

Christensen, P. and A. Prout (2002) 'Working in Ethical Symmetry in Social Research with Children', *Childhood*, 9 (4), 477–97.

Christopoulou, N., I. Rydin, D. Buckingham and L. de Block (2004) *Children's Social Relations in Peer Groups: Inclusion, Exclusion and Friendship* (London: European Commission/CHICAM).

Closs, A., J. Stead and R. Arshad (2001) 'The Education of Asylum-Seeker and Refugee Children', *Multicultural Teaching*, 20 (1), 29–33.

Cohen, S. (2002) 'The Local State of Immigration Controls', *Critical Social Policy*, 22 (3), 518–43.

Cohen, S. (2003) *No One Is Illegal: Asylum and Immigration Control Past and Present* (Stoke-on-Trent: Trentham Books).

Cohen, S. (2006) *Deportation is Freedom! The Orwellian World of Immigration Controls* (London and Philadelphia: Jessica Kingsley Publishers).

Cole, E. (2003) *A Few Families Too Many: The Detention of Asylum-Seeking Families in the UK* (London: Bail for Immigration Detainees).

Coleman, J. (1988) 'Social Capital in the Creation of Human Capital', *American Journal of Sociology*, 94 (S1), 95–120.

Collinson, S. (1993) *Beyond Borders: West European Migration Policy towards the 21st Century* (London: Royal Institute of International Affairs).

Corbett, J. (1999) 'Inclusive Education and School Culture', *International Journal of Inclusive Education*, 3 (1), 53–61.

Crawley, H. (2005) 'Developing DFID's Policy Approach to Refugees and Internally Displaced Persons.' Thematic Paper II: The UK, The EU and Forced Migration. (Oxford: Refugee Studies Centre).

Crawley, H. (2006) *Child First, Migrant Second: Ensuring That Every Child Matters.* ILPA Policy Paper (London: ILPA).

Crawley, H. and T. Lester (2005) *No Place for a Child. Children in UK Immigration Detention: Impacts, Alternatives and Safeguards* (London: Save the Children).

Croucher, S. L. (2004) *Globalization and Belonging: The Politics of Identity in a Changing World* (Lanham: Rowman and Littlefield).

Crowley, J. (1999) 'The Politics of Belonging: Some Theoretical Considerations', in A. Geddes and A. Favell (eds), *The Politics of Belonging: Migrants and Minorities in Contemporary Europe* (Aldershot: Ashgate), 15–41.

DCSF (2008) *Personalised Learning – A Practical Guide*, DCSF ref: 00844-2008DOM-EN (Nottingham: DCSF Publications), available online at: http://publications. teachernet.gov.uk/default.aspx?PageFunction=productdetails&PageMode= publications&ProductId=DCSF-00844-2008&, last retrieved 1 December 2009.

Dell'Olio, F. (2002) 'The Redefinition of the Concept of Nationality in the UK: Between Historical Responsibility and Normative Challenges', *Politics*, 22 (1), 9–16.

Dell'Olio, F. (2005) *The Europeanization of Citizenship: Between the Ideology of Nationality, Immigration and European Identity* (Aldershot: Ashgate).

DfES (2002a) *Educating Asylum-Seeking and Refugee Children: Guidance on the Education of Asylum-Seeking and Refugee Children* (London: DfES Publications).

DfES (2002b) *Good Practice Guidance on the Education of Asylum Seeking and Refugee Children* (London: DfES Publications).

DfES (2002c) *Guidance for Local Education Authorities on Schools Collection and Recording Data on Pupils' Ethnic Background (in Compliance with the Data Protection Act and the 2001 National Population Census)* (London: DfES Publications).

DfES (2002d) *School Admissions Code of Practice* (London: DfES Publications).

DfES (2003a) *Every Child Matters; Change for Children in Schools* (London: DfES Publications).

DfES (2003b) *Managing Pupil Mobility – Guidance* (London: DfES Publications).

DfES (2004a) *Aiming High: Raising the Achievement of Minority Ethnic Pupils* (London: DfES Publications).

DfES (2004b) *Aiming High: Guidance on Supporting the Education of Asylum Seeking and Refugee Children – A Guide to Good Practice* (London: DfES Publications).

DfES (2004c) *Vulnerable Children Grant: Guidance for Financial Year 2004–5* (London: DfES Publications).

DfES, DoH, and Home Office (2003) *Keeping Children Safe. The Government's Response to The Victoria Climbié Inquiry Report and Joint Chief Inspector's Report Safeguarding Children* (London: The Stationery Office).

Dobson, J., G. McLaughlan and J. Salt (2001) 'International Migration and the United Kingdom: Recent Patterns and Trends', Research Development Statistics Occasional Paper No. 75. Home Office ON-line Report. Retrieved 16 September 2009 from www.homeoffice.gov.uk/rds/pdfs/occ75.pdf

Durkheim, E. (1893[1997]) *De La Division du Travail Social: Etude sur l'Organisation des Societies Superiores* (Paris: Altan).

Düvell, F. and B. Jordan (2003) 'Immigration Control and the Management of Economic Migration in the United Kingdom: Organisational Culture, Implementation, Enforcement and Identity Processes In Public Services', *Journal of Ethnic and Migration Studies*, 29 (2), 299–336.

Essed, P. and R. Wesenbeek (2004) 'Contested Refugee Status: Human Rights, Ethics and Social Responsibility', in P. Essed, G. Frerks and J. Schrijvers (eds), *Refugees and the Transformation of Societies: Agency, Policies, Ethics, and Politics* (Oxford: Berghahn Books) 53–68.

Fekete, L. (2009) *A Suitable Enemy: Racism, Migration and Islamophobia in Europe* (New York: Pluto Press).

Fix, M. and L. Laglagaron (2002) *Social Rights and Citizenship: An International Comparison*. A Report of the Working Group on Social Rights and Citizenship of the Carnegie Endowment for International Peace Comparative Citizenship Project (Washington, DC: The Urban Institute).

Flynn, D. (2005) 'New Borders, New Management: The Dilemmas of Modern Immigration Policies', *Ethnic and Racial Studies*, 28 (3), 463–90.

Gedalof, L. (2004) 'Unhomely Homes: Women, Family and Belonging in the UK, Discourses of Migration and Asylum.' Paper presented at the Racism, Sexism and Contemporary Politics of Belonging Conference, London, 25–27 August.

Geddes, A. (2005) 'Immigration and the Welfare State', in E. Guild and J. van Selm (eds), *International Migration and Security: Opportunities and Challenges* (London and New York: Routledge), 159–73.

Germann Molz, J. and S. Gibson (2007) 'Introduction: Mobilizing and Mooring Hospitality', in J. Germann Molz and S. Gibson (eds.), *Mobilizing Hospitality: The Ethics of Social Relations in a Mobile World* (Aldershot: Ashgate), 1–26.

Gibney, M. (2004) *The Ethics and Politics of Asylum: Liberal Democracy and the Response to Refugees* (Cambridge: Cambridge University Press).

Gibney, M. and R. Hansen (2003) *Deportation and the Liberal State: The Forcible Return of Asylum Seekers and Unlawful Migrants in Canada, Germany and the United Kingdom* (Geneva: UNHCR).

Gibney, M. J. (2001) 'The State of Asylum: Democratization, Judicialisation and the Evolution of Refugee Policy', in S. Kneebone (ed.), *The Refugee Convention 50 Years On: Globalization and International Law* (Aldershot: Ashgate), 19–46.

Gibson, S. (2007) '"Abusing Our Hospitality": Inhospitableness and the Politics of Deterrence', in J. Germann Molz and S. Gibson (eds), *Mobilizing Hospitality: The Ethics of Social Relations in a Mobile World* (Aldershot: Ashgate), 159–76.

Gigauri, G. (2006) 'Resolving the Liberal Paradox: Citizen Rights and Alien Rights in the United Kingdom', RSC Working Paper No. 31, Working Paper Series (Oxford: University of Oxford, Refugee Studies Centre).

Gilbert, P. (2005) 'Introduction and Outline', in P. Gilbert (ed.), *Compassion: Conceptualisations, Research and Use in Psychotherapy* (London: Routledge), 1–8.

Gillborn, D. (2008) *Racism and Education: Coincidence or Conspiracy?* (London: Routledge).

Gillborn, D. and D. Youdell (2000) *Rationing Education: Policy, Practice, Reform and Equity* (Buckingham: Open University Press).

Giner, C. (2006) 'Asylum and Childhood in the UK: A Highly Political Relationship.' RSC Working Paper No. 34, Working Paper Series (Oxford: University of Oxford, Refugee Studies Centre).

Giner, C. (2007) 'The Politics of Childhood and Asylum in the UK', *Children & Society,* 21 (4), 249–60.

Goodwing-Gill, G. S. (2004) 'Refugees and Their Human Rights.' RSC Working Paper No. 17. Working Paper Series (Oxford: University of Oxford, Refugee Studies Centre).

Graham, D. T. (2000) 'The People Paradox: Human Movements and Human Security in a Globalising World', in D. T. Graham and K. N. Poku (eds), *Migration, Globalisation, and Human Security* (London: Routledge), 185–214.

Greenslade, R. (2005) 'Seeking Scapegoats: The Coverage of Asylum in the UK Press.' Asylum and Migration Working Paper No. 5 (London: Institute for Public Policy Research).

GTC (2006) *The Statement of Professional Values and Practice for Teachers: The GTC Statement* (London: GTCE).

GTC/GSCC/NMC (2008) *Values for Integrated Working with Children and Young People*: www.gscc.org.uk/NR/rdonlyres/D2517B64-E968-43B3-83E7-CA8AED2DEB02/0/ Keyattributes.pdf, accessed 27 November 2009.

Hamilton, R., and D. Moore (eds) (2004) *Educational Interventions for Refugee Children: Theoretical Perspectives and Implementing Best Practice* (New York: RoutledgeFalmer).

Hammarberg, T. (1995) 'Preface' in B. Franklin (ed.), *The Handbook of Children's Rights: Comparative Policy and Practice* (London: Routledge), ix–xiii.

Hammer, T. (2000) *Democracy and the Nation State: Aliens, Denizens and Citizens in a World of International Migration* (Aldershot: Avebury).

Hardwick, N. J. and Rutter (1998) 'The Asylum White Paper – What This means for Schools and Local Authorities', *Multicultural Teaching,* 17 (1), 6–7.

Harris, C. I. (1993) 'Whiteness as Property', *Harvard Law Review,* 106 (8), 1707–91.

HMIP (2005) *Report of an Announced Inspection of Yarl's Wood Immigration Removal Centre,* 28 February–4 March 2005 (London: HMIP).

HMIP (2008) *Report on an Announced Inspection of Yarl's Wood Immigration Removal Centre,* 4–8 February by HM Chief Inspector of Prisons (London: HMIP).

Home Office (2002) *Secure Borders, Safe Haven: Integration with Diversity in Modern Britain* (London: The Stationery Office).

Home Office (2003) *Home Office Departmental Report 2003.* Retrieved 16 September 2009 from www.archive2.official-documents.co.uk/document/ cm59/5908/5908. htm

Home Office (2004a) *Asylum Statistics United Kingdom 2004* (London: The Stationery Office).

Home Office (2004b) *Home Office Targets: Autumn Performance Report 2003,* ON-line Report. Retrieved 16 September 2009 from www.archive2.official-documents.co.uk/document/cm60/6057/6057.htm

Home Office (2004c) *Indicators of Integration – Final Report* (London: The Stationery Office).
Home Office (2005a) 'Controlling Our Borders: Making Migration Work for Britain', Press Release Search, ON-line Report. Retrieved 16 September 2009 from http://press.homeoffice.gov.uk/press-releases/Controlling_Our_Borders_Making_
Home Office (2005b). *Integration Matters: A National Strategy for Refugee Integration* (London: Home Office).
Home Office (2005c) *Integration Matters: A National Strategy for Refugee Integration – A Draft for Consultation* (London: The Stationery Office).
Home Office (2006) 'A New Model for National Refugee Integration Services in England', Consultation paper, ON-line Report, retrieved 16 September 2009 from www.ukba.homeoffice.gov.uk/sitecontent/documents/aboutus/consultations/closedconsultations/nationalrefugeeintegration/consultation_document.pdf?view=Binary
Home Office (2008) *Managing our Borders* (London: The Stationery Office).
House of Commons Education and Skills Committee (2005) *Every Child Matters: 9th Report of Sessions 2004–2005* (London: Every Child Matters).
Hume, D. (1748[1975]) *Enquiries Concerning Human Understanding and Concerning the Principles of Morals* (Oxford: Oxford University Press).
Humpage, L. and G. Marston (2006) 'Recognition, Respect and Rights: Refugee Living in Temporary Protection Visas (TPVs) in Australia', in N. Yuval-Davis, K. Kannabirān and U. Vieten (eds), *The Situated Politics of Belonging* (London: Sage Publications), 113–26.
ICAR (2004) 'Media Image, Community Impact. Assessing the Impact of Media and Political Images of Refugees and Asylum Seekers on Community Relations in London.' Report of a pilot research study (London: ICAR). Retrieved 16 September 2009 from www.icar.org.uk/publications
IRR (Institute of Race Relations) (2000) *European Race Bulletin*. Retrieved 16 September 2009 from www.irr.org.uk/2000/
Isin, E. F. (2002) *Being Political: Genealogies of Citizenship* (Minneapolis: University of Minnesota Press).
Janaway, C. (1994) *Schopenhauer* (Oxford: Oxford University Press).
Joint Chief Inspectors, The (2005) *Safeguarding Children: The Second Joint Chief Inspectors' Report on Arrangement to Safeguard Children*. Retrieved 16 September 2009 from www.hmica.gov.uk/files/safeguards_imagefree.pdf
Joppke, C. (1999) *Immigration and the Nation-State: The United States, Germany, and Great Britain* (New York: Oxford University Press).
Jordan, B. and F. Düvell (2002) *Irregular Migration: The Dilemmas of Transnational Mobility* (Cheltenham and Northampton: Edward Elgar).
Kahin, M. H. (1998) 'Somali Children: The Need to Work in Partnership with Parents and Community', *Multicultural Teaching*, 17 (1), 14–16.
Kao, G. (2004) 'Social Capital and Its Relevance to Minority and Immigrant Populations', *Sociology of Education*, 77 (2), 172–5.
Kendall, S., A. Johnson, C. Gulliver, K. Martin and K. Kinder (2004) *Evaluation of the Vulnerable Children Grant, National Foundation for Education*. DfES Research Report 592. Available at www.nfer.ac.uk/research-areas/pims-data/summaries/vcg-evaluation-of-the-vulnerable-children-grant.cfm
King, G. and C. Murray (2000) 'Rethinking Human Security', *Political Science Quarterly*, 116 (4), 585–610.

Kirp, D. L. (1980) *Doing Good by Doing Little* (Berkeley: University of California Press).

Koser, K. and C. Pinkerton (2002) *The Social Networks of Asylum-seekers and the Dissemination of Information about Countries of Asylum* (London: Home Office).

Kundnani, A. (2001) 'In a Foreign Land: The New Popular Racism', *Race & Class*, 43 (2), 41–60.

Kunz, E. F. (1981) 'Exile and Resettlement: Refugee Theory', *International Migration Review*, 15 (1/2), 42–51.

Lea, J. (2000) 'The Macpherson Report and the Question of Institutional Racism', *Howard Journal of Criminal Justice*, 39 (3), 219–33.

Leaning, J. and Arie, S. (2000) 'Human Security: A Framework for Assessment in Conflict and Transition', Working Paper (Cambridge, MA: Harvard Center for Population and Development Studies).

Lewis, G. and S. Neal (2005) 'Introduction: Contemporary Political Contexts, Changing Terrains and Revisited Discourses', *Ethnic and Racial Studies*, 28 (3), 423–44.

Lewis, H. (1998) 'Embracing the Holistic/Constructivist Paradigm and Sidestepping the Post-Modern Challenge', in C. Clark, A. Dyson and A. Millward (eds), *Towards Inclusive Education?* (London: David Fulton Publishers), 90–105.

Loizos, P. (2000) 'Are Refugees Social Capitalists?', in S. Baron, J. Field and T. Schuller (eds), *Social Capital: Critical Perspectives* (Oxford: Oxford University Press), 124–41.

Lynn, N. and S. Lea (2003) '"A Phantom Menace and The New Apartheid": The Social Construction of Asylum-Seekers in the United Kingdom', *Discourse and Society*, 14 (4), 425–52.

Macaskill, S. and M. Petrie (2000) *"I Didn't Come Here for Fun": Listening to the Views of Children and Young People who are Refugees or Asylum-Seekers in Scotland* (Edinburgh: Save the Children).

Macpherson, W. (1999) *The Stephen Lawrence Inquiry: Report of an Inquiry by Sir William Macpherson of Cluny* (London: HMSO).

Malkki, L. H. (1996) 'Speechless Emissaries: Refugees, Humanitarianism, and Dehistoricization', *Cultural Anthropology*, 11 (3), 377–404.

Malloch, M. S. and E. Stanley (2005) 'The Detention of Asylum Seekers in the UK: Representing Risk, Managing the Dangerous', *Punishment & Society*, 7 (1), 53–71.

Marfleet, P. (2006) *Refugees in a Global Era* (Basingstoke: Palgrave Macmillan).

Marland, M. (1998) 'Refugee Pupils: A Headteacher's Perspective', *Multicultural Teaching*, 17 (1), 17–22.

Martin, C. (1997) *The Holistic Educators: Education for the 21st Century* (Nottingham: Educational Heretics Press).

McDonald, J. (1998) 'Refugee Students' Experiences of the UK Education System', in J. Rutter and C. Jones (eds), *Refugee Education: Mapping the Field* (Stoke-on-Trent: Stylus Publishing), 149–70.

McKnight, A., H., H. Glennerster and H. Lupton (2005) 'Education, Education, Education ...: An Assessment of Labour's Success in Tackling Educational Inequalities', in J. Hills and K. Stewart (eds), *A More Equal Society?: New Labour, Poverty, Inequality and Exclusion* (London: Policy Press), 47–68.

Melzak, S. (1997) *Meeting the Needs of Refugee Children*. Unpublished training material from the Medical Foundation for the Care of Victims of Torture.

Melzak, S. and R. Warner (1992) *Integrating Refugee Children in Schools* (London: Minority Rights Group).

Ministry of Justice (2008) *Lord Goldsmith QC: Citizenship, Our Common Bond.* Retrieved 16 September 2009, from www.justice.gov.uk/reviews/docs/citizen-ship-report-full.pdf

Moran, A. (2005) *Australia: Nation, Belonging, and Globalization* (New York: Routledge).

Morris, L. (2003) 'Managing Contradiction: Civic Stratification and Migrants' Rights', *International Migration Review*, 37 (1), 74–100.

Mott, G. (2000) *Refugees and Asylum Seekers: The Role of the LEAs* (Slough: Education Management Information Exchange, National Foundation for Educational Research in England).

MRCF (2007) *Strategic Plan 2007–2010: 'Immigration, Inclusion, Integration vs. Immigration, Ignorance, Intolerance'* (London: Migrants and Refugee Communities Forum). Retrieved 16 September 2009 from www.mrcf.org.uk/docs/plan.pdf

Muller, B. (2004) 'Globalization, Security, Paradox: Towards a Refugee Biopolitics', *Refuge: Canada's Periodical on Refugees*, 22 (1), 49–57.

Myers, K. (2009) 'The Ambiguities of Aid and Agency: Representing Refugee Children in England 1937–38', *Cultural and Social History*, 6 (1), 29–46.

NASS (2004a) *Dispersal Guidelines*, Policy Bulletin No. 31. Retrieved 16 September 2009 from www.asylumsupport.info/bulletin31.htm

NASS (2004b) *Funding for Disbenefited Families with Children*, Policy Bulletin No. 52. Retrieved 16 September 2009 from www.asylumsupport.info/bulletin52.htm

Nelles, W. (2003) 'Introduction', in W. Nelles (ed.), *Comparative Education, Terrorism and Human Security: From Critical Pedagogy to Peacebuilding?* (New York: Palgrave Macmillan), 1–7.

Nussbaum, M. C. (1998) 'Morality and Emotions', in E. Craig (ed), *Routledge Encyclopaedia of Philosophy* (London and New York: Routledge). Retrieved 16 September 2009 from www.rep.routledge.com/article/L064SECT5

Nussbaum, M. C. (2001) *Upheavals of Thought: The Intelligence of Emotions* (New York: Cambridge University Press).

O'Neill, M. and R. Harindranath (2006) 'Theorising Narratives of Exile and Belonging: The Importance of Biography and Ethno-Mimesis in "Understanding" Asylum', *Qualitative Sociology Review*, 2 (1), 39–53.

O'Neill, M. and T. Spybey (2003) 'Global Refugees, Exile, Displacement and Belonging', *Sociology*, 37 (1), 7–12.

Ofsted (2003a) *The Education of Asylum-seeker Pupils* (London: Ofsted Publications Centre).

Ofsted (2003b) *Inspecting Schools: Framework for Inspecting Schools* (London: Ofsted Publications Centre).

Ofsted (2008) *Safeguarding Children* (London: Ofsted Publications Centre).

Pallon, A., D. Massey, M. Ceballos, K. Espinosa and M. Spittel (2001) 'Social Capital and International Migration: A Test Using Information on Family Networks', *American Journal of Sociology*, 106 (5), 1262–98.

Parekh, B. (2000) *The Parekh Report: The Future of Multi-ethnic Britain* (London: The Runnymede Trust and Profile Books).

Patton, M. Q. (2002) *Qualitative Research and Evaluation Methods* (Thousand Oaks: Sage Publications).

Pettigrew, T. (1998) 'Reactions toward the New Minorities of Western Europe', *Annual Review of Sociology*, 24 (1), 77–103.

Phillimore, J. and L. Goodson (2008) *New Migrants in the UK: Education, Training and Employment* (Stoke-on-Trent: Trentham Books).

Pinson, H. and Arnot M. (2010) 'Local Conceptualisations of the Education of Asylum-Seeking and Refugee Students: From Hostile to Holistic Models', *International Journal of Inclusive Education*, 14 (1), 1–20.

Pirouet, L. (2001) *Whatever Happened to Asylum in Britain?* (Oxford: Berghahn Books).

Prout, A. (2002) 'Researching Children as Social Actors', *Children & Society*, 16 (2), 67–76.

Prout, A. (2005) *The Future of Childhood* (London: RoutledgeFalmer).

Reakes, A. and R. Powell (2004) *The Education of Asylum Seekers in Wales: Implications for LEAs and Schools* (Slough: National Foundation for Educational Research in England and Wales).

Refugee Council (2008) 'Beyond the School Gates: Supporting Refugees and Asylum Seekers in Secondary School'. Retrieved 16 September 2009 from www.refugeecouncil.org.uk/Resources/Refugee%20Council/downloads/researc hreports/inclusiveschools_may08.pdf

Remsbery, N. (2003) *The Education of Refugee Children: Policy and Practice in the Education of Refugee and Asylum-seeker Children in England* (London: Pupil Inclusion Unit, National Children's Bureau).

Richman, N. (1998) *In the Midst of the Whirlwind: A Manual for Helping Refugee Children* (Stoke-on-Trent: Save the Children and Trentham Books).

Richmond, A. H. (1993) 'Reactive Migration: Sociological Perspectives on Refugee Movements', *Journal of Refugee Studies*, 6 (1), 7–24.

Richmond, A. H. (1994). *Global Apartheid: Refugees, Racism and the New World Order* (Toronto: Oxford University Press).

Ringrose, J. (forthcoming) 'Beyond Discourse? Using Deleuze and Guattari's Schizoanalysis to Explore Affective Assemblages, Heterosexually Striated Space, and Lines of Flight Online and at School', *Educational Philosophy and Theory*.

Roberts, A. (1998) 'More Refugees, Less Asylum: A Regime in Transformation', *Journal of Refugee Studies*, 11 (4), 375–95.

Robinson, V. (1990) 'Into the Next Millennium: An Agenda for Refugee Studies', *Journal of Refugee Studies*, 3 (1), 3–15.

Robinson, V. and J. Segrott (2002) *Understanding the Decision-making of Asylum Seekers* (London: Home Office).

Rose, N. (1990) *Governing the Soul: The Shaping of the Private Self* (London: Routledge).

Rothschild, E. (1995) 'What is Security?' *Daedalus*, 124 (summer), 53–98.

Rutter, J. (1998) 'Refugee Children in the Early Years', *Multicultural Teaching*, 17 (1), 23–6.

Rutter, J. (2001) 'EMAG and Refugee Children: Perpetuating Discrimination?', in C. Jones and C. Wallace (eds), *Making EMAG Work* (Stoke-on-Trent: Trentham Books), 29–44.

Rutter, J. (2006) *Refugee Children in the UK* (Buckingham: Open University Press).

Rutter, J. and M. Candappa (1998) *Why Do They Have to Fight? Refugee Children's Stories from Bosnia, Kurdistan, Somalia and Sri Lanka (A Reader for Children aged 11–13)* (London: The Refugee Council).

Rutter, J. and T. Hyder (1998) *Refugee Children in the Early Years: Issues for Policy-Makers and Providers* (London: The Refugee Council and Save the Children).

Rutter, J. and C. Jones (1998) *Refugee Education: Mapping the Field* (Stoke-on-Trent: Trentham Books).

Rutter, J. and R. Stanton (2001) 'Refugee Children's Education and the Education Finance System', *Multicultural Teaching*, 19 (3), 33–9.

Sales, R. (2002) 'The Deserving and the Undeserving? Refugees, Asylum Seekers and Welfare in Britain', *Critical Social Policy*, 22 (3), 456–78.

Sales, R. (2005) 'Secure Borders, Safe Haven: A Contradiction in Terms?', *Ethnic and Racial Studies*, 28 (3), 445–62.

Save the Children (2002) *Starting Again: Young Asylum-Seekers' Views on Life in Glasgow* (Glasgow: Save the Children Scotland).

Save the Children (2004) *My Mum Is Now My Best Friend* (Edinburgh: Save the Children).

Schools against Deportations (2005) *Declaration on the Deportation of Children and Young People from Schools and Colleges under Immigration Act Powers*, available at: www.irr.org.uk/sad/schools_petition.pdf, or www.schoolsagainstde-portations.org, accessed 27 November 2009.

Schopenhauer, A. (1837[1995]) *On the Basis of Morality*, trans. E. F. J. Payne, revised edn (Indianapolis: Hackett).

Sen, A. (2000) 'Why Human Security?' Paper presented at the International Symposium on Human Security, Tokyo, 28 July.

Shafir, G. (2004) 'Citizenship and Human Rights in an Era of Globalization', in A. Brysk and G. Shafir (eds), *People out of Place: Globalization, Human Rights, and the Citizenship Gap* (New York and London: Routledge), 11–28.

Shire, G. (2008) 'Introduction: Race and Racialisation in Neo-liberal Times', in S. Davison and J. Rutherford (eds), *Race, Identity and Belonging: A Soundings Collection* (London: Lawrence and Wishart), 7–18.

Silove, D., Z. Steel and R. Mollica (2001) 'Detention of Asylum Seekers: Assault on Health, Human Rights, and Social Development', *The Lancet*, 357 (9266), 1436–7.

Sivanandan, A. (2001) 'UK: Refugees from Globalism', *Race & Class*, 42 (3), 87–91.

Smith, J. and C. Jenkins (2003) 'Introduction', in J. Smith and C. Jenkins (eds), *Through the Paper Curtain: Insiders and Outsiders in the New Europe* (London and Malden, MA: Blackwell/Royal Institute of International Affairs, European Programme), 1–14.

Solomos, J. and L. Schuster (2001) *Migration, Citizenship and Globalization: A Comparison of Trends in European Societies*. Social Science Research Papers, No.12 (London: South Bank University).

Sporton, D. and G. Valentine (2007) *Identities on the Move: The Integration Experiences of Somali Refugee and Asylum Seeker Young People* (University of Sheffield/University of Leeds: ESRC).

Stalker, P. (2002) 'Migration Trends and Migration Policy in Europe', *International Migration*, 40 (2), 151–79.

Stanley, K. (2001) *Cold Comfort: Young Separated Refugees in England* (London: Save the Children).

Stanley, K. (2002) *Cold Comfort: The Lottery of Care for Young Separated Refugees in England* (London: Save the Children).

Statham, P. (2003) 'Understanding the Anti-Asylum Rhetoric: Restrictive Policies or Racist Publics?', *Political Quarterly*, 74 (1), 163–77.

Stead, J., A. Closs and R. Arshad (2002) 'Invisible Pupils: The Experience of Refugee Pupils in Scottish Schools', *Education and Social Justice*, 4 (1), 49–55.

Stewart, E. (2004) 'Deficiencies in UK Asylum Data: Practical and Theoretical Challenges', *Journal of Refugee Studies*, 17 (1), 29–49.

Suhrke, A. and A. R. Zolberg (2002) 'Issues in Contemporary Refugee Policies', in A. Bernstein and M. Weiner (eds), *Migration and Refugee Policies: An Overview* (London: Continuum International Publishing Group), 143–80.

Summers, D. (2004) 'More Secure than Safe', retrieved 16 September 2009 from www.notinmyname-uk.org/index.htm

Swann, Lord (1985) *Report of the Committee of Enquiry into the Education of Children from Ethnic Minority Groups* (The Swann Report) (London: Her Majesty's Stationery Office).

Taylor, D. (2008) 'My Classmates Came To The Rescue When I Was Threatened With Deportation', *Independent on Sunday*, 14 September: at www.independent. co.uk/news/people/profiles/my-classmates-came-to-the-rescue-when-i-was-threatened-with-deportation-926525.html, accessed 27 November 2009.

Teuber, A. (1982) 'Simone Weil: Equality as Compassion', *Philosophy and Phenomenological Research*, 43 (2), 221–37.

Thomas, C. (2000) *Global Governance, Development and Human Security: The Challenge of Poverty and Inequality* (London: Pluto).

Tomlinson, S. (1987) *Ethnic Minorities in British Schools: A Review of the Literature 1960–1982* (London: Heinemann).

Turton, D. (2002) 'Forced Displacement and the Nation-State', in J. Robinson (ed.), *Development and Displacement* (Oxford/Milton Keynes: Open University Press/Oxford University Press), 19–76.

Turton, D. (2003) 'Conceptualizing Forced Migration', Working Paper Series, Working Paper No. 12 (Oxford: University of Oxford, Refugee Studies Centre).

UNCHR (2008) *2008 Global Trends: Refugees, Asylum-seekers, Returnees, Internally Displaced and Stateless Persons*, retrieved 16 September 2009 from www.unhcr. org/4a375c426.html

UNCRC (1989) *United Nations Convention on the Rights of the Child*, available at http://untreaty.un.org/English/TreatyEvent2001/pdf/03e.pdf

UNDP (1994) *Human Development Report* (New York: UN Development Programme).

UNICEF Innocenti Research Centre (2007) *Report Card 7: Child Poverty in Perspective: An Overview of Child Well-being in Rich Countries: A Comprehensive Assessment of the Lives and Well-being of Children and Adolescents in the Economically Advanced Nations* (Florence: United Nations Children's Fund), available at www.unicef-irc.org/publications/pdf/rc7_eng.pdf

Van Selm, J. (2005) 'Immigration and Regional Security', in E. Guild and J. van Selm (eds), *International Migration and Security Opportunities and Challenges* (London and New York: Routledge Research in Transnationalism), 11–27.

Vincent, C. and S. Warren (1998) *Supporting Refugee Children: A Focus on Home–School Links* (Warwick: University of Warwick).

von Bredow, W. (1998) 'The Changing Character of National Borders', *Citizenship Studies*, 2 (3), 365–76.

Wade, J., F. Mitchell and G. Baylis (2008) *Unaccompanied Asylum Seeking Children: The Response of Social Work Services* (London: BAAF).

Waghid, Y. (2005) 'Action as an Educational Virtue: Toward a Different Understanding of Democratic Citizenship Education', *Educational Theory*, 55 (3), 323–42.

Watts, M. (2004) 'Telling Tales of Torture: Repositioning Young Adults' Views of Asylum Seekers', *Cambridge Journal of Education*, 34 (3), 315–29.

Weil, S. (1970) *First and Last Notebooks* (London: Oxford University Press).

Weiner, M. (1995) *The Global Migration Crisis* (New York: Longman).

Whitaker, R. (1998) 'Refugees: The Security Dimension', *Citizenship Studies*, 2 (3), 413–34.

Williams, C. R. (2008) 'Compassion, Suffering and the Self: A Moral Psychology of Social Justice', *Current Sociology*, 56 (1), 5–24.

Wolton, S. (2006) 'Immigration Policy and the Crisis of British Values', *Citizenship Studies*, 10 (4), 453–67.

Xenos, N. (1996) 'Refugees: The Modern Political Condition', in M. J. Shapiro and H. R. Alker (eds), *Challenging Boundaries: Global Flows, Territorial Identities* (Minneapolis: University of Minnesota Press), 233–46.

Yuval-Davis, N. (2005) 'Racism, Cosmopolitanism and Contemporary Politics of Belonging', *Soundings*, 30 (1), 166–78.

Yuval-Davis, N. (2008) 'Racism, Cosmopolitanism and Contemporary Politics of Belonging', in S. Davison and J. Rutherford (eds), *Soundings on Race, Identity and Belonging: A Soundings Collection* (London: Lawrence and Wishart), 101–13.

Yuval-Davis, N., F. Anthias and E. Kofman (2005) 'Secure Borders and Safe Haven and the Gendered Politics of Belonging: Beyond Social Cohesion', *Ethnic and Racial Studies*, 28 (3), 513–35.

Yuval-Davis, N., K. Kannabirān and U. Vieten (2006) 'Introduction', in N. Yuval-Davis, K. Kannabirān and U. Vieten (eds), *The Situated Politics of Belonging* (London: Sage Publications), 1–14.

Zhou, M. (1997) 'Segmented Assimilation: Issues, Controversies, and Recent Research on the New Second Generation', *International Migration Review*, 31 (4), 975–1008.

Index

[]

Williams, Christopher R. 26, 28
Wolton, Suke 51

Yarl's Wood 61, 62, 63, 64, 188,
Youdell, Deborah 76
youth culture
  and bullying 152
  English language issues 153
  and friendships 152
  gendered nature of 153–4

and Otherness 151, 152, 166–7,
  168
youth 'speak' 162
youth values
  and belonging 166–7
  and friendships 167
  respect 168
  and security/safety 168–9
Yuval-Davis, Nira 31–2, 144–5,
  209–10

Lightning Source UK Ltd.
Milton Keynes UK
UKOW06n0633170116

266525UK00017B/400/P